Cooking
Without Milk

Milk-Free and Lactose-Free Recipes

FLORENCE E. SCHROEDER

CUMBERLAND HOUSE PUBLISHING

NASHVILLE, TENNESSEE

Published by
  Cumberland House Publishing, Inc.
  431 Harding Industrial Drive
  Nashville, TN 37211
  www.cumberlandhouse.com

Cover design: Unlikely Suburban Design
Text design: Lisa Taylor

Library of Congress Cataloging-in-Publication Data

Schroeder, Florence E., 1941–
    Cooking without milk : milk-free and lactose-free recipes / Florence E. Schroeder.
        p. cm.
Includes index.
    ISBN 1-48182-309-6 (pbk.)
1. Milk-free diet—Recipes. I. Title.
    RM234.5 .S37 2002
    641.5'63—dc21   2002012220

Printed in Canada
1 2 3 4 5 6 7 8 — 07 06 05 04 03 02

For those of us who must prepare meals without lactose—
with no milk or milk by-products.

Sometimes we need a reminder that variety is still
available and easily accessible.

Cooking is still fun, and variety the spice of life....

—FES

Contents

✖ ✖ ✖ ✖ ✖ ✖ ✖ ✖ ✖ ✖ ✖ ✖ ✖ ✖ ✖ ✖ ✖ ✖ ✖ ✖

Acknowledgments

✕ ✕ ✕ ✕ ✕ ✕ ✕ ✕ ✕ ✕ ✕ ✕ ✕ ✕ ✕ ✕ ✕ ✕ ✕

For my family who encouraged my efforts, especially my children who encouraged me to experiment, tasted my recipes, and laughed uproariously at my early draft typos.

Introduction: Pay Attention

✖ ✖ ✖ ✖ ✖ ✖ ✖ ✖ ✖ ✖ ✖ ✖ ✖ ✖ ✖ ✖ ✖ ✖

Food and nourishment are not necessarily synonyms. Eating is not always coexistent with nutrition. And intelligence at a physiologic level can seem quite obscure at a cognitive level. For a moment let us try to take that lofty cognitive intelligence down to the level of our intestinal tract as it tries to nourish us on a daily basis. Our intestinal tract, or gut, is made up of three layers. The inner absorptive layer consists of cube-shaped cells that are packed tightly together. If this membrane layer were stretched out flat it would cover the size of a tennis court. Now, imagine a garbage man as he backs his truck up to the tennis court and sprays it with about a quarter of an inch of partially digested food, garbage, and a variety of sundry chemicals and toxins. And just as that truck is pulling away, the septic man pulls up with his truck and sprays your tennis court with about an inch of raw sewage. Now you commission this single-cell membrane with the job of keeping all the garbage and sewage on one side of the membrane while selecting all of the potential organic nutrients out from that mess and putting them on the other side of the membrane. And after the membrane has selected out all of the good stuff, it has to clean off all the sewage and garbage and remove it (and it cannot take too long to do it) because our friendly delivery men are going to be back tomorrow with a fresh load of sewage and garbage so this process can happen all over again. And don't forget, this membrane has to be so good at this job that the organic material it extracts from this mess is enough to build and sustain life.

Actually, the real life situation is even more complicated than our present imaginary membrane. Real gut membranes secrete a rich mucus coat, with all manner of different molecules and chemicals in it, to help it do its job. Furthermore, there has developed an amazing symbiotic relationship between the cells lining the gut and the bacteria that are found there. These bacteria contribute a great deal to the healthy functioning of the gut lining. All this is truly an incredible miracle, but it is the saga that unfolds day after day within your own gut. Most of the time this miracle goes on and on without even a hint of effort, but other times the gut has a way of making itself known. Imagine again if this membrane was somewhat less than perfect. What would happen if it leaked? The membrane certainly would not be able to fulfill its commission, with sewage leaking onto the good side of the membrane and the hard-searched-for nutrients seeping back into the garbage. While this system is almost perfect, it can, and does, develop problems. Most of these problems start by leakiness in the gut lining.

This is why you need to pay attention to the material presented in this cookbook! In developed countries a leaky gut is most often caused by poor quality foods and food intolerance (in Third World countries the problem is often from infection). Dairy heads the list of these food intolerances. Food intolerance can definitely turn that quiet, efficient, miracle worker of a gut into a living nightmare. To make matters dramatically worse, symptoms of food intolerance are not limited to the gut but can become generalized throughout the body. Thus the list of symptoms from food intolerance is long, including, but not limited to, abdominal cramps, gas, heartburn, diarrhea, constipation, inflammatory bowel disease, arthritis, muscle aches, headaches, behavioral and personality changes, endocrine dysfunction, fatigue, weight gain, weight loss, edema, osteoporosis and other nutrient deficiencies, and it is at least a contributor to a host of other diseases including heart disease and cancer.

To understand how food intolerances can have such dramatic and wide-ranging effects, we have to add more complexity to our single membrane model of gut function. This single-celled membrane, which constitutes our gut lining, is backed up by a secondary immune-mediated defense system. These immune cells have an incredible ability to search and destroy any material that it determines should not be there. So imagine again our leaky membrane, garbage and sewage pouring through the membrane, and these immune cells are your next line of defense. This is grueling hand to hand combat, each toxin must be identified and dealt with individually and often at the expense of many of our own immune cells. This job is so consuming that the gut employs 60 percent of our entire immune system. These immune cells, called lymphocytes, are delicately tuned instruments that when overstressed can lose their balance. They are also very powerful destroyers and when this kind of power gets out of control you have set the stage for a multitude of problems that have the potential to destabilize your entire immune system.

So it definitely behooves you to pay careful attention to the effect of food on your gut. Being attentive to your gut is called conscious eating, and it is the foundation of holistic health. It embraces the concept that the internal organs of your digestive system possess intelligence. Is this an outrageous concept? Not according to modern concepts of neurophysiology. Embedded within the wall of the gut, from the mouth to the anus, is an interacting web of nerve cells whose complexity is rivaled only by that of the brain itself. This web is connected to the brain, as well as to the rest of our internal organs, by the vagas nerve, which is the largest autonomic nerve in the body. These nerves in the gut, just like those in the brain, communicate with each other by secreting tiny amounts of very specialized chemicals called neurotransmitters. Serotonin is just one of those select chemicals. This neurotransmitter is the focus of most of the newer anti-depressants and is at the center of the emerging concepts behind the neurobiology of intelligence and emotion. Yet a little-appreciated fact is that 90 percent of the body's serotonin lies within the gut, not within the brain. It can only be concluded that our gut, to which we rarely give a passing thought unless we are on the toilet, is rich in all the paraphernalia that underlies intelligence. Our problem, of course, is not that the gut lacks intelligence, but that our other locus of intelligence, the brain, is not smart enough to listen to it. We would be a lot healthier if our gut had just a little more intelligence, enough to be able to speak. Then it could just say, "Don't eat that junk food, you idiot." As it is, the gut only speaks in terms of a variety of aches, pains, cramping, and bloating. It would seem that it would not be easy to ignore this language but we make an incredibly valiant effort in this direction.

This book will help you to understand the language of your digestive tract as it gives you feedback on what you eat, especially in the area of dairy foods. Before you eat, while eating, and after you eat, rely upon the intelligence inherent in your gut and let it tell you what to eat, when to eat, and how much to eat. Listen to those groans and pains and relate them to what you have eaten and act accordingly. It can well be said that the key to healthy eating and healthy dieting is not in the counting of calories but in the connection of consciousness between the gut and brain. While this book will get you started on this great adventure, there are volumes written on issues relating to conscious eating; such topics as would include food allergies, elimination diets, body and digestive typing, techniques of eating, and many more.

I hope you enjoy this cookbook as I have and reap its many blessings not only in its delicious foods but also in its sage advice. I wish you good eating and good health.

—David Salter, M.D.

✖ ✖ ✖ ✖ ✖ ✖ ✖ ✖ ✖ ✖ ✖ ✖ ✖ ✖ ✖ ✖ ✖

FAQs and Facts about Digestion

What is lactose intolerance?

Lactose is the major sugar of milk. Lactose is a disaccharide, which means two sugar molecules (in this case, one glucose and one galactose) joined together into one larger molecule. Lactose intolerance is the inability to digest lactose, and the symptoms of lactose intolerance include nausea, cramps, bloating, gas, and diarrhea.

How does lactose intolerance differ from milk allergy?

Lactose intolerance is the inability to digest lactose into its component sugars. The symptoms and discomfort arise from the excessive growth of bacteria in the gut. A milk allergy, on the other hand, is a reaction by the body to the proteins or other components of the milk (or other substance) that the body recognizes as foreign and therefore to be "killed." Allergic reactions are inflammatory reactions and involve a long series of immunological reactions. The bottom line for our discussion is that people with lactose intolerance may be able to eat food that contains partially digested milk, like cheese or yogurt, while people with more severe intolerances and true milk allergies must avoid all milk products at all times.

Is milk the ideal food?

Milk is the ideal food for infant mammals; it has sugar (lactose), fats, and proteins, including antibodies from the mother, that provide the baby with all the energy and nutrients that the young animal needs to grow. The milk produced by each species differs, and is ideal for that species' young. Human milk is ideal for human babies; cow's milk is ideal for calves. Humans are able to ingest cow's milk, but cow's milk is not the perfect food for humans. Cow's milk differs from human milk in several ways, including more protein, a higher ratio of fat to protein, and less lactose than human milk.

Milk and dairy products are not "normal" foods for adult mammals. In fact, only humans (and some of their pets) regularly consume dairy products. While infant mammals have the lactase enzyme needed to digest lactose, the sugar in milk, most adult mammals lose the lactase enzyme from their digestive system. Instead they have enzymes that digest sugars found from plant materials (primarily sucrose, glucose, and galactose).

Humans in some areas of the world started using milk products from their domesticated animals, like cows, sheep, goats, and yaks thousands of years ago. People whose ancestors ingested a lot of milk products for thousands of years continue to express the lactase enzyme into adulthood. People whose ancestors ate little or no milk products lose the lactase enzyme with maturity, as do other mammals. Therefore, many adults have little or no tolerance for lactose.

In many cases, low lactose foods like cheese and yogurt are tolerated by people without the lactase enzyme, while high lactose foods such as milk and ice cream are not. The food industry has responded with predigested, lactase-treated milk and lactase-containing over-the-counter pills to help these people digest lactose. Lactase-treated products and lactase pills, however, are expensive.

For those people who are unable to tolerate the milk proteins, lactase-treated products are just as intolerable as untreated dairy products.

Normal digestion

All foods, whether sugar, fat, or protein, are composed of polymers of smaller nutrient molecules joined covalently into larger molecules. Digestion is the process of breaking the large polymers of sugars, amino acids, or fatty acids into the individual molecules, which can then be absorbed by the body. There are three types of food: carbohydrates, proteins, and fats.

The simplest *carbohydrates* are sugars, which are either monosaccharides (one sugar molecule) or disaccharides (two sugar molecules joined chemically). Table sugar is composed of one glucose molecule attached to one fructose molecule, while lactose is a glucose attached to a galactose molecule. There are different enzymes to break each disaccharide down into its component monosaccharides. Starches are more complex polysaccharides, and can have hundreds of sugar units combined into a single large molecule. There are specific enzymes that break the large polymers down to the disaccharides, which are then handled like simple sugars by the body. Cellulose, or insoluble fiber, is the most abundant molecule on the earth, and makes up the cell walls of plants. It is completely indigestible by animals; herbivorous animals, like cows, can get energy from cellulose only because the microbes in their guts digest the cellulose for them.

Proteins are large molecules made of hundreds of amino acids. Enzymes called peptidases break proteins down into individual amino acids.

Dietary fats consist of three fatty acid molecules chemically attached to a glycerol molecule. Lipases are the enzymes that break fats down into their component fatty acid molecules. Fats and cholesterol are necessary for making lipid membranes, and also serve as a concentrated source of calories to tide organisms over periods of famine.

Digestion starts in the mouth

When you put a piece of food in your mouth, the digestion process begins immediately. Not only is the food broken down mechanically by chewing, but the salivary glands secrete enzymes into the saliva that start to break down large molecules like starches (polysaccharides) into smaller molecules (maltose, a disaccharide). When food is swallowed, it enters the stomach.

The stomach contains a very acidic solution, which causes heartburn and acid reflux disease if it escapes the stomach. The purpose of the acid is to break down most food molecules into smaller molecules. There are also some specific peptidases that work in the stomach to start the digestion of proteins.

When the partially digested food leaves the stomach and enters the small intestine, it is neutralized by the bile acids, which are secreted by the liver. Bile acids not only neutralize the stomach acid, they are also detergents that solubilize fat molecules. Digestive enzymes from the pancreas mix with the food to continue digesting the peptides to amino acids, the disaccharides to monosaccharides, and fats to fatty acids.

The small intestine also has receptor molecules that recognize and bind to various small food molecules. The digested food molecules bind to the receptors and are absorbed into the bloodstream. Once the amino acids, fatty acids, and monosaccharides are in the blood, they are distributed throughout the body to supply the energy and building blocks needed to keep the body going.

When the contents of the gut reach the large intestine, it usually contains mostly water and the indigestible insoluble fiber that laxative commercials tell us so much about. The role of the large intestine is to absorb the water so that the final waste product is relatively solid, minimizing water loss. There are bacteria in the large intestine. When sugar (lactose) is not digested in the small intestine, the bacteria in the large intestine digest the sugars, grow to large population densities, and cause the gas, bloating, and diarrhea that are common symptoms of lactose intolerance.

Lactose digestion in infants, adults, and lactose-intolerant individuals

Infants of all mammals make high levels of the enzyme lactase, which breaks lactose down into glucose and galactose, its component monosaccharides. This makes milk an ideal food for the young animal. The adults of most mammals stop making the lactase enzyme as they mature and start to make other digestive enzymes needed to break down the components of their normal adult diet. For instance, carnivores would start to make lots of proteases, while herbivores would start to express a suite of enzymes to digest the carbohydrates that make up the bulk of their diet.

Lactose intolerance therefore is not a defect, but the normal state for most adult mammals. It is the inability to digest lactose, or to break it down into the galactose and glucose monosaccharides. The result is a lot of sugar that cannot be absorbed by the small intestine; hence the sugar passes into the large intestine, where it feeds the normal gut bacteria, allowing them to overgrow. The result is many more bacteria than normal, and all those bacteria are digesting the sugars and releasing gas into the intestine. The extra sugars also prevent the large intestine from absorbing as much water as it normally would. The symptoms, therefore, are gas and diarrhea and bloating and discomfort.

How does being milk or lactose intolerant affect diet?

On the side of the refrigerator of my daughter's daycare there is a list of food preferences and restrictions. In this group of eighteen toddlers, there are four who are not to have cow's milk, and/or cheese and yogurt. Inside the fridge are boxes of soy and rice milk with those children's names on them. What a difference from 30 years ago when my mom discovered that she was unable to have milk and milk products.

In the 1970s, ulcer patients were placed on a "bland" diet, which consisted of lots of milk and pudding. My father had bleeding ulcers, and was placed on that bland diet, which changed the diet of our entire family. The increase in milk products made Mom very ill, and after a few inconclusive days in the hospital, she decided to stop eating all milk products to see if it would help. It did. But eliminating milk products from the modern American diet is a very difficult process, especially for those, like my mom, who can't tolerate milk proteins or milk sugars.

My siblings and I were in the preteen/teenage years, which means picky eaters, when Mom discovered that she could not have any milk products. Suddenly we needed *three* different meals every night for dinner: milk-free for Mom, the milk-rich bland diet for Dad, and something that we kids would eat. The recipes in this cookbook saved us from the three-meal meals. They were adapted from the "regular" foods that we had always eaten, modified to make them milk-free. The process of cooking without milk is easier today, with the milk substitutes and the nondairy margarines that are now readily available.

What should a lactose-intolerant person eat, and what should they not eat?

Everyone knows that a balanced diet is important. Studies have shown that low-fat fiber-rich diets that include plenty of fresh fruits and vegetables help people live longer and healthier lives. True, there are studies showing that yogurt seems to help some people live to an extreme old age in good health; but that does not mean that yogurt will help a lactose-intolerant person, so do not feel that you are missing out. After all, no one says that a person who is allergic to peanuts should eat peanut butter, even if it is a good source of protein. Just be sure that you eat a variety of the foods you can have every day.

There are many foods that a lactose-intolerant person can eat, from all the food groups (yes, even chocolate, as long as it is from the chocolate recipes in this book or a dark chocolate that is not made with milk—read the labels!). Vegan diets, by definition do not contain milk products, but they are difficult for even dedicated people to follow. It is not necessary to follow a vegan diet, although a balanced vegan diet will not hurt you. The recipes in this book include meats, eggs, fruits and vegetables, and grains. There are desserts and beverages of many types. And all of them have been developed by and tested on the author (an extremely milk-intolerant person) and her family. This book will have recipes for your family, too.

Sources of calcium

There are many green leafy vegetables that have calcium. A few good calcium sources are beans (all types), green leafy vegetables, dried figs, hummus, and tofu. Calcium-fortified orange juice is also a good choice. There is a list of calcium-rich foods in this book (see pg. 256). There are also many lists available showing how much calcium various foods have, and there are calcium supplements available; just be sure that if you take calcium tablets you also have Vitamin D to help absorb the calcium.

Daily challenges

Restaurants: As this book notes, any restaurant you go to wants you to leave happy, so that you will come back again. They should be happy to tell you what is in any dish, and help you find items on the menu that are milk-free. However, not all wait staff will know what lactose intolerance is, or what you can and cannot eat. I have watched wait staff say that perfectly safe items are not okay, and that salads sprinkled with cheese are okay. Ultimately you have to take responsibility for what you eat. Most important, if something arrives at the table that you cannot eat, do not hesitate to send it back. If it comes back two minutes later with most of the cheese scraped off, send it back again. It does not matter if the cook and waiters think you are picky, all that matters is that you leave the restaurant after a good meal that does not give you pain or discomfort. After all, *you* are paying them to provide you with a meal. Insist on one that you can eat.

Social occasions

Friends and family also want to have you feel good when you leave after a meal, but unless they have experience cooking for a lactose-intolerant person, you will have to remind them about your diet limitations. Not everyone will understand or be helpful. My grandmother kept a stash of cold hard-boiled eggs in her refrigerator for Mom since she was convinced that if there were no tasty alternatives, my mom would give up her silly ideas and eat the good food she cooked. In a case like that you can either refuse all invitations (not always possible), or bring something that you can enjoy eating—a salad or a casserole. If your host is not willing to cook milk-free for you, do not feel bad about "insulting" them by bringing a contribution to the meal. Consider the situation a potluck if it makes you feel better, but do not let yourself get so hungry that you eat something that makes you sick!

The work environment

This can also be a tough situation to deal with many times there will be an office party, whether for a birthday or to celebrate meeting a goal. It is important that you do participate in the social aspects of these events, even if you cannot participate in the gustatory portion of the proceedings. If it is possible, volunteer to go get the food, that way you can be sure that there will be something you can eat. If your office does birthday parties, make sure that your coworkers know that you are milk/lactose intolerant and will not be able to eat carrot cake with cream cheese frosting. No one's feelings will be hurt if they know that they should get you an angel food cake with fresh berries instead of the ice cream cake that might show up on other occasions.

The importance of this cookbook—anyone can use it.

This cookbook will serve as an important, basic tool for people who discover that they or someone they cook for can't tolerate milk, whether because of the sugars or the proteins. It will help lactose-intolerant and milk-allergic people by providing a large number of recipes that do not need milk or cheese to taste good. Moreover, this book will teach you how to convert your own favorite recipes to milk-free versions. But, this book is not restricted to lactose- and milk-intolerant people; all these recipes can be made with real milk and/or butter for people who want to have alternatives to cheese-drenched high-fat foods. Even more important, I know from personal experience that you will find child-friendly foods in this cookbook, and sometimes that is the most important consideration of all, as I have learned from my own three-year-old daughter!

Enjoy using this book.

—Roxann Schroeder, Ph.D.

Cooking Without Milk

Living with Milk or Lactose Intolerance

✗ ✗

This cookbook is a common sense guide to milk-free cooking. The ingredients called for in these pages are products found in the average grocery store. You do not have to find specialty products to cook milk-free. This is not a vegan or vegetarian cookbook; the recipes are milk and lactose free, not meat, egg, or wheat free. The thing you will be reminded of throughout this work is to **read the labels**. I will also remind you of what to look for when you do that.

Common sense of milk or lactose intolerance

I am extremely lactose intolerant. I was confirmed lactose intolerant in 1972 and spent the better part of a year feeling sorry for myself. Most of my favorite foods were responsible for a very uncomfortable biological idiosyncrasy. I could no longer have cheese, butter, ice cream, or yogurt. Worst of all, no buttermilk—that was really a blow. Actually, I shouldn't have been eating these food anyway, I just didn't know that at the time.

As a child I was painfully thin, and as a teenager I had a bleeding ulcer, for no apparent reason. No one, all those years ago, thought of milk as a problem. When I became a mother, I was treated by my doctor as one who was having "woman problems." Later, when my children were still at home and years away from leaving for college, my doctor decided that my distress was empty nest syndrome. I didn't go to the doctor often with my discomfort—you can see why.

I also struggled for years with what was diagnosed as arthritis in the early 1970s. The problem was so severe that I was given several shots of cortisone, over a period of two to three years, for the swelling in the finger joints and my hip. I was told by my doctor that I would need a hip replacement by the time I was forty. This was when I was in my early thirties. I believed it would be necessary since I had chronic pain and an inability to use my joints. It hasn't been necessary. To be fair to the medical community, I only sought help when the symptoms became severe. I had been embarrassed too many times by doctors who could find nothing, physically, wrong. We know now that the symptoms of milk/lactose intolerance can mimic many physical and emotional problems.

I suspect that many people are not sure if they are milk or lactose intolerant. If you're not sure, some of the ideas in this book may help you decide. After checking with a medical professional to make sure nothing else is going on, think about the possibility that milk, in some form or other, may be causing chronic discomfort. Being milk or lactose intolerant isn't simple, but it is normal. It is up to you to consider the possibilities, make the decision, and take the steps that may be able to make you more comfortable.

This is a cookbook. If you want to know about milk/lactose intolerance, there is a lot of information on the internet or at your local library. The information on the internet is a mixed bag. Some want to tell us that it is all our imagination, some want to convince us that milk is lethal, and more want to sell us something—lots of somethings. If you do go digging, among other information you will find that your system needs lactase, a digestive enzyme, to break down the lactose into its separate components in order to digest it. And that for 70 percent, or more, of the world's population the sugars in milk cause an intolerance or allergy.[1] It would seem that it is more normal not to be able to tolerate cow's milk than otherwise.

Some health professionals do not seem to grasp the range of discomforts that ingesting any form of lactose can cause. Again, the reason for this is that symptoms of lactose intolerance can mimic many other physical and emotional problems, and, in fact, may be the cause of them. No matter how careful or caring, any doctor is capable of missing what later proves to be the obvious. Don't be impatient, but don't quit until you know for sure that there is no major illness. The symptoms are not your imagination, and they can be controlled.

It's difficult to diagnose milk or lactose intolerance because milk is extremely common in the American diet, making it difficult for some to simply stop drinking milk and eating milk products. How else will you get calcium? Doesn't milk have natural vitamin D to help us absorb the needed calcium? In fact, vitamin D is required to be added by the dairy industry to cow's milk, but vitamin D is not required in any other milk product such as cheese, yogurt, and ice cream. Cow's milk naturally comes with a relatively small amount of vitamin D, enough for the animal, which has been absorbed through the cow's skin. We get vitamin D the same way, simply by exposing ourselves—even just the hands and face—to the sun for fifteen to twenty minutes three times a week.[2] Besides, like calcium, vitamin D is abundant in other foods.[3]

Milk has been a valuable source of calcium and vitamin D in the U.S.; use it if you can but don't worry about it if you, or your child, can't. No one has yet proven a need for cow's milk. There are many more sources of calcium than milk that are more easily absorbed into our systems.[4] Take a look at the world at large. Countries that don't normally have a diet high in milk products produce beautiful healthy people with strong bones and teeth.[5] What that tells us is the typical Western-world diet includes milk because we have bought into two areas: The continuous, powerful, and all too often effective advertising of the milk industry; and strong government encouragement of that industry—*not* because milk is essential for human health.

When trying to avoid milk and milk by-products, be aware that every year millions of pounds of milk, dried and liquid, are made into protein additives for foods and pharmaceuticals. That the milk industry is successful in getting their products used in the form of additives in such a wide variety of foods is becoming a problem for many people. Foods that *were* perfectly good for milk- and lactose-intolerant people, are now inconsumable for many of us who are milk/lactose sensitive or intolerant.

Milk or lactose intolerance

Milk allergy and milk intolerance are caused when the person ingesting the product reacts to the sugars and/or proteins in the milk. Be aware that lactose or milk reactions range from mild to very serious. Not everyone reacts the same way. Symptoms can be stomach or bowel discomfort; diarrhea or constipation (it can cause either or both); almost constant gas; bloating, burping, and heartburn; pain in the back or side; nausea; swollen joints; depression or weepiness; an inability to concentrate or communicate; fatigue; elevated temperature; headaches.[6] These are fairly common problems.

Lactose can also cause skin rash, colic, vomiting, diarrhea, and bronchitis in babies. Followed by allergy, asthma, bronchitis, coughing, sneezing, constipation or diarrhea, gastroesophageal reflux, vomiting, hives, or poor growth in children.[7] Due to possible swelling of joints, you may feel other symptoms such as arthritic-like pain when ingesting milk. Some people may become emotional or have trouble thinking clearly. Some intolerant systems may mimic irritable bowl syndrome. Headaches and the inability to concentrate may be the result of milk or lactose. An additional problem is that not all reactions occur immediately, and there is no one set of symptoms that say "milk reaction" to the medical community.

Are you intolerant?

Few in-depth studies have been done that focus on milk-induced illness in adults. Whether one wants to call what we are feeling an intolerance or an allergy is of little consequence to those who have the symptoms. However, there is evidence to suggest that milk sugar (lactose) does play a major role in human disease at all ages.[8]

That's where common sense comes in; it is the best thing available to the millions of us who have varying degrees of intolerance. What is the only thing that can be done about milk or lactose intolerance? *Avoid milk and milk by-products!* At this time, there is not a cure—only avoidance. Individuals may have to avoid all milk, or just some. That's what you have to find out for yourself: can you tolerate a small amount?

If you're not sure if milk may be causing problems, and if a doctor can not find the cause of your discomfort, try the avoidance test. Really eliminate all milk products for two to three weeks. You must wait because lactose builds up in one's system. After **no milk** for at least **two weeks**, after your system is completely cleared of all residues, try a glass of milk or a bowl of ice cream. Then wait at least two or three days again before eating more, and see what happens. Remember, it takes days for your system to rid itself of the substance. And all the while it's there, you are likely to feel, if not actual physical discomfort, like you're on an emotional roller coaster.

Avoid all milk? Might you face skepticism, criticism, or even ridicule? Well—probably not, certainly not as much as thirty years ago. Nonetheless, it's hard for most people, even family and doctors, to understand a biological phenomenon that does not affect them, or that they cannot readily see. More and more we are realizing what ingesting the wrong thing can do to people. If nothing else has worked, try a *completely* milk- and lactose-free test. There is information on calcium and other sources of calcium in the back of this book. If you are intolerant you will be fine without milk if you eat a balanced diet.

There are suggestions for replacing fresh milk products with fermented milk products. It is thought that fermented products, such as yogurt, buttermilk, acidophilus milk, some cheeses such as cheddar, Edam, and Parmesan can be tolerated by anyone. This is assumed to be so because some of the lactose has been predigested. This may be possible for some, but I have noticed that latent reactions are not considered at all, and some symptoms don't show up for four to five days. I suspect that's how lactose intolerance is often missed. If you try these foods, see how you feel in a few days, including your emotional/mental side. Despite the fact that a declaration has been made that yogurt is safe because it comes predigested, carefully consider how you feel after ingesting it, then *you* decide. I've tried it at different times, and it does not work for me.

What is called "delayed pattern milk allergy" is not obvious but produces chronic distress that is seldom diagnosed, except maybe as your imagination. Unfortunately, children are assumed to outgrow lactose intolerance when they haven't.[9] Patterns of illness change and parents, as well as doctors, can be confused about what is happening. Milk/lactose intolerance is especially dangerous because it is so hard to diagnose and mimics other illnesses. Studies have been, and are being done, to help understand the chemical/biological reactions to milk, but none that I know of are working to create a tolerance for milk.

Diet and other aspects of day-to-day living

There are aspects of daily living and milk/lactose intolerance that do not mesh well. What to do when dining out at a restaurant or friend's home, for instance. We know that lactose intolerance doesn't kill immediately. It's not scary to other people, like a shellfish or peanuts, or a serious allergy to milk would be. But it does make one ill and can become serious. Should we just put up with occasional discomfort and eat whatever is put before us? Or should we simply decline all engagements where food may be part of the occasion? No—just eat whatever is safe for you. If you don't, you will be out of sorts and you will hurt later.

Don't decline invitations because you will cause "extra work" or "trouble."

If people don't care to take a little extra time for you, they won't invite you in the first place. But—it is up to you to let the hostess or host know that you are limited in what you can eat; no one is a mind reader. You wouldn't serve a friend walnuts if you have been told that he/she cannot tolerate tree nuts—right?

Restaurants can be a problem with any food allergy and milk or lactose intolerance is no exception. But don't let your food limitations stop you; enlist the aid of the restaurant personnel. Most will be understanding and sympathetic. If a waitperson does not know what is in a particular dish, have them check with the chef or cook. If they don't know either, have a fresh salad or fruit plate. If you want breakfast out, and the eggs are fried in butter or margarine, ask for poached eggs. Make certain they cook them in water; a few people use milk for poached eggs. Tell them not to dab butter on the eggs (some cooks do), or on toast served with them. Some cooks put the eggs on top of buttered toast as a matter of habit. If there is no lactose-free bread, tell them to hold the toast. Many commercial English muffins and bagels are made with milk—be aware of that. If the bread is milk-free, tell them absolutely no butter, and remember, no margarine unless they have the ingredients and you can see that there are no milk by-products. Most jellies are fine. *If a meal comes out wrong—send it back.* I've had to do this frequently, especially when traveling. It's okay, no restaurant owner, cook, or chef wants to have a customer become ill because of a simple misunderstanding.

Other things to remember? Ask if they put cheese in the spaghetti sauce. Are the bread sticks made with milk? What do they serve that is milk and lactose free? Make sure that others understand what lactose and milk and milk by-products means. I have had people say, "That food is okay, it only uses dried milk." Others say, "That's no good, it has eggs in it." At that point you can help them understand and they will be better informed next time the situation arises. There is a lactose guide on pages 253–254.

Latté or coffees? Perhaps you've checked with some of the stores and the clerk said yes, we use a nondairy creamer. However, follow up the question with this one: Do you use separate steamers, or wash the machine between milk and the non-milk? I have, and the answer has always been "no," with a look of sheer dumbfoundedness—they never thought about that. Don't be shy about asking, then purchase black coffee if you want something.

Typically, Japanese, Korean, Chinese and some other Oriental restaurants don't use milk in their cooking. You will find that European foods tend to be heavily milk-based. Food prepared in India and Vietnamese restaurants may use milk that is not noticeable at first glance. Ask! Also, don't assume because a restaurant seems to be kosher or pareve that there will be no problem. If it is not owned and run by a serious adherent of Judaism, they may not obey the laws of kashrut absolutely; ask to be safe.

Can I rely on kosher symbols to determine if a product is milk-free?

The Jewish community uses a system of product markings to indicate whether a food is kosher, or accordance with Jewish dietary rules. There are two kosher symbols that can be of help for those with a milk allergy: A "D," or the word *dairy*, on a label next to "K" or "U" (usually found near the product name) indicates presence of milk protein, and a "DE" on a label indicates the product was produced on equipment shared with dairy.

If the product contains neither meat nor dairy products, it is pareve. Pareve-labeled products are milk-free according to religious specifications. *Be aware that under Jewish law a food product may be considered pareve even if it contains a very small amount of milk.* Therefore, a product labeled as pareve could potentially have enough milk in it to cause a reaction in a milk-allergic individual.

What else?

Once you are no longer ingesting lactose you will feel much better, but you will still be susceptible to other health problems. You must be sure that you and your doctor are aware of what is in the medicines you may need to take. Most medicines today are based on lactose and some have casein. If you're not careful, the medicine can make you sicker. I've asked both the doctor and the pharmacist to check medications for me. At times we've found it difficult to find appropriate medicines without lactose. Be aware also that over-the-counter products can contain lactose, casein, or some other milk by-product. Check the various items you use such as toothpaste, allergy medications, pain pills, vitamins, etc.

Hospitalization may pose a problem, also. If you do have to be hospitalized, plan ahead if possible. Perhaps you can speak with the staff nutritionist in advance. It should help to ensure that you will not be given milk-laden food while there. If that is not an option, be very careful of what you ask for from the hospital's menu. Perhaps, if you are extremely sensitive, you will want to have food brought in. It may seem strange, but you will get better sooner if you're not subjected to foods that cause you problems.

Read labels

This is a common sense, basic cookbook with recipes based on what is available at any modern grocery store. Being milk/lactose intolerant does not mean that you can only shop at specialty stores; it *does* mean that you have to read labels—carefully. And do remember, companies will change ingredients from time to time. That means you have to *keep* reading labels, and if something causes trouble, avoid it. If the label says "flavorings," "natural flavoring," or "artificial flavoring," but not what the flavoring is, I would avoid it. At this time, manufacturers and food processors do not have to list any ingredient that is less than 2 percent of the whole. You can contact the manufacturer and find out what is in a particular product. You're not asking for trade secrets, all you have to ask is "does that small percentage, or the unnamed additions, have milk or milk by-products?" Then expect an answer. If one is not forthcoming, perhaps you shouldn't use the product. Another good source of food ideas? The vegan cookbooks.

When purchasing food, think of the possible problems. Many in-store delis cut the lunchmeat and cheeses on the same slicers. They usually do not wash the blade between foods, only wipe it off, and sometimes not even that. A wiping action does not remove the cheese residue or the lactose. You can ask that the store change their procedures, but it is unlikely to happen. In fact, a store that shall remain unnamed here, advertised the use of separate machines, but did not adhere to their own rules. Watch to make sure of what is actually happening. The store was busy and the clerks simply did not think; they used the slicing stations interchangeably. Throughout the book and the recipes you will find constant reminders to *read the label*. That is what you must do for yourself or the person you cook for. You will find other important information at the end of the recipes.

One more thought. The predigestants do not work for me. Even taking several, I still cannot comfortably tolerate milk in any form. When I have inadvertently gotten milk or lactose somewhere, and it happens, I have discovered a source of help. I find that taking a very small amount of vinegar helps to ease the pain. The vinegar appears to act as an acid that I, at least, am lacking. I don't know if it will help you. But hey—if it works. . . .

Again—read the label!

Almost any food can have lactose, or other milk by-products. Whey solids and casein, for instance, are used as an inexpensive filler in a wide variety of foods. It can be found in breads, cookies, syrups, canned meats and vegetables, frozen dinners, and more. *Read labels!* For instance, I suffered intermittent distress for several days until my daughter read the label on a dill pickle jar. I had not found our usual brand, nor did I read the label—I now know that at least one brand of dills has lactic acid in them. So do green olives and most maraschino cherries. Lactic acid is a substance that comes from souring milk. Lactic acid is not lactose, however, it is a milk by-product, and you may or may not be sensitive to it. It's something to be aware of and to think about.

Some cereals have both whey solids and dry milk solids. *Read the labels.* Kosher products labeled "pareve" are lactose-free and may be safe (see pg. 9). Many snack foods have milk by-products and some sodas (pops) as well. If a label says it has "natural" or "artificial" flavors, be aware of how you feel after ingesting the product for the first time.

You decide

Make reading labels a habit and check frequently on your old standbys. There are times when a change in a product you have come to rely on as safe can cause serious problems.

In the late '70s, the U.S. Congress passed a bill to require strict labeling of all ingredients, or at least most of them if over a certain percentage of the whole. As producers became aware of the numbers of people, not only those who are milk or lactose intolerant, who need to know what is in all products they eat, labeling is becoming more accurate; however, not 100 percent. If you or the person you prepare meals for find a particular food questionable, don't use it.

Intolerant people do not all have the same reactions, some are far less sensitive than others. A milk by-product may be in such small percentages as not to be required on the label. However, even a minute amount of the by-product can cause a severely milk-intolerant person distress. Be your own judge. Where you or the person you care about is concerned, you are the decision maker about what product will be used in meal preparations.

Food preferences are acquired

There are items in this book that are substitutes for foods that children like. I want to make a strong point about something here. People who are accustomed to milk products may not like the taste of nondairy substitutes. *Don't tell that to the child who has no choice.* I have friends who have made a wry face about my cereal "milk" and said, "That doesn't taste right to me. How can you eat it?"

Don't do that folks, especially not to children, nor even to adults who have no choice—*just don't say anything.* Remember, many tastes are acquired, such as for spinach. And personally, I still don't like liver and onions.

We all need good food and calcium

These recipes are good for everyone, not, as some might say, "some gathering of zwieback marvels served with weak tea." Family members and guests can drink milk with their meal, or have cheese on a salad, burger, or sandwich. Milk can be a good source of calcium and protein for those who can tolerate it well. Everyone, even those who tolerate milk, should be aware that animal protein should be consumed in moderation (see pg. 255).

Those who cannot ingest milk in any form may need to supplement their calcium. Preferably by a balanced diet, but if that's not possible, I don't suggest antacid tablets. I've yet to find one with vitamin D. I feel that if someone needs tummy comforters regularly, he needs to either be more careful about what is being ingested, or find out why he is hurting.

If you choose to use calcium tablets to make up for lack of calcium in your diet, get calcium with vitamin D so the calcium will be properly absorbed into your system. The recipes in this book are well balanced, and I've noted good sources of calcium. Nonetheless, I can't force anyone to eat the fresh vegetables or other calcium-rich foods available. I can only make the suggestion.

Milk/lactose intolerant? Allergy?

The recipes that start from scratch in this collection use a minimum of fat, and will call for less salt than you may be used to using with standard recipes.

Over the years I have found that I can better tolerate foods with less salt and fat than foods which use amounts suggested in most standard recipes.

I also don't tolerate high sugar foods very well. It would seem that the inability to digest milk sugar also limits my ability to efficiently utilize other sugars as well. Perhaps your biological system will be happier with less of the aforementioned culprits, too.

Where practicable, there are recipes in this book that ask you to choose the amount of sugar you will use. The reason being the same for most of us; we don't do well with sugars in large quantities. The finished product may not be to your liking if you do use less sugar, so again, it's up to you.

Whys and wherefores

Most people have formed cooking habits before they, or a person they are responsible for, were found to be lactose intolerant. This set of recipes may be a major change from your present method of meal preparation.

For instance, if you want to fry eggs for breakfast, you will find a suggestion for heating the pan, spraying it with a vegetable shortening, and then using a tablespoon or two of water rather than fat. The eggs are very good and the habit of frying in butter or bacon fat is all that needs to be considered. You will find that sautéing vegetables with water and a nondairy margarine in a covered pan, is as good as "sautéing in fat or oil to cover the bottom of pan."

None of these recipes is written is stone, however. Each individual should prepare foods in whatever manner is personally preferable. Just be aware that small changes in cooking habits can make big changes in one's physical comfort. That is the main thrust of this book—be aware and experiment. Most any dietary limitation can be served with a tasty variety of foods that are readily available.

For those who must cook with no milk, key words are put in quotation marks. Rather than using brand names for lactose-free milk substitutes, this book calls for "milk," "butter," etc. I know from experience that brand names are not always found everywhere.

"Milk" does not mean only the liquid product obtained from cows, or even goats, it has many other names (see pg. 254). Be certain, if you are severely sensitive or allergic, to read labels to avoid milk and all milk by-products.

These recipes are good simple fare for all family members or guests. I hope they will help a lot of people to feel more comfortable physically, be able to think more clearly, and feel their best emotionally as well.

"butter" - milk-free margarine with the same fat content as butter.

"buttermilk" - 2 tablespoons fresh lemon juice, plus "milk" to make 1 cup.

butter substitute – find a product with at least 80 percent fat. If not available use a combination of margarine and shortening.

brown bananas – can still be used though very ripe; use less sugar, ripening increases banana natural sugars.

chocolate - read the label on chips, semi-sweet, unsweetened, and sweet chocolate. Always melt chocolate in a double boiler or over low heat to prevent burning or scorching.

"cream" - regular nondairy creamer with high fat content.

flour - presifted white flour.

heat skillet, then spray with vegetable spray - the same rule applies for oil. Heat the skillet, then add cooking medium. Keeps medium from becoming too hot or burning before cooking process begins.

julienne - to cut food into thin match-like strips.

line pans with waxed paper - when baking cakes instead of spraying or greasing the pan, line it with a sheet of waxed paper that has been cut to fit the bottom of the pan. When cake is cooled loosen the sides with a table knife and peel the paper from the bottom. Layers are nice and even using this method.

margarine - milk-free, lactose-free margarine or butter-flavored shortening if tolerated.

mayonnaise - some contain various forms of milk or lactose, so read the label.

"milk" - liquid nondairy creamer. Make sure it is milk/lactose free. My product of choice is Mocha Mix nondairy Creamer®. I find the taste most acceptable, and it is **not** packaged on a line that is also used for cow's milk.

Mocha Mix® - A nondairy frozen dessert much like ice cream but milk-free. Used in "Ice Cream" Pies.

nondairy - does not always mean milk-free, there is milk *protein* in many items marked milk-free. Read the labels carefully.

nondairy/whipped topping - read the label and choose one with no cream.

oats - uncooked rolled oats.

oil - vegetable oil or olive oil.

preheat - the oven should always be preheated when baking.

punch-down - after dough has risen, push down with fist to release air bubbles.

remove bread from pan immediately – to wire racks to allow proper cooling and prevent sogginess.

ring of foil or brown paper – tear foil or brown paper a little larger than pie; fold in fourths and cut a small area from center. Unfold and place on pie during baking to prevent a burnt crust.

shortening + "butter" - butter-flavored shortening and "butter." If severely milk intolerant, do not use butter-flavored shortening; use plain shortening or margarine with same fat content as butter.

"soured milk" - 2 tablespoons vinegar, plus "milk" to make 1 cup.

tender-crisp - cook just until done; serve while the vegetables are still crisp or firm.

tests done - a clean stainless steel table knife will come out clean when custard pies are done. For cakes and quick breads a toothpick will come out clean. Yeast breads will sound hollow when thumped lightly with a finger.

MOCHA MIX® NONDAIRY CREAMER VS. MILK
CALORIE COMPARISON
(PER 8-OZ. SERVING; CALORIES APPROXIMATE)

2% milk . . . . *140 calories*
Original Mocha Mix®. . . . . *160 calories*
Fat Free Mocha Mix® . . . . *80 calories*

12-oz. package chocolate chips	=	***2 cups of chips***
14-oz. package coconut	=	*5½ cups, loosely packed*
18 squares graham crackers	=	***1½ cups of crumbs***
10-oz. package shelled walnuts	=	*2½ cups of nuts*
2-lb. package powered sugar	=	***7½ cups of sugar***

Meats & Main Dishes

✖ ✖ ✖ ✖ ✖ ✖ ✖ ✖ ✖ ✖ ✖ ✖ ✖ ✖

Roast Beef ✖ Pot Roast ✖ Oven Beef Stew ✖ Beef Stew Variation ✖ Pot Roast with Vegetables ✖ Beef Stew ✖ Beef Stew with Dumplings ✖ Steak and Mushroom Sauce ✖ Chili—Fast! ✖ Quick Chop Suey with Ground Beef ✖ Ground Beef with Rice and England Boiled Dinner ✖ Corn Beef and Cabbage ✖ Glazed Corn Beef ✖ Stuffed Pork Chops ✖ Roast Pork Loin ✖ Hearty Chops and Rice ✖ Butterfly Pork Chops ✖ Sweet and Sour Pork ✖ Roast Turkey ✖ Bread Stuffing ✖ Stuffing with Lemon Roger's Stir-Fried Chicken ✖ Stir-Fried Beef ✖ Chicken and Noodles ✖ Chicken and Dumplings ✖ Quick Baked Fish ✖ Fish and Orange ✖ Fish and Stuffing ✖ Broiled Fish ✖ Boston Baked Beans with Ham ✖ Steamed Rice ✖ Simple Green Rice ✖ Pasta ✖ Macaroni Goulash ✖ Spaghetti Pasta with Hot Dogs ✖ AND MORE . . .

✖ ✖ ✖ ✖ ✖ ✖ ✖ ✖ ✖ ✖

Though this is not a vegetarian cookbook, I don't suggest meat at every meal nor every day. Whether one has problems with milk or not, meats should be eaten sparingly (see calcium section on pg. 255).

As a general rule for roasting meats, place the fat side up on a rack in an open pan. Set the oven temperature at 325° for beef and veal and at 350° for pork roasts. Preheating the oven is not absolutely necessary for long-cooking meats and main dishes, but it is for any other baking. Keep that in mind and use your preference as the deciding factor here in the first section. If you want to be energy efficient, don't preheat for meats.

When browning meats, heat the pan *then spray* with a vegetable shortening. If you prefer to brown in the traditional way, I suggest using vegetable or olive oil or a vegetable shortening sparingly.

Fresh meats and fresh vegetables have a flavor that does not need a lot of additional spices to be enjoyable. The combinations of vegetables and/or seasonings in the following recipes are all good, and I am sure you will enjoy them. However, don't be timid about trying a favorite spice or a favorite vegetable combination of your own. These recipes lend themselves to change and experimentation to complement your own tastes and preferences.

To Roast Beef

Beef roast of size needed; no seasoning is needed, but sprinkle with salt and pepper to taste. Spray roasting pan and rack with vegetable spray; place meat fat side up on rack in open pan. Roast at 325° as suggested below.

	minutes per pound	*thermometer temperature*
Rare	.22–26	140°
Medium	.27–30	160°
Well done	.33–36	170°

For rolled roast add 10 minutes per pound.

Pot Roast

1   3-pound rump (or other   ½ to 1 cup water
cut of beef)

1. Choose a pan with a tightly fitting cover; heat and then spray well with vegetable spray.
2. Brown meat on all sides; add water and cover. Simmer for 2½–3 hours, adding water as needed.

Or roll roast in seasoned flour:

½ cup flour   ½ teaspoon garlic powder (or
½ teaspoon salt   paprika if preferred)
¼ teaspoon fresh ground pepper

Proceed as above, except use a small amount of oil to brown well.

✖   ✖   ✖   ✖   ✖

Oven Beef Stew

2   pounds stew beef (½″ pieces)   ½ large rutabaga, diced
2   cups diced carrots   ½ teaspoon salt, optional
2   cups chopped celery   ½ teaspoon fresh ground pepper
1   large chopped onion   1 tablespoon dry mustard
4   medium potatoes with skins,   1 tablespoon instant tapioca,
washed and diced   optional—thickens stew if used

1. Spray a large pot with vegetable spray; place all ingredients in pot or slow cooker; sprinkle with spices and tapioca. Mix well.
2. Cover and bake at 275° for 4½–5 hours. This is slow cooking; stirring is not necessary.

Beef Stew Variation

2	pounds stew beef	2	medium carrots, diced
4	cups water	2	stalks celery, diced
4	beef bouillon cubes	1	small parsnip, diced
1	small turnip, diced	1	green bell pepper, diced
2	medium onions, diced	4	red potatoes, cubed

Proceed as above. Use tapioca, if preferred, to thicken broth.

Pot Roast with Vegetables

1	4- to 5-pound beef roast	2	bay leaves
2	large onions, quartered	4	1arge potatoes, quartered
4	large carrots, quartered	1	small parsnip, diced
4 to 6	celery stalks, cubed	½	rutabaga, diced

Proceed as with Pot Roast (see pg. 19), but allow 3½–4 hours for larger roast; 30–45 minutes before roast is done, add prepared vegetables and fresh ground pepper.

Variation: Add green bell pepper, diced fresh tomatoes, or small whole onions. Using an ovenproof pan with a tight cover, combine all ingredients and cook in the oven at 275° for 4-5 hours for a 5- to 6-pound roast.

Beef Stew

2	pounds cubed stew beef	1	bay leaf
4	cups beef broth *	4	large carrots, chunked
1	teaspoon Worcestershire sauce	3	medium potatoes, chunked
1	clove garlic, minced	2	medium onions, chopped
			2 stalks celery, chunked

1. Spray large pot with vegetable spray; place all ingredients in pot and stir to combine. Bring to a simmer.

2. Cover and simmer over low heat 4–5 hours or until meat is tender.

* *Or use 4–5 beef bouillon cubes and 4 cups water.*

Variation: Spray pan with vegetable spray and brown the meat; add 4 cups hot water and bouillon cubes, simmer for 2–2½ hours. Dice vegetables and add to meat and liquid during last 30–45 minutes. Add more water if necessary. No salt is needed, bouillon cubes are salty. This version gives crisper vegetables and the length of cooking time will depend on how tender you prefer your vegetables.

Beef Stew with Dumplings

1½ pounds stew beef (or chuck), cut into 1″ cubes	¼ cup chopped parsley
¼ cup flour	2 bay leaves
2 tablespoons oil	½ teaspoon fresh ground pepper
1 cup sliced onion	1½ cups cubed carrots
2 garlic cloves, minced	½ cup sliced celery
5 cups water	2 cups cubed potatoes
	½ cup chopped green bell pepper

Dumpling Mix

1½ cups flour	3 tablespoons shortening
¼ teaspoon salt	¾ cup "milk"
2 teaspoons baking powder	

1. Dredge beef in flour. Spray large pan with vegetable spray and brown the beef in oil. Remove meat from pan and set aside.
2. Cook onion and garlic in the oil until tender, adding a tablespoon or two of water if needed, then return meat to pan. Add water, parsley, bay leaves, and pepper; bring to a simmer and cover.
3. Simmer 1 hour, stirring occasionally.
4. Add vegetables, return to simmer, and cook 15 minutes. Add more water if needed to cook dumplings. Meanwhile, mix dry ingredients for

dumplings. Cut in shortening and blend in "milk." After the vegetables have simmered about 15 minutes, (dip spoon into stew liquid then into dumpling mixture), drop dumplings by tablespoonful onto bubbling stew. Simmer uncovered 10 minutes. Cover with domed lid and simmer 10 minutes more.

5. Serve immediately.

Steak and Mushroom Sauce

1	1½-pound round steak (or stew beef)	2	cans beefy mushroom soup (read the label)
1	medium onion, chopped	1	clove garlic, minced (or ¼–½ teaspoon garlic powder)
2	4-oz. cans mushroom stems and pieces + liquid		Pepper and salt to taste

1. Heat skillet; spray with vegetable spray. Cut meat into bite-sized pieces and brown.
2. Add remaining ingredients; cover and simmer until tender, stirring occasionally, 2½–3 hours. Add a little water near end of cooking if you want a thinner sauce.

Beef and Bell Pepper

2	pounds round steak or stew beef	¼	teaspoon salt
2	celery stalks, sliced	2	tablespoons cornstarch combined with ¼ cup cold water
1	medium onion, sliced	2	medium green bell peppers, cut into bite-sized pieces
1	cup cold water		
¼	teaspoon fresh ground pepper		Hot cooked rice

1. Heat skillet; spray with vegetable spray. Brown meat thoroughly.
2. Remove meat to baking dish sprayed with vegetable spray; keep warm.
3. Place celery and onion in skillet with ¼ cup water and cook until tender, stirring occasionally. Stir in ¾ cup water and salt and pepper; bring to a

boil. Add combined cornstarch and water mixture and boil 2 minutes, stirring constantly.

4. Pour sauce over meat in baking dish; cover and bake at 375° for 1¼ hours, or until meat is fork-tender. Occasionally baste meat with the sauce.
5. Remove cover; add green bell pepper to meat mixture and mix in well. Bake uncovered 15 minutes longer.
6. Serve over hot rice.

- Serves 8 -

✖   ✖   ✖   ✖   ✖

Fork-Tender Swiss Steak

1 *3-pound round steak, 2″ thick*	¼ *teaspoon salt*
1 *cup flour*	2 *tablespoons olive oil*
¼ to ½ *teaspoon fresh ground pepper*	2 *onions, sliced*
	2 *cups diced fresh tomatoes* *

1. Place steak on cutting board. Combine flour and seasonings, sprinkle some on steak. Pound flour into meat with meat hammer or edge of a heavy saucer. Continue by turning and pounding flour into meat until all the flour is used.
2. Heat large skillet; spray with vegetable spray. Place oil in skillet and brown onions. Remove onions and brown steak on both sides. Place onions on top of meat; add tomatoes, cover, and cook slowly for about 3 hours, until fork-tender. **Or** bake at 350° until tender.

* Use canned tomatoes if fresh aren't available.

Swiss Steak

1 1½-pound round steak, about ¾″ thick	1 carrot, shredded
1 medium onion, sliced	¼ to ½ cup flour seasoned with fresh ground pepper
1 stalk celery, diced	1 15-oz. can tomato sauce

1. Cut the steak into serving pieces; place on counter or cutting board, and sprinkle with flour. Pound the flour into the meat with a meat hammer or edge of saucer until all flour is used.
2. Place meat and vegetables in a pan sprayed with vegetable spray and cover with tomato sauce; combine well. Bring mixture to a simmer. Cover and cook over low heat for 2½–3 hours or until meat is tender.

✻　✻　✻　✻　✻

To Broil Meats

Spray the broiler pan and rack with vegetable spray for ease of clean-up. Arrange the rack so the meat is 3–5″ from the heat. Broil until the meat is browned on one side then turn halfway through cooking time to brown the other side.

Preheat an electric broiler, but it is not necessary to preheat a gas broiler.

After broiling meat, season to taste and serve immediately on a preheated platter to keep meat hot.

Suggested Broiling Time for Steaks

	1″ thick	2″ thick
Rare	4–5 minutes each side	14–16 minutes each side
Medium	5–6 minutes each side	16–18 minutes each side
Well done	7–8 minutes each side	18–20 minutes each side

Broiled Round Steak

1	1½-pound round steak	½	medium onion, sliced
½	cup oil	1	clove garlic, crushed
½	cup wine vinegar	½	teaspoon thyme
2	tablespoons steak sauce	½	teaspoon fresh ground pepper
	(read the label)	¼	teaspoon salt

1. Trim excess fat from meat and **marinate in mixture 4 hours or overnight.**
2. Combine all ingredients except steak.
3. Preheat broiler if electric; spray broiler pan with vegetable spray and place meat on rack. Broil to desired doneness, using marinade to baste and turning only once, halfway through the cooking time.

Broiled Marinated Chuck Steak

1	2½- to 3-pound chuck steak, about 1½" thick	3	tablespoons Worcestershire sauce
		2	tablespoons vegetable oil
¾	cup soy sauce	1	teaspoon ground ginger
¼	cup vinegar	½	teaspoon fresh ground pepper
¼	cup brown sugar		

1. Trim excess fat from steak. Mix all ingredients except the steak in a 9 x 13" dish or in a large plastic bag. Add steak; cover completely or close; **place in refrigerator to marinate about 4 hours or overnight**, turning meat occasionally if using a dish.
2. Preheat broiler if electric. Spray broiler and rack with vegetable spray and place steak on rack about 3–5" from heat. Brush meat frequently with marinade and cook about 30 minutes for medium rare, turning only once.

- Serves 6–10 -

Lemon Flank Steak

1	pound flank steak	¼	cup water
3	tablespoons fresh lemon juice	¼	teaspoon dill weed
1	tablespoon vegetable oil	¼	teaspoon fresh ground pepper

1. Combine all but steak. Trim steak; place in dish, or plastic bag and pour marinade over steak, coating completely.
2. **Cover and refrigerate 6–8 hours or overnight**, turning meat at least once if in a dish.
3. Preheat broiler if electric. Spray broiler with vegetable spray. Place meat 3–4" from heat and broil 10–14 minutes, or to desired doneness. Brush occasionally with marinade and turn meat once, halfway through the cooking time.

> ### GENERAL RULE
> *Carve broiled steak thinly across the grain.*
> ✗ ✗ ✗ ✗ ✗ ✗ ✗

Oven Barbecue Steaks

1	3-pound round steak, ¾" thick	½	cup vinegar
1	small onion, chopped	1	tablespoon prepared mustard
¾	cup catsup	1	tablespoon Worcestershire sauce
¾	cup water	¼	teaspoon fresh ground pepper
		1	tablespoon brown sugar

1. Cut meat into serving-sized pieces. Heat large skillet, spray with vegetable spray and brown the meat; remove to baking dish sprayed with vegetable spray. Add remaining ingredients to skillet and simmer for 5 minutes.
2. Pour the mixture over meat; cover and bake at 350° for 2 hours or until meat is tender.

Variations:

BBQ Hamburgers: *For hamburgers use only ¼ cup vinegar (rice vinegar is good, but experiment) in the sauce recipe. Cook the patties in a skillet until firm; remove fat from skillet. Add the sauce, cook 15-20 minutes to allow flavor to meld with the meat.*

Broiled Hamburgers: *Broil 3-5″ from heat; turn once. Season and serve.*

Note: *If your broiled burgers are not juicy add ½ cup of water per 1 pound of ground meat; mix in bowl before forming patties.*

✖ ✖ ✖ ✖ ✖

Meatballs

1½ pounds ground beef	¼ cup chopped green bell pepper
⅔ cup rolled oats	1 cup salsa (or catsup)
1 small onion, chopped	¼ teaspoon fresh ground pepper
1 egg, lightly beaten	

1. Mix all ingredients; shape into balls using about 1 tablespoon mixture for each.
2. Spray a baking dish with vegetable spray and bake the meatballs for 20-25 minutes until done.

For Meat Loaf: *Use meatball ingredients. Spray a loaf pan with vegetable spray; press above mixture in pan. Bake 1½ hours or until done. Drain fat, remove loaf to board or platter, and slice.*

Note: *To add flavor to most any ground beef dish, add ½ pound of ground sausage for each pound of ground beef.*

Sweet & Sour Meatballs

1½ pounds grounds beef	½ cup brown sugar
⅔ cup crushed cracker crumbs	1 13-oz. can crushed pineapple
⅓ cup minced onion	⅓ cup vinegar
1 egg	1 tablespoon soy sauce
¼ teaspoon ginger	⅓ cup chopped green bell pepper
¼ cup mayonnaise (read the label)	Hot cooked rice
2 tablespoons cornstarch	

1. Crush cracker crumbs. Combine first 6 ingredients, shape into balls using about 1 tablespoon mixture for each. Heat skillet, spray with vegetable spray, and cook meatballs until browned all around. Remove from skillet and keep warm; drain fat from skillet.
2. Drain pineapple, reserve liquid. Combine cornstarch and brown sugar. Stir in pineapple juice, vinegar, and soy sauce until smooth. Pour into skillet and heat to boiling, stirring constantly; boil until thickened, about 1 minute.
3. Add meatballs, crushed pineapple, and bell pepper. Heat thoroughly.
4. Serve over hot rice.

Meat Loaf

1½ pounds ground beef	½ teaspoon garlic powder
25 saltine crackers, crushed	½ cup grated carrot
1 8-oz. can tomato sauce	½ cup chopped celery
2 eggs, lightly beaten	⅓ cup chopped onion
1 teaspoon marjoram	⅓ cup chopped green bell pepper
¼ teaspoon fresh ground pepper	

1. Crush cracker crumbs; blend all ingredients thoroughly.
2. Spray loaf pan with vegetable spray and press meat mixture into it.
3. Bake at 350° for 1½ hours or until done.

- Serves 6-8 -

Meat Loaf II

1½ pounds ground beef
1 medium onion, chopped
1 small carrot, grated
1 stalk celery, chopped
1 egg, lightly beaten

½ cup rolled oats
¼ cup wheat germ, optional
1 clove garlic, minced
½ cup mayonnaise (read the label)
Salt and pepper, if desired

1. In a large bowl mix all ingredients.
2. Spray loaf pan with vegetable spray and place mixture into it and press firmly. Bake at 350° for 1 to 1½ hours or until done.

- Serves 6-8 -

✖ ✖ ✖ ✖ ✖

Good Chili-Fast!

1 pound ground beef
1 28-oz. can tomatoes
3 15-oz. cans kidney beans *
1 teaspoon garlic powder
1 tablespoon onion powder

1 tablespoon flour
½ teaspoon fresh ground pepper
½ teaspoon sugar
½ teaspoon salt
1 to 3 tablespoons chili powder,
     or to taste

1. Brown beef and drain fat. Meanwhile, place tomatoes into a large pan, crush or break if whole; add beans and bring to a simmer.
2. Combine flour and spices well and add to drained beef; mix well.
3. Transfer beef/spice mixture to tomato and beans, mix well, and bring to a simmer. Cook for 10 minutes.
4. Serve hot.

- Serves 6-8 -

* Or use a combination of beans.

Quick Chop Suey with Ground Beef

1	pound ground beef	1	beef bouillon cube
2	cups sliced celery	1/4	cup soy sauce
1/2	cup sliced onion	1/4	teaspoon salt
1 1/2	cups water	1	16-oz. can bean sprouts
2	tablespoons cornstarch	4	cups cooked rice

1. Heat skillet; spray with vegetable spray. Cook celery, onion, and meat until meat is browned, drain fat.
2. Blend cornstarch with water until smooth and stir into beef mixture. Add bouillon, soy sauce, and salt.
3. Heat, stirring constantly, until sauce is thick and clear. Stir in sprouts; heat about 3 minutes.
4. Serve over hot rice.

- Serves 4-6 -

Ground Beef with Rice & Vegetables

1	pound ground beef	1	cup uncooked white rice
1	medium chopped onion	2	cups water
1/2	cup chopped green bell pepper	2	cups chopped fresh tomatoes
1/3	cup sliced celery	1/4	teaspoon fresh ground pepper
1	small clove garlic, minced	1/4	teaspoon salt

1. In a large skillet brown beef and drain. Meanwhile, spray a small covered saucepan with vegetable spray; cook vegetables, except tomatoes, with a small amount of water until tender. Do not overcook.
2. Add vegetables, tomatoes, and remaining ingredients to cooked and drained beef, mixing well; bring to a simmer. Cover and simmer on reduced heat 20–35 minutes (depending on type of rice), until rice is done, stirring occasionally.

- Serves 4-6 -

Quick Stuffed Peppers

4 to 6	large green bell peppers	1	package Spanish Rice mix*
1	pound ground beef	2	cups chopped fresh tomatoes
1	small onion, chopped	2	cups hot water

1. Cut tops from peppers; remove seeds & parboil peppers and tops 4–6 minutes. Meanwhile, in a large skillet brown beef; drain fat. Add Spanish rice and remaining ingredients except peppers and tops; simmer about 15 minutes.
2. Spray appropriate-sized baking dish with vegetable spray and arrange bell peppers so they support each other; fill each with portion of mixture and put a pepper top on each. Cover dish and bake at 350° for 20–25 minutes.

* Read label as directed on the package of Spanish Rice mix for the correct amount of water and for any possible milk or milk by-product such as lactose, sodium caseinate, etc.

Note: Green peppers are good for freezing & reheating; when you make Quick Stuffed Peppers, make some extra.

PARBOILING BELL PEPPERS

Parboiling is to partially cook the peppers in boiling water; then the water can be used as a nutritious stock for beef or vegetable soups.

Not only is the water well flavored, but the vitamins and other nutrients that have leached during the parboiling will be in the soup. (The microwave will create the same results as parboiling, without the water, if you prefer to use it.) Also, since the water for the peppers is boiling you can use it to make peeling the tomatoes much easier. (If you wish to make stock of the water, wash the tomatoes carefully first.) Put the fruit into the boiling water for one minute, then into cold water and simply slip off the skins. Then make soup or store the stock in covered containers in the refrigerator.

x x x x x x x x

Meat Pie

½ cup chopped onion
¼ cup chopped green bell pepper
2 cups diced vegetables, in
    amounts of your choice *
2 cups beef bouillon **

2 cups cooked chopped meat ***
2 tablespoons cornstarch, plus
    ¼ cup cold water
Dough for ½ Biscuit Recipe (see
    pg. 54)

1. Place onion and bell pepper in pan with ¼ cup water and sauté until onion is transparent. Add remaining vegetables and bouillon and bring to a simmer. Simmer 15 minutes.
2. Add cooked meat; bring to boil and add cornstarch mixture. Stir constantly for about 1 minute.
3. Spray a baking dish with vegetable spray and transfer hot mixture to dish then cover with prepared biscuit dough. Place as individual biscuits, or to fit the dish with slits cut to allow steam to escape.
4. Bake at 400° for 20 minutes, or until nicely browned.

  * Celery, peas, carrots, corn, turnips, parsnip, etc.
  ** 2 cups water and 2–3 bouillon cubes according to taste, or canned bouillon. Whichever you use, read the label.
*** This is a good way to use any leftover meat.

Ground Beef Pie

1 pound ground beef
½ cup chopped onion
2 cups fresh green beans,
    cut as desired

1 10-oz. can tomato soup *
1 teaspoon brown sugar
¼ teaspoon fresh ground pepper
¼ teaspoon salt, optional

1. Brown meat and onion in skillet until meat is cooked; remove accumulated fat. Stir in remaining ingredients. Pour into pastry-lined pie pan. Add top crust and remember to cut slits for steam to escape.

2. Bake at 400° for about 25 minutes, or until nicely browned.

Pastry

2	cups flour	1	teaspoon onion powder
⅔	cup shortening	¼ to ⅓ cup cold water

Make as normal double-crust pie (see pg. 220).

* Read the label for milk or milk by-product.

Traditional New England Boiled Dinner

4	pounds corned beef	12	small white onions
5	medium beets	2	pounds cabbage, cored
12 to 16 small potatoes			and quartered
6	small carrots	2	tablespoons minced parsley

1. Place beef in a large pot and cover with water 2" over the top of meat.
2. Bring to boil; skim off any foam that accumulates; cover pot and allow to simmer 3–4 hours, or until fork-tender. Add water if necessary to keep meat covered.

Cook beets separately:
1. Scrub beets; leave about an inch of stem, cover with water and bring to a boil. Simmer ½ to 1 hour (depending on size of beets), until tender.
2. Allow to cool slightly, then slip off skins.

In the meantime prepare the other vegetables:
1. 25–35 minutes before serving, add carrots, onions, and potatoes to pot with meat; return to simmer, then cover and cook 5 minutes.
2. Add cabbage, return to simmer and cook last 15 minutes.
3. To serve, slice beef (across grain) and arrange along center of a heated platter. Surround with vegetables and sprinkle with minced parsley.

Corned Beef & Cabbage

1	3- to 4-pound beef brisket	3	medium carrots, quartered
2	quarts water	2	medium potatoes, quartered
1	6-oz. can tomato sauce	1	medium cabbage, cut in wedges
3	medium onions, quartered		

1. In large pot with cover place corned beef, onions, water, and tomato sauce; bring to a simmer. Cover and simmer 2–2½ hours, until meat is fork-tender.
2. Add potatoes and carrots; return to simmer, cook 10–15 minutes.
3. Add cabbage, simmer another 15 minutes.
4. Remove meat from pot and slice thinly across the grain.
5. Serve with the hot vegetables as above. Cooking time for vegetables always depends on how crisp or tender you like them.

Glazed Corned Beef & Vegetables

1	4- to 6-pound beef brisket	8	small potatoes, washed
1	tablespoon pickling spices	½	pound small Brussels sprouts
⅓	cup orange marmalade	4 to 6	small carrots, sliced
2	tablespoons brown sugar	¼	cup sliced green onion
2	tablespoons prepared mustard	1	small bell pepper, cut in rings

1. Place corned beef in pan; cover with water; add spices and simmer 3–4 hours or until tender. Transfer meat to rack in open roasting pan, reserving liquid.
2. Meantime, prepare glaze. Heat marmalade, brown sugar, and mustard in a small pan; bring to boil, stirring often. Use this mixture to brush over beef. Bake at 350° for 20 minutes, occasionally brushing with glaze.
3. Cook potatoes, carrots, and Brussels sprouts in reserved liquid until tender-crisp, 15–20 minutes, then add green onions, and cook an additional 2–3 minutes.
4. To serve, place sliced beef on heated platter and arrange vegetables around it, using thinly sliced bell pepper rings as garnish for top.

Braised Pork Chops

1" chops . . . . .cook 30–35 minutes
½" chops .cook 20–25 minutes
Thinner than ½" chops . . . . .watch them

1. Trim excess fat from chops. Use skillet with tightly fitting cover to cook slowly and keep moist.
2. Heat skillet; spray with vegetable spray. Brown chops slowly, about 3–4 minutes on each side. Add up to ¼ cup water for thick chops; if/as needed for thin chops.
3. Cover and cook until well done. Season lightly with salt and fresh ground pepper after cooking.

Stuffed Pork Chops

6 pork chops, 1" thick	½ teaspoon sage
1 cup soft bread crumbs	1 cup finely chopped apple
¼ teaspoon fresh ground pepper	½ cup raisins
⅛ teaspoon salt	¼ cup water

1. Trim excess fat from chops; make a pocket in each by cutting into chop along the bone. (Cutting from bone side holds stuffing best.)
2. Mix bread, spices, and fruit; pour water over all and mix well. Stuff about ¼ cup mixture into each chop.
3. Heat large skillet; spray with vegetable spray. Brown chops on both sides. Pour off any drippings. (If well trimmed, there may not be any.)
4. Cover tightly and cook slowly 45 minutes to 1 hour on rangetop, or in 350° oven, until done.
5. Season with salt and pepper before serving if desired.

- Serves 6 -

Variation: *Use Bread Stuffing with sage (see pg. 39). Proceed as above.*

Roast Pork Loin

1   4- to 6-pound pork loin roast

1. Spray roasting pan and rack with vegetable spray for ease of clean-up.
2. Place roast, fat side up, on rack in an open roasting pan. No need to add
   water or cover roast. Roast at 325°
   for 30–35 minutes per pound, or
   2½–3½ hours. If using meat
   thermometer it should read 170°
   when roast is done.

*4- to 6-pound boneless loin roast: treat as
above.*
*7- to 10-pound boneless smoked fully
cooked ham: treat as above.*
Cook 2-2½ hours or to 130–140° on the thermometer.

SAUCES
Plum sauce is very good with roast pork. Orange glaze is nice on a baked ham, and marmalade glaze goes well with ham.
✗ ✗ ✗ ✗ ✗ ✗ ✗

Note: *If you like, brush the roast with your choice of glaze several times during cooking. For sauces and glazes, see pgs. 126–139.*

Hearty Chops & Rice

4	pork chops	2	tablespoons brown sugar
¼	cup sliced celery	½	teaspoon salt
½	cup chopped onion	½	teaspoon basil
2	8-oz. cans tomato sauce	1	cup uncooked white rice
1½	cups water		

1. Trim excess fat from chops. Heat large skillet; spray with vegetable spray.
   Brown the chops well. (Drain fat if any accumulates). Set chops aside,
   keeping warm.
2. Cook onion and celery in skillet until tender, adding small amount of
   water if necessary. Stir in remaining ingredients; add chops and bring to
   a simmer. Cover and simmer 25–30 minutes.

- Serves 4 -

Butterfly Pork Chops

6 to 8 butterfly chops, ¾–1″ thick
¼ cup water

1. Trim excess fat. Heat skillet, spray with vegetable spray. Brown chops well. Add water; cover tightly and simmer 45 minutes to 1 hour, or until done.
2. Remove cover and allow to rebrown if preferred. Season after cooking, as desired.

- Serves 6-8 -

Sweet & Sour Pork

2 pounds boneless pork shoulder, cut into 1″ cubes
3 medium green bell peppers
1 26-oz. can pineapple chunks

¼ cup cornstarch
½ cup sugar
½ cup vinegar
¼ cup soy sauce
3 cups cooked rice

1. Heat skillet; spray with vegetable spray. Brown pork on all sides. Cover pan tightly and cook slowly for 30 minutes, adding a small amount of water if necessary. Meanwhile, remove seeds from bell pepper, cut into 1″ squares and boil 5 minutes in water to cover; save water.
2. Drain pineapple, reserving liquid. Add enough pepper water to pineapple juice to make 1 cup liquid. Combine meat, bell pepper, and pineapple chunks with ¼ cup pepper water, bring to a simmer; cover and simmer 5 minutes.
3. In small sauce pan, mix together cornstarch and sugar; stir in pine-apple/pepper liquid, vinegar, and soy sauce. Bring to boiling point, stirring constantly. Boil about 2 minutes, or until mixture clears. Pour over meat mixture and stir lightly. Simmer 4-5 minutes.
4. Serve with plenty of hot rice.

- Serves 4-6 -

Roast Turkey

Prebasted turkeys are very good, just read the label to be certain that no milk by-product or lactose was used if you are cooking milk-free meals. Most of the prebasted birds that I've seen use a vegetable shortening for basting. It is *not* necessary to rub the cavity with salt prior to roasting. Sprinkle a small amount into the cavity if you wish but it is not a necessity. Stuff just before roasting if you use stuffing.

1. Spray roasting pan with vegetable spray. Place the bird on a rack. After about two-thirds of the suggested roasting time is up, cut the cord or skin that holds the legs to allow the heat to reach the inner portion of the thigh. This insures even cooking of the thicker portions of the bird. (I have forgotten to do this simple task more than once; the bird does not cook as well if left uncut.)

> **GRAVY PACKETS**
>
> *If you are cooking milk-free* **do not** *use the gravy that comes with the birds without first reading the label.*
>
> ✗ ✗ ✗ ✗ ✗ ✗ ✗

2. A 4- to 6-pound bird takes about 3-3½ hours to cook. If using a thermometer it should read 190°. The drumstick will move easily, so it will twist out of joint when done. Be sure to protect fingers when making the twist test. This is slow roasting, so cook thoroughly.

Note: A tent of aluminum foil will help the bird to brown very nicely without basting. Chicken and duck are roasted in the same manner as turkey.

Chicken:	*4–5 lbs.*	*1½–1¾ hours at 375°*
	5+ lbs.	*1¾–2 hours at 375°*
Duck:	*3–5 lbs.*	*3–3½ hours at 325°*
Turkey:	*6–8 lbs.*	*3½–4 hours at 325°*
	8–12 lbs.	*4–4½ hours at 325°*
	12–16 lbs.	*4½–5½ hours at 325°*

Bread Stuffing

¼	cup minced onion	1	teaspoon sage, or to taste
½	cup chopped celery	¼	teaspoon fresh ground pepper
⅓	cup water (or broth)		Poultry seasoning to taste
4	cups bread crumbs		

Bread Stuffing with Lemon

1	cup chopped celery	⅔	cup parsley
¾	cup chopped onion	1	tablespoon grated lemon rind
½	cup water (or broth)	¼	teaspoon fresh ground pepper
10	cups bread crumbs	½	teaspoon salt, optional

1. Spray small skillet with vegetable spray; cook celery and onion in water until onion is translucent. Meanwhile, in large bowl mix bread crumbs and remaining ingredients. Add cooked vegetables and water, mixing thoroughly.
2. Bake 20 minutes at 325°, or use to stuff bird.

Note: *Use more liquid for moist dressing, less for dry.*

Giblet Stuffing*

1. Make bread stuffing except: Simmer heart, gizzard, and neck in water to cover until tender, 1 to 2 hours. Add onion, celery, and liver; cook an additional 15 minutes. Chop giblets and remove meat from neck bones; add meat, vegetables, and liquid to crumbs; mix well.
2. Bake at 325° for 20 minutes, or use to stuff bird.

If lactose intolerant, see asterisked note on pg. 253.

Turkey-Pumpkin Stew

10″ pumpkin (or squash)	1 medium onion, diced
1 tablespoon cornstarch	2 medium carrots, cubed
¼ teaspoon ginger	1 small yellow squash, sliced
1 cup chicken bouillon	¾ pound fresh green beans
2 pounds turkey meat, cubed	

1. Slice 1" from top of pumpkin and reserve for lid. Scoop seeds (roast them if you like) and remove pumpkin until sides are about ¾" thick. Cut into uniform pieces and reserve.

2. Heat a skillet; spray with vegetable spray. Precook turkey cubes, turning to sear all sides. Combine cornstarch and ginger with the bouillon; mix thoroughly. Add reserved pumpkin and rest of ingredients to the turkey and bring to a simmer, stirring constantly. Simmer about 10 minutes.

This is not only a tasty stew it's a fun way to use pumpkins. It's also an unusual recipe that turns out well the first time.

✗ ✗ ✗ ✗ ✗ ✗ ✗

3. Place pumpkin shell on a baking pan and pour the turkey mixture into it, then cover with the reserved lid. Pour about 1 cup of water into the baking pan (not into the pumpkin); bake at 350° for 1-1½ hours until flavors meld and pumpkin pieces are cooked thoroughly.

4. To prevent darkening of the pumpkin skin, cover with foil after half an hour or so.

Cranberry Sauce

	Sugar Free		Sugared
2	packages cranberries	2	packages cranberries
2	cups water	2	cups water
½	cup fructose (or other sugar substitute)	1¼	cups sugar

1. Sort and rinse cranberries. Mix ingredients in saucepan; bring to a simmer and simmer 5–7 minutes, until the skins pop on the berries.
2. Serve hot or cold.

Note: Cranberry sauce is good with turkey and chicken any way you fix them.

✖ ✖ ✖ ✖ ✖

Stir-Fried Chicken

2	cups chicken, cut in strips	1	medium summer squash, sliced thin
2	cups fresh cut green beans	1	medium tomato, sliced thin
2	tablespoons minced onion	¼	teaspoon curry powder
2	stalks celery, sliced		Hot cooked rice
1	medium zucchini, sliced thin		

1. Remove fat, skin, and bones from chicken; cut into strips. Heat skillet; spray with vegetable spray. Cook and stir chicken until it is white. Set aside; keep warm.
2. Place fresh green beans in skillet with small amount of water. Cook, stirring frequently, about 5 minutes. Remove from pan; set aside with chicken; keep warm. Put onion, celery, zucchini, and squash in pan, add a small amount of water. Sprinkle on half of the curry powder and stir while heating for about 3 minutes.
3. Add tomatoes with the remaining curry powder and stir while heating vegetables through, about 2 minutes; return beans and chicken to pan and heat thoroughly.
4. Serve immediately over hot rice.

Broiled Chicken with Orange Sauce

Broiler chicken, split—as many as you need

1. Preheat broiler if electric. Remove fat and skin from chicken, rinse, and pat dry. Place meaty side down on broiler rack and put in broiler about 5" from heat. Broil, turning every 10 minutes, about 35–40 minutes, or until chicken is tender. You may want to brush with olive oil or melted "butter" during cooking. While chicken is cooking make the Orange Sauce.
2. Serve with hot rice and Orange Sauce.

Orange Sauce

1	11-oz. can mandarin oranges	1/4	cup slivered almonds
1	tablespoon cornstarch	1	tablespoon fresh lemon juice
1/3	cup orange juice	1/4	teaspoon allspice
		1/8	teaspoon ginger

1. Drain oranges and reserve liquid. Blend orange juice, liquid from oranges, and cornstarch in saucepan. Bring to boil, stirring constantly; simmer 2 minutes.
2. Remove from heat; stir in reserved orange pieces, almonds, lemon juice, and spices.
3. Serve hot over chicken.

Roger's Stir-Fried Chicken

2	tablespoons olive oil	1	pound snow pea pods
1	pound chicken, cut in strips	1/3	cup pineapple sweet & sour sauce (read the label)
4 to 5 fresh mushrooms			
1	onion, chopped	1½	tablespoons soy sauce
1	green bell pepper, chopped	1	cup peanuts
			Hot cooked rice

1. Heat olive oil in large skillet. Clean and slice mushrooms. Sauté lightly; remove from skillet; set aside.
2. Cook chicken with about half the onions and ½ tablespoon soy sauce, until chicken is white. Add remaining ingredients and cook over low heat while stirring.
3. Shortly before serving, add the peanuts and mushrooms. Do not overcook the vegetables.
4. Serve over hot rice.

✖ ✖ ✖ ✖ ✖

Stir-Fried Beef

2 tablespoons olive oil	⅓ cup pineapple sweet & sour sauce (read the label)
1 pound beef marinated *	
4 to 5 fresh mushrooms	3 tablespoons soy sauce
1 onion, chopped	1 cup peanuts
1 green bell pepper, chopped	Hot cooked rice
1 pound snow pea pods	

1. In large skillet heat olive oil. Lightly sauté well-cleaned, sliced mushrooms; remove from skillet and set aside.
2. Brown beef in skillet with about half the onions and 1 tablespoon soy sauce.
3. After beef is browned add remaining ingredients and cook over low heat while stirring. Just before serving add mushrooms and peanuts. Do not overcook.
4. Serve over hot rice.

Marinate beef strips in papaya juice with crushed garlic; use enough seasoned juice to cover the meat. Buy marinated beef if you wish, but read the label.

Easy Oven Chicken

¼ to ½ cup olive (or vegetable oil),		1	cup flour
	enough to cover bottom	½	teaspoon salt
	of baking pan evenly	¼	teaspoon fresh ground pepper
1	2- to 3-pound chicken, cut up	2	teaspoons paprika

1. Place oil in 425° oven to preheat. Mix dry ingredients in paper or plastic bag.
2. Remove skin and excess fat from chicken, rinse in cold water, and pat dry with paper towel. Shake 2 to 3 pieces of chicken at a time in bag of seasoned flour, coating each thoroughly.
3. Place chicken in single layer on hot oil, meaty side down. Bake about 20 minutes at 425°. Turn meaty side up and bake about 20 minutes longer, or until done.

Chicken Pot Pie

1	3- to 4-pound chicken, cut up	1	medium onion, chopped
2	bay leaves	1	small green bell pepper, chopped
1	tablespoon parsley flakes	3 to 4	medium potatoes, diced
¼	teaspoon garlic powder	6	cups water
¼	teaspoon fresh ground pepper		Cornstarch and water
½	teaspoon salt		Pastry or biscuit topping
3	stalks celery, sliced		(see pgs. 162 & 220)

1. Remove skin and fat from chicken; rinse with cold water. In a large pot combine water, chicken, and spices and bring to a simmer. Simmer about 50 minutes to 1 hour, or until chicken is tender and the meat is easily separated from the bones.
2. Remove the chicken and add vegetables to the broth; cook for about 15–20 minutes, depending on size of vegetable pieces. Meanwhile, remove the bones from the chicken. Return meat to the broth after the vegetables have cooked.

3. Mix about ¼ cup cornstarch with 1 cup water; use as much as needed to thicken broth to desired consistency.
4. Spray an appropriate-sized baking dish with vegetable spray and place chicken mixture into it; cover with a pastry or biscuit topping. Bake at 450° about 20 minutes, or until crust is browned and completely cooked.

Braised Chicken

1. Remove skin and fat from chicken, rinse in cold water, and pat dry with paper towel. Heat a proper-sized skillet (one that will allow all pieces to be in a single layer after searing) over medium heat; spray with vegetable spray. Sear the dried chicken in the hot pan, turning frequently to sear all around. This is to keep meat moist.
2. When pieces are seared, put all into skillet, add ¼–½ cup water and your choice of seasonings, such as fresh pepper and sage or thyme. Cover and cook on low heat about 15 minutes; turn chicken and add a little more water if necessary. Cover pan and continue cooking another 15 minutes, or until done.
3. Chicken is done when thickest pieces are tender and no trace of pink appears when pricked with fork.

Braised Chicken & Vegetables

2½ pounds chicken pieces	1 large green bell pepper, cut in strips
2 cups sliced onions	
1 clove garlic, minced	¼ teaspoon fresh ground pepper
1 large red pepper, cut in strips *	½ teaspoon thyme (or other seasonings of your choice)

1. Remove skin and fat from chicken, rinse, and dry. Braise as directed above. While chicken is cooking, steam onions in ¼ cup water until translucent.
2. Add minced garlic and pepper strips; cook slightly, adding small amount of water if necessary; season with fresh pepper and thyme.

When chicken has 5–7 minutes left to cook, pour vegetables on top and baste everything with the chicken juices. Cover and finish cooking.

* *Pimiento strips are good if you don't find red bell peppers.*

Quick Chicken Cacciatore

2½ to 3 pounds chicken pieces
1   16-oz. can stewed tomatoes
½   medium onion, minced
½   cup chopped green bell pepper
2   tablespoons chopped parsley

1   clove garlic, minced
½   teaspoon oregano
1   cup sliced ripe olives *
Hot cooked spaghetti

1. Heat large skillet; spray with vegetable spray. Braise chicken. Add remaining ingredients except olives. Bring to a simmer and lower heat. Simmer 25 minutes, add olives, and cook about 10 minutes longer or until chicken is fork-tender.
2. Serve over hot spaghetti.

* ***Do not*** *substitute green olives—most have lactic acid.*

Oriental Chicken

2   chicken breasts—remove skin, fat, and bones
1   cup fresh or frozen peas, thaw if frozen
1   8-oz. can bamboo shoots, drained
2   green onions, sliced

1   tablespoon pimiento, sliced
1   tablespoon cornstarch
1¼ cups chicken bouillon (or water + 2 bouillon cubes)
¼   cup slivered almonds
Hot cooked rice

1. Cut chicken into 1" pieces. Heat skillet; spray with vegetable spray. Cook meat until tender, adding water if necessary.

2. Remove chicken from skillet and keep warm; add vegetables to skillet and cook 1 minute. Sprinkle with cornstarch; add bouillon and simmer until thickened. Add almonds and chicken; heat thoroughly.
3. Serve over hot rice.

Creole Chicken

2	pounds chicken pieces	½	cup chopped onion
1½	cups water	1	teaspoon basil
¾	cup tomato juice	¼	teaspoon fresh ground pepper
1	cup fresh sliced mushrooms	1½	cups quick-cooking rice, uncooked

1. Heat skillet; spray with vegetable spray and brown chicken.
2. Add remaining ingredients except rice.
3. Cover and cook over low heat for 30 minutes.
4. Add uncooked rice and cook an additional 15 minutes or so, stirring occasionally.

✖ ✖ ✖ ✖ ✖

Chicken Cacciatore

2½ to 3 pounds chicken pieces		2	teaspoons oregano
2	medium onions, diced	1	teaspoon basil
2	garlic cloves, minced	2	bay leaves
1	16-oz. can tomatoes	½	teaspoon celery seed
2	6-oz. cans tomato paste	¼	cup water (or white wine)
½	teaspoon salt		Cooked spaghetti (or vermicelli)
½	teaspoon fresh ground pepper		

1. Remove skin, fat, and bones from chicken. Combine all ingredients; bring to a simmer and simmer 2–3 hours, or until chicken is fork-tender.
2. Serve over spaghetti or vermicelli.

Chicken and Noodles

3 to 4 pounds chicken pieces *	½ teaspoon salt
6 cups chicken broth **	½ teaspoon fresh ground pepper
2 carrots, shredded	1 bay leaf
2 onions, diced	1 teaspoon basil
2 stalks celery, diced	1 10-oz. package egg noodles

1. Remove skin, fat, and bones *** from chicken.
2. Place chicken and broth in pot and bring to a simmer. Remove foam if it accumulates. Add remaining ingredients, except noodles, return to simmer; simmer 1½–2 hours, longer if chicken is tough, or until tender.
3. When chicken is tender, bring broth to boil and add noodles; stir well and cook until noodles are just done, 15–20 minutes. Enjoy.

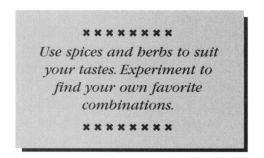

✗ ✗ ✗ ✗ ✗ ✗ ✗
Use spices and herbs to suit your tastes. Experiment to find your own favorite combinations.
✗ ✗ ✗ ✗ ✗ ✗ ✗

* Purchase chicken pieces, or if you prefer, buy a cut-up or whole chicken of appropriate weight.

** Make broth with bouillon cubes if necessary; omit salt.

*** If you prefer, cook chicken with bones in. When meat is tender remove chicken from broth. Bring broth to boil and add noodles to begin cooking them. Meanwhile, remove bones from cooked chicken and return the meat to the pot when noodles have about 5 minutes left to cook.

Chicken and Dumplings

3 to 4 pounds chicken pieces	1 tablespoon minced parsley
2 stalks celery, sliced	½ teaspoon fresh ground pepper
2 medium carrots, shredded	½ teaspoon salt
1 medium onion, minced	2 bay leaves
⅓ cup chopped green bell pepper	Water

1. Remove skin and fat from chicken; place meat, vegetables, and spices in kettle with water to cover. Simmer until chicken is tender 1½–2 hours, or longer if necessary, adding more water if needed.
2. When thoroughly cooked, remove chicken from broth and remove bones. Return meat to pot and bring to boil to cook dumplings.

Dumplings

1½	cups flour	3	tablespoons shortening
2	teaspoons baking powder	¼	cup "milk"
¼	teaspoon salt		

1. Blend dry ingredients; cut in shortening; blend in "milk."
2. Dip spoon into hot broth before dipping up dough to help dumpling slide easily. Slide spoonfuls of dough into chicken and boiling stock.
3. Cook uncovered for 10 minutes, then 10 minutes longer, covered. Use a kettle with a domed lid so moisture does not drip on dumplings.
4. Place dumplings and chicken, if large pieces, on platter or in bowl and keep hot while thickening stock for gravy. Do this quickly; you don't want the dumplings to cool.

Gravy

3	tablespoons cornstarch	¼	cup water for each 2 cups of stock

Mix the cornstarch and cold water thoroughly. Have the stock boiling and carefully stir the mixture into the stock, stirring constantly. Boil 2 minutes.

Variation: Thoroughly mix ½ cup cornstarch with 1 cup cold water. Add a little at a time to boiling stock, stirring constantly, until the desired thickness is reached. Serve over Chicken and Dumplings.

Note: Sometimes the stock is thick enough for gravy, making the gravy step unnecessary. Simply serve and enjoy.

FISH

Fish should be cooked briefly. There is no tough muscle that needs time to become tender, so be careful not to overcook. Fish is done when it can be easily flaked with a fork.

To bake fish, preheat oven to 350°. Spray a shallow baking pan with vegetable spray; sprinkle fish lightly with fresh ground pepper, dot with "butter," and sprinkle overall with fresh lemon juice.

APPROXIMATE BAKING TIMES:

15 minutes per pound for whole fish

20 minutes per pound for fillets

30 minutes per pound for steaks

Tartar Sauce

1 cup mayonnaise *(read the label)*	1 teaspoon fresh lemon juice
¼ cup onion minced	¼ teaspoon paprika
2 to 3 tablespoons minced dill pickle	

Mix all ingredients thoroughly; add "milk" or water for thinner sauce.

Quick Baked Fish

1 pound fish fillets	1 10-oz. can tomato soup
4 slices lemon	*(read the label)*

1. Spray shallow baking dish with vegetable spray. Place fish in single layer and top with lemon slices. Bake 15 minutes at 350°.
2. Add soup and blend with liquid around fish; baste fish gently and bake 10 minutes longer or until done.

Note: If using frozen fillets you may get better flavor if you rinse the fish under cold water and pat dry with paper towel before cooking.

Fish and Orange

1	pound flounder fillets	1	scallion, sliced thinly
¼	teaspoon fresh ground pepper	1	medium tomato, sliced thinly
¼	teaspoon ginger	3	tablespoons minced bell pepper
½	cup fresh orange juice	2	tablespoons "butter," softened
	Juice of 1 lemon	2	oranges, peeled and sliced

1. Place fish in bowl or shallow dish and sprinkle with pepper and ginger. Combine orange and lemon juices, pour over fish; marinate 20 minutes.
2. Spray shallow baking dish with vegetable spray and place fish in it. Save the juices.
3. Place scallion, tomato, and bell pepper on fish, drizzle with melted "butter." Bake at 350° for 15 minutes, then pour the juices over the fish and top with orange slices. Bake an additional 15 minutes, or until fish flakes easily.

- Serves 4 -

✳ ✳ ✳ ✳ ✳

Fish and Stuffing

1. Use whole boned fish, or fillets, and bread stuffing.
2. If using whole fish, stuff the cavity two-thirds full and close with skewers or stitch closed. With fillets, place the stuffing between 2 layers of fish and hold together with toothpicks.
3. Spray a shallow baking dish with vegetable spray. Sprinkle the fish with fresh ground pepper, dot with "butter," and sprinkle with fresh lemon juice if desired. Bake according to time chart, adding 4-5 minutes to assure the stuffing is done.

✳ ✳ ✳ ✳ ✳

To Broil Fish

Spray broiler pan with vegetable spray. Dip fillets in melted "butter" and lemon juice; broil 6" from source of heat for about 4-5 minutes. Turn and broil 4-5 minutes more, or until flaky.

✖ ✖ ✖ ✖ ✖

Salmon Loaf

2 16-oz. cans salmon	3 cups cracker crumbs (read the label)
2 eggs, lightly beaten	2 tablespoons fresh lemon juice
Salmon liquid + enough "milk" to make 1½ cups liquid	2 tablespoons minced onion
	¼ teaspoon fresh ground pepper

1. Spray a 9 x 5" loaf pan with vegetable spray. You do not have to remove bone and skin from salmon,* remove the skin if you prefer.
2. Mix all ingredients well and press lightly into prepared pan. Bake at 350° for 45 minutes.

* Bones in canned salmon are soft and edible, making it an excellent source of calcium.

Seasoned Salmon Loaf

1	large can salmon	1	medium onion, chopped
3	eggs, lightly beaten	1	tablespoon "butter," softened
1½	cups "milk"	1	tablespoon fresh lemon juice
2	cups soft bread crumbs	¼	teaspoon poultry seasoning

1. Drain and flake salmon; mix all ingredients well.
2. Spray loaf pan with vegetable spray and place mixture into it, patting lightly into loaf shape. Bake at 325° for 45–50 minutes.

*Note: Salmon Loaf is good with Dijon mustard or horseradish. And for those with **no** problem ingesting milk, a cheese sauce is good on salmon loaf.*

✖   ✖   ✖   ✖   ✖

Tuna Casserole

1	cup uncooked noodles	½	cup sliced mushrooms
3	cups Medium White Sauce *	⅓	cup sliced ripe olives
1	large can tuna	¼	cup minced onion
⅓	cup slivered almonds	2	tablespoons fresh lemon juice

1. Cook noodles; make Medium White Sauce.
2. Combine all ingredients and pour into baking dish sprayed with vegetable spray.
3. Bake at 350° for 20-25 minutes.

* See pg. 122.

Tuna Pasty

1	12-oz. can tuna	¼	teaspoon fresh ground pepper
1	small onion, minced	1	tablespoon prepared mustard,
1	stalk celery, minced		optional
¼	cup mayonnaise (read	1	Biscuit Recipe (below)
	the label)		

1. Prepare biscuit dough and divide into 3–4 balls, set aside. Drain tuna and mix with remaining ingredients.
2. Roll out biscuit dough into 8" squares. Place one-third to one-fourth of the tuna mixture on each dough square; bring up corners to meet in middle and press closed. Repeat for remaining dough and tuna mixture.
3. Lightly spray a baking sheet with vegetable spray; place pasties so they don't touch and bake at 375° for 15–20 minutes, or until browned.

Biscuit Recipe

2	cups flour	¼	cup shortening
¼	teaspoon salt	¾	cup "milk"
3	teaspoons baking powder		

1. Mix dry ingredients; cut in shortening; add "milk" and stir just enough to hold dough together.
2. Place on lightly floured surface; knead lightly and proceed with pasties.

Vicki's Tuna Pocket

Use a favorite pasty, yeast, or quick biscuit dough.

1	6½-oz. can tuna	1	tablespoon prepared mustard
1	teaspoon onion powder	1	tablespoon Dijon mustard
⅛	teaspoon fresh ground pepper		

1. Follow directions for tuna pasty.
2. Vary by using the tuna, onion powder, and fresh ground pepper only and placing a slice of American cheese on the tuna before folding over. ***Only*** for those who can ingest cheese of course. Remember, be careful if baking on one baking sheet. Keep cheese from melting onto the noncheese pocket or pasty.

Scalloped Potatoes with Ham

4	cups sliced potatoes	1/4	teaspoon fresh ground pepper
1	ham slice, precooked	1	tablespoon "butter"
1	medium onion, minced	1 1/4	cups hot "milk"

1. Thoroughly wash potatoes; peel or not (looks best to most people if peeled); slice thinly. Cut ham into small cubes and mince onion.
2. Spray a 1½-qt. baking dish with vegetable spray and place a layer of potatoes in bottom. Sprinkle with a layer of minced onion, ham, and pepper; continue layering, then dot top with "butter." Pour hot "milk" over all and bake uncovered at 350° for 75 minutes.

Boston Baked Beans with Ham

1	package navy beans (4 cups)	2	teaspoons dry mustard
2	medium onions, minced	1/2	teaspoon fresh ground pepper
1/2	cup molasses	4	cloves
1/2	pound cubed ham pieces		Water to cover

1. Sort and rinse the beans, then place in pot with water to cover and bring to boil. Boil for 2 minutes; remove from heat and let soak for 1 hour; drain and rinse.*
2. Add remaining ingredients and fresh water to cover beans, stirring well.

> ✗ ✗ ✗ ✗ ✗ ✗ ✗ ✗
> *Brown Beans with Rice is a tasty, nutritious way to use leftover beans. Add 1 cup cooked rice to each cup of the leftover beans and heat through.*

3. Spray bean pot or covered baking dish with vegetable spray; pour bean mixture into pot; cover and bake at 250° for 5–5½ hours, or until beans are nicely tender.

* This is an exception to the rules. Generally try to utilize the water vegetables are cooked in, in order to preserve the vitamins and minerals. By discarding the original bean water, you are discarding the major cause of the discomfort many people feel after eating baked beans or bean soup. By boiling the beans, the gases that beans contain are released into the water. When you drain and rinse you get rid of a large amount of these gases.

Steamed Rice
(Long- and Short-Grained)

1½ cups water
1 cup rice

½ teaspoon salt, optional

1. Bring water to boil and add rice; or combine ingredients in saucepan with tight-fitting cover; bring to boil. Cover and turn heat to *low*.
2. Cook 20–25 minutes for long-grained rice; 25–30 minutes for short-grained rice.
3. Remove from heat, fluff, and enjoy.

> **RINSE THE RICE?**
> *As a general rule, **do not** rinse rice, or pastas, after cooking. You rinse away the vitamins and minerals.*
>
> ✗ ✗ ✗ ✗ ✗ ✗ ✗ ✗

Note: *To steam brown rice, use 1¾ cups water and steam for 40 minutes. Cooking time for rices varies, so follow package directions.*

Simple Green Rice

Toss one of the following with the hot rice: Slightly steamed chopped spinach, chopped parsley, sprigs of watercress, or sliced scallions with the cooked rice. Use 1 cup of greens for each 1 cup of uncooked rice; steam together about 2 minutes.

Pasta

1 cup pasta
5 to 6 cups water

1 tablespoon vegetable or olive oil

1. Use no salt, or very little, and about 1 tablespoon of oil in the water to keep the pasta from sticking together.
2. Bring water and oil to boil; add pasta and cook uncovered at a slow boil. Cook until barely tender. Don't overcook; test after 6 minutes, it should be tender not mushy.
3. Drain in colander and serve with choice of sauces, or add to other ingredients. Rinsing is not necessary unless you wish to cool the pasta for a cold salad.

Note: Follow package directions for pastas; cook about 6-7 minutes for thin pastas, longer for thicker pastas.

Macaroni Goulash

1 pound ground beef
2 medium onions, chopped
2 stalks celery, minced
¼ green bell pepper, minced
3 cups chopped fresh tomato
1 clove garlic, minced

¼ teaspoon fresh ground pepper
½ teaspoon salt, optional
4 to 5 mushrooms, sliced
½ cup sliced ripe olives
1½ cups uncooked macaroni (or other pasta)

1. Heat skillet, spray with vegetable spray. Brown beef. Meanwhile, steam onion, celery, bell pepper, and garlic in ¼ cup water. Drain fat from beef; add steamed vegetables, tomatoes, and spices; simmer about 30 minutes.
2. Add mushrooms and black olives; simmer additional 15 minutes. Cook macaroni separately during this last cooking period. When pasta is still firm but cooked, drain. Combine ingredients and heat 2-3 minutes.

Spaghetti and Meatballs

1	pound ground beef	¼	teaspoon fresh ground pepper
1	cup cracker crumbs	½	teaspoon garlic powder
1	medium onion, minced	¼	cup "milk" (or mayonnaise)
2	eggs, lightly beaten	1	tablespoon minced parsley
¼	teaspoon salt		

1. Combine all ingredients and shape into 1" meatballs.
2. **Either** heat skillet, spray with vegetable spray, and brown meat on all sides, draining as fat collects, **or** spray a baking pan with vegetable spray and bake at 350°, about 20 minutes, turning once after 10 minutes, or until browned and cooked through.
3. Remove meatballs from pan with a slotted spoon.
4. Add meatballs to a spaghetti sauce and heat to blend flavors at least 20 minutes, while cooking spaghetti separately.
5. In a large bowl combine all, **or** on a warmed platter place hot spaghetti and top with sauce and meatballs. For those who can ingest cheese, have grated Parmesan cheese to top their individual portions.

Pasta with Hot Dogs

1½	cups macaroni	¼	cup minced onion
2	cups spaghetti sauce with mushrooms (read the label)	¼	cup thinly sliced celery
		¼	cup minced green bell pepper
1	large carrot, grated	2	hot dogs, sliced (read the label)
2	tablespoons "butter"		

1. Cook macaroni just until tender; drain and add warmed spaghetti sauce and grated carrot.

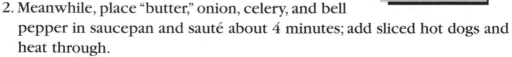

Kids love it!
✗ ✗ ✗ ✗

2. Meanwhile, place "butter," onion, celery, and bell pepper in saucepan and sauté about 4 minutes; add sliced hot dogs and heat through.
3. Combine all ingredients and heat to blend flavors. Serve hot.

Vegetables

✖ ✖ ✖ ✖ ✖ ✖ ✖ ✖ ✖ ✖

SPINACH DIP ✖ FRIED EGGPLANT ✖ STEAMED EGGPLANT ✖ SWEET POTATOES WITH

MARSHMALLOWS ✖ BAKED YAMS ✖ BAKED POTATO ✖ STUFFED POTATOES ✖ MASHED

POTATOES ✖ STEAMED POTATOES ✖ CRISP BROILED POTATOES ✖ FRIED POTATOES ✖

CARROTS ✖ CARROTS AND PINEAPPLE ✖ CHINESE CABBAGE ✖ STUFFED EGGPLANT ✖

STEWED TOMATOES ✖ BROILED TOMATO ✖ VEGETABLE MÉLANGE ✖ STEAMED SUMMER SQUASH

✖ ACORN SQUASH ✖ SPAGHETTI SQUASH ✖ AND MORE . . .

✖ ✖ ✖ ✖ ✖ ✖ ✖ ✖ ✖ ✖

Vegetables are the original snack foods. Strips of carrot, celery, green bell pepper, cauliflower pieces, etc., keep well on a tray covered with plastic wrap and kept handy in the refrigerator. They also stay crisp when stored in a tightly covered container of any sort. Keep them handy as a choice for an after-school snack for the children.

If you don't regularly eat a variety of vegetables, experiment more. The dark green vegetables are a source of calcium, important to all of us and especially for those of us who can not get our calcium from milk products. If you or the people you prepare foods for don't find vegetables exciting, dress them up a bit. Use dips, serve them with various nuts, spread peanut butter on them, or do whatever appeals to you.

Buy fresh vegetables that are firm, have no signs of spoilage, and have good color. Most stores light their produce sections to maximize the appearance of their wares; keep that in mind when buying. Take your time when purchasing fresh produce—it's worth your while, taste and nutrition wise, to choose the best available to you.

When fresh vegetables are cooked in water, some of the vitamins and minerals are dissolved and lost. It's best to use a minimum of water and

TESTING PRODUCE FOR QUALITY

To test fresh produce for ripeness or quality is easy. Simply hold the fruit or vegetable in your hand and feel it—don't squeeze it. Squeezing produce may result in later damage if pressed too hard. A tomato, peach, or nectarine for instance, needs only to be hefted and felt. They should feel firm, neither overly hard nor mushy. When testing for some fruit, such as melons, use a sniff test. If a fresh melon smell wafts up, it is ready to use.

✖ ✖ ✖ ✖ ✖ ✖ ✖ ✖

cook just until tender-crisp to retain the nutrients your body needs. Do not overcook—vegetables look and taste best when tender but still crisp.

Be aware that potatoes, onions, broccoli, turnips, Brussels sprouts, cabbage, and corn on the cob do not need to be cooked in large quantities of water. These vegetables are very good steamed or cooked with a minimum of water. Like cooking with no milk, it's a matter of getting accustomed to cooking with steam or small amounts of water, and well worth the effort.

Also, do not use salt when cooking your vegetables. It's not simply that salt isn't good for us, it's that the texture is best if *unsalted* water is used. Salt tends to toughen vegetables when used in the cooking water.

Experiment with herbs and spices on your cooked vegetables. Popular herbs to use on veggies are: basil; parsley; coriander or caraway; garlic powder; mace or marjoram; dill weed; rosemary; sage or savory; thyme or tarragon. Tomatoes are good with basil, fennel, oregano, sage, tarragon or marjoram, or yes, salt.

Sprinkle vegetables with fresh lemon juice, especially dark greens. Use a touch of vinegar, wine vinegar, balsamic, etc., or slivered almonds. Sliced hard-cooked eggs are good with some vegetables; or mash the yolks for color and flavor. Try bacon bits (read the label), or occasionally try crisp, crumbled bacon.

Making vegetables interesting makes them more enjoyable. Many people think of vegetable dips as sour cream–based. Not necessarily; use low-calorie or regular mayonnaise and fresh lemon or lime juice as a base for vegetable dips.

Spinach Dip

2 cups mayonnaise	1 clove garlic, minced
1 small onion, minced	1 cup minced fresh spinach
2 tablespoons fresh lemon juice	$\frac{1}{3}$ cup minced fresh parsley
$\frac{1}{4}$ teaspoon fresh ground pepper	

1. Place everything in a blender and blend on high until finely chopped.
2. Refrigerate covered about 4 hours.

Or: Simply mince the spinach and parsley, blend all ingredients thoroughly, and refrigerate in covered container about 4 hours to blend flavors.

Create your own dips, but if using dry soup mixes read the label! Try a favorite spaghetti sauce, which is good with celery, green onions, or cauliflower. And, of course, remember peanut butter spread on celery sticks, apples, or carrots, etc., is many children's favorite snack; it's tasty and adds some protein to the diet.

To Steam or Sauté Vegetables

For the following vegetables, steam or sauté, and serve tender-crisp. Add "butter," pepper, or lemon on the hot vegetables just before serving, or at the table; salt is optional. You can use a bamboo steamer, a stainless steel steamer, or a covered skillet that allows single or shallow layers of vegetables. If using a steamer, heat the water to a boil and place steamer with vegetables on top of it. Cook to tender-crisp.

If using a skillet, use about ¼–½ cup of water to steam the vegetables. Place the vegetables and water in the skillet; bring to simmering point; cover pan; reduce heat and steam until tender-crisp. Make sure you don't run out of water while steaming.

Have a sharp tined fork, or use the tip of a paring knife, to check for tenderness. You should not expect a long cooking time. Keep watch until you are accustomed to steaming vegetables. There is a short time between attractive vegetables, with nice color, and mushy vegetables with the color leached out.

As a general rule:
> *Cook 4–6 minutes for thin or cubed vegetables*
> *Cook 8–12 minutes for thick vegetables or chunks*
> *Cook 20–30 minutes or longer for large whole vegetables*

Asparagus is good with minimal seasoning, or try a bit of garlic powder or lemon juice. It's also good with almonds sprinkled on top. Steam whole 10–20 minutes, depending on size.

Beets do not need salted water, but a bit of vinegar in the water seems to preserve a lovely color. Serve plain, or sprinkle with lemon juice, vinegar, dill, or coriander.

Broccoli is good in fresh vegetable platters, or steamed until tender-crisp and served with fresh ground pepper and lemon juice. Make 1 or 2 cuts through the stems of the broccoli if they are thick.

Brussels Sprouts should be steamed until fork-tender, 5-8 minutes. Don't overcook or the taste and the color will suffer. Serve with lemon or "butter."

Cabbage is good as slaw or in tossed salads. It is also good if steamed 3-4 minutes, and served with "butter" and fresh pepper. A bit of lemon or caraway in the cooking are also nice touches for cabbage.

Cabbage, Cauliflower, and Celery are often overcooked. They are not appealing when offered as a mushy substance. Not only do these vegetables taste best when steamed, they look good when not overcooked.

Carrots are always best if not overcooked and are the nemesis of many children when mushy or over sweetened. Steam until easily pierced. Serve plain or with a touch of "butter" and fresh ground pepper.

Cauliflower is good in salads or fresh vegetable platters. To cook it, steam only until tender-crisp and serve with fresh pepper and lemon juice or "butter." To prepare the whole head, remove the core and steam for 15-20 minutes, or until tender. Cook flowerets 8-10 minutes.

Celery is most often used in salads, or cooked in and with other dishes, or as a soup. If steamed only until tender-crisp, celery is a tasty vegetable that stands on its own merits. Serve with lemon juice or "butter" and fresh ground pepper.

Corn on the Cob is another much-abused vegetable by millions of us! Cook it as soon as possible after buying; don't store it a week or even a few days if you can help it. Steam in a kettle of water for only 4 minutes. Serve hot either plain or with "butter," fresh pepper, and a little salt at the table.

Green Beans are good with "butter," or serve with bacon bits. Steam, sprinkle with thyme, savory, or marjoram.

Mushrooms should be washed gently. I rarely cook them, but when I do, I try not to drown them in the cooking medium. They are a very good garnish for meats when cooked and served hot. Fresh mushrooms are excellent in salads and on vegetable platters. When used in gravies, mushrooms will end up thoroughly cooked, of course.

Onions, when mild, are one of my favorite tossed salad ingredients. They're good steamed, boiled, sautéed, fried as tempura, or baked. Serve plain, creamed, or in other dishes. It is a versatile vegetable. To sauté vegetables like onions or mushrooms, heat a small saucepan and spray with vegetable spray; add 1 tablespoon of "butter" and ⅛ cup water per 1 cup of vegetables. Cook until tender, not soft.

Parsnips are good in stews, but also steamed and mashed. Serve with "butter" and fresh pepper. Or grate some raw for an interesting addition to green salads.

Peas are another abused vegetable, more often overcooked than not. Peas are excellent when "just cooked"—not mushy—unless they are meant to be pea soup. Serve hot with "butter" and fresh ground pepper, or add fresh minced onion before serving. Or combine with tiny onions before cooking. Also try fresh shelled peas in salads. Try frozen peas right out of the freezer as a special treat. I like it better than ice cream.

Peppers go well in fresh salads, scrambled eggs, or sautéed and served plain with "butter" and slivered toasted almonds. If leaving whole to stuff, parboil 4 minutes before stuffing. (Use the water you parboil them in to make soup.)

Potatoes, White and Red, need only enough water to keep them moist. Cover and steam until tender, yet crisp, for boiled potatoes, or until softened if using for mashed potatoes. If making gravy, use a bit more water, then save it to use in the gravy. You use all the water and thereby all the nutrients in that water. Leave the skins on whenever possible. Occasionally wash well, slice, and serve on a fresh vegetable platter. Serve immediately; potatoes do have a tendency to discolor quickly. *Do not store onions and potatoes in the same bin. They tend to begin rotting more quickly if stored together.*

Pumpkin is often overlooked as a vegetable, but it is good served mashed, with "butter" and fresh pepper, just as squash or yams would be served.

Rutabagas go well in soup and stews and are also good mashed with "butter," fresh ground pepper, and salt to taste. When cooking a vegetable in order to mash it, cook it thoroughly (until softened) but in a small amount of water so the vitamins and minerals will be retained. You should be able to mash without draining. If you intend to make gravy, use more water for making it, that way you will retain the vitamins and minerals in the gravy.

Squash, **Summer** (Zucchini, Yellow, and White Squashes) are excellent in salads; just wash and slice. They are equally as good steamed, tender-crisp, served with "butter" and fresh pepper, or with a sprinkling of herbs. Also try in stir-fry recipes.

Squash, **Winter** (Hubbard, Acorn, Butternut, etc.) do require a long cooking time. These are tasty served plain with "butter" only, or with "butter" and brown sugar.

Sweet Potatoes and Yams require longer cooking times, also, to break down the fibers for our digestion. They are good if baked in the skins, then sliced and served hot. Unlike white or red potatoes, the cooked skins are not edible.

Tomatoes can be prepared in many ways, including diced, sliced, or cut into wedges for salads. Steam in covered saucepan, no water need be added, and serve with "butter," fresh pepper, and a touch of salt. Broil until heated through, 3–5 minutes; or prepare stewed tomatoes. To *peel* a tomato, put into boiling water for 1 minute, then remove and plunge into cold water. The skins will slip off easily. Do not leave in the boiling water too long or thick layers of pulp will peel off with the skin. *Store fresh tomatoes at room temperature, not in the refrigerator.*

Turnips are good in soups or stews, or mashed and served with "butter," fresh ground pepper, and salt. Boil or steam whole 20–30 minutes or dice and steam 12–15 minutes.

✖ ✖ ✖ ✖ ✖

WASHING GREENS

Greens, such as spinach, beet tops, watercress, dandelion greens, etc., must be washed thoroughly to be pleasing. Fine grains of sand love to cling to these leaves, so you get the grittiness we all dislike if you don't clean them with care. Rinse in a sink or pan of water to cover and plunge the leaves up and down gently. Discard the water and repeat 2 or 3 times if sandy. Then rinse under running water and shake or spin the water out. Tear for salads. To cook, steam in just the water that clings after washing; cut with scissors, or a sharp knife, if you want even-sized pieces. Serve hot with "butter" and fresh pepper, with fresh lemon juice, or with vinegar.

✖✖✖✖✖✖✖

Fried Eggplant

1. Wash and slice eggplant; peel only if skin is tough. Dip slices in flour, then in lightly beaten egg, then in more flour or cracker crumbs. Heat skillet; spray with vegetable spray. Add eggplant and cook until browned and tender, 5–7 minutes, turning once.
2. Serve hot.

Note: Use a small amount of oil if your pans are not the nonstick variety.

Steamed Eggplant

1	medium eggplant, cubed	1	clove garlic, minced
4	tomatoes, chopped	¼	teaspoon fresh ground pepper
1	onion, chopped	¼	teaspoon salt
1	green bell pepper, chopped	6	slices crisp bacon, optional

1. Heat skillet; spray with vegetable spray.
2. Place all ingredients in skillet and add ¼ cup water; cook until vegetables are tender-crisp.

Note: Have grated Parmesan cheese on the table for those who can eat it. It goes very nicely with eggplant. If bacon is used, cook until crisp, drain well, and crumble.

Potatoes

Potatoes are a versatile food. The bad part of potatoes, if there is one, is what we choose to put on or in them after they are cooked, or the manner in which we cook them.

For instance, most sweet potato recipes ask for 1 cup of syrup and ½ cup of brown sugar, plus a marshmallow topping. That is not sweet potato, in my opinion, it's potato-flavored syrup. Vegetables and other foods have a very lovely flavor when not hidden under sugars. If sweet is traditional, try the following:

Sweet Potatoes with Marshmallows

4 yams/sweet potatoes
   cooked,* peeled, and
   mashed

¼ cup brown sugar
   Mini marshmallows

1. Boil potatoes until thoroughly cooked. Remove skins and mash with brown sugar to give the flavor we remember.
2. Spray a baking pan with vegetable spray; place mashed potatoes in pan with a layer of marshmallows on top.
3. Bake at 350° for 15–20 minutes.

To cook, wash but do not peel; boil until tender, drain, then slip off skins.

Baked Yams

2 to 3 medium yams

1. Wash yams thoroughly and pierce with fork to ensure that steam escapes.
2. Place in 375° oven; bake until tender and easily pierced with fork.
3. Slice with sharp knife and serve hot.

Note: *The skin is not edible so it must be carefully peeled before being served to young children.*

Baked Potato

1 medium-sized potato per person

1. Wash potatoes thoroughly; prick with fork several times to allow steam to escape; bake at 400° for 40–50 minutes or until easily pierced with fork or skewer.
2. Serve hot with "butter" and fresh pepper; a touch of fresh lemon is also very good. Perhaps sour cream on the side for those who can have it.

Stuffed Potatoes

1. After baking potatoes, reduce oven temperature to 350°. Slice a shallow piece from the top of each potato; scoop out with a spoon, keeping shell intact. Mash hot potatoes in a bowl with 1 tablespoon "butter" and 1 tablespoon "milk" for each potato. Refill skins, or combine with other ingredients, then refill.
2. Bake an additional 15 minutes at 350°. Serve hot.

Chili Stuffed: Combine a can of chili without beans with mashed potatoes; refill shells. Bake at 350° for 15 minutes. Serve hot.

Bacon Stuffed: Combine crisp bacon and minced onion with mashed potatoes; refill shells. Bake at 350° for 15 minutes. Serve hot.

Tuna Stuffed: Combine drained flaked tuna, mayonnaise, and coriander with mashed potatoes; refill shells. Bake at 350° for 15 minutes. Serve hot.

Note: Peeling potatoes is unnecessary, except when making mashed potatoes. If you do peel them, peel very thinly. Using a vegetable peeler will help assure minimum thickness of peels. Children can safely use most vegetable peelers. This is a good way to include them to preparing a family or holiday meal.

DON'T DISCARD THE SKINS!

White and red potato skins are edible and should be enjoyed often. The skins add their own subtle flavor when eaten with the rest of the vegetable. Plus you get the benefit of the nutrients that are stored near the surface of the potato.

✳ ✳ ✳ ✳ ✳ ✳ ✳ ✳

Mashed Potatoes

Potatoes   "Butter"
Water   "Milk"

1. Wash and peel potatoes; cube and steam until thoroughly cooked. Drain if necessary—or use water to make gravy. Mash, using "butter" and "milk" to taste.
2. Whip well, until light and fluffy.
3. Serve hot.

Steamed Potatoes

1. Wash potatoes thoroughly and cut into quarters.
2. Place in pan with ¼–½ cup water, depending on amount of potatoes. Bring to a simmer, cover and reduce heat; steam until tender-crisp. (Be careful, it's easy to get "browned" potatoes.)
3. Serve hot.

Crisp Broiled Potatoes

1. Thoroughly wash potatoes; cut into lengthwise strips approximately ½" thick. Spray broiler pan with vegetable spray; place strips of potatoes on pan; place under heat for 10–15 minutes. Stir frequently for even browning.
2. Serve hot with a light sprinkling of salt if desired.

Fried Potatoes

1. Wash and slice potatoes; spray skillet thoroughly with vegetable spray and place potatoes in pan. Add about ¼ cup water; cover and steam 10–15 minutes. Remove cover and brown over medium-low heat, turning to brown evenly.
2. Add minced onion to potato while steaming if desired. A tablespoon or so of "butter" will help the potatoes to brown and add a bit of flavor.

Carrots

Carrots   *Water to steam carrots*

1. Peel or thoroughly wash carrots with a vegetable brush. These vegetables have an outer layer that holds soil very well.
2. Spray saucepan with vegetable spray; slice carrots and place in pan with a small amount of water. Steam until tender-crisp do not overcook. **Or** cook in steamer.
3. Toss with "butter" and serve hot.

Carrots and Pineapple

½ cup pineapple chunks   ⅛ teaspoon fresh ground pepper
2 cups cooked sliced carrots   1 tablespoon "butter"
1 tablespoon cornstarch and
     ¼ cup water

1. Drain pineapple and reserve liquid. Cook carrots in ½ cup water; drain and reserve liquid. Meanwhile, mix cornstarch and ¼ cup cold water thoroughly. Combine carrot and pineapple liquids to make 1 cup. In saucepan combine juices and cornstarch mixture; heat to boiling point.
2. Add remaining ingredients and heat through.

Chinese Cabbage

3 cups shredded cabbage   1 green bell pepper, sliced thin
2 stalks celery, sliced   1 medium onion, sliced
2 tablespoons water

1. Prepare vegetables by shredding or slicing in thin strips.
2. Heat skillet, then spray skillet with vegetable spray. Drop in vegetables and water, stirring well; cover tightly and bring to a simmer. Steam 5 minutes, stir, and serve hot.

Stuffed Eggplant

1	large eggplant	1	tablespoon cornstarch
1	cup sliced mushrooms	¼	cup pimiento
¼	cup minced onion	¼	teaspoon fresh ground pepper
¼	cup minced green bell pepper	¼	teaspoon salt
1	clove garlic, minced	2	tablespoons "butter" + ¼ cup cracker crumbs

1. Wash eggplant, cut off a lengthwise slice. Remove and cube pulp. Place eggplant, onion, green bell pepper, and garlic in saucepan with ¼ cup water; steam 10 minutes.
2. Stir cornstarch, pimiento, and seasonings into vegetable mixture; fill shell with mixture. Top with crumbs and "butter."
3. Bake at 350° for 20–25 minutes.

Stewed Tomatoes

4 medium tomatoes, chopped	2 tablespoons minced bell pepper
1 small onion, minced	¼ teaspoon fresh ground pepper
1 stalk celery, minced	¼ teaspoon each: salt and sugar

Combine ingredients and bring to a simmer. Simmer about 10 minutes.

Note: Include ½ cup bread crumbs for "traditional" stewed tomatoes.

PEELING TOMATOES

Place tomatoes in boiling water for 1 minute, then plunge into cold water. Skins will slip off. Don't leave in boiling water beyond 1 minute. The longer the tomato is in the hot water the more pulp comes off with the peel.

✗ ✗ ✗ ✗ ✗ ✗ ✗

Broiled Tomato

Tomato	*Fresh ground pepper*
Basil	*"Butter"*
Oregano	*Salt, optional*

1. Wash tomato and cut in half.
2. Sprinkle tomato halves with basil, oregano, and fresh ground pepper; top with a bit of "butter."
3. Broil at low temperature for about 4 minutes. Salt after cooking if you wish.

Vegetable Mélange

1	*small onion, sliced*	*1*	*medium zucchini, sliced*
1	*medium bell pepper, sliced*	*1*	*small summer squash, sliced*
1	*clove garlic, minced*	*¼*	*cup "butter"*
4	*medium tomatoes, sliced*	*½*	*cup almonds, optional*

1. Heat skillet; spray with vegetable spray. Melt "butter" and add onion, bell pepper, and garlic. Sauté until onion begins to become transparent.
2. Add remaining vegetables carefully. Heat through until squash are just tender. Sprinkle with almonds and serve.

Steamed Summer Squash

1. Wash and cut unpeeled squash (crookneck, zucchini, etc.), into ½" slices.
2. Spray skillet with vegetable spray; add 2 tablespoons to ¼ cup "butter" (depending on amount of squash used), and slices of squash. Cook, just until tender but still crisp, 6–8 minutes.
3. Serve hot.

Acorn Squash

1. Wash squash; cut in half and remove seeds.
2. Spray a baking pan with vegetable spray; place squash halves cut side down in pan; pour water to about ¼" depth around squash. Bake at 400° for 30 minutes.
3. Turn squash upright; continue baking until thoroughly cooked, another 20–30 minutes.
4. Serve each half as an individual serving with "butter" and seasonings on the table. *Or* scoop squash from shells; mash with "butter" and fresh ground pepper to taste. Serve hot.

*A popular way to serve squash: ***
When you turn the squash over after 30 minutes, put brown sugar and "butter" into each and continue baking until done. Each shell is an individual serving. You can do each shell a different way to please individual tastes and needs.

* Not suggested for diabetic diets unless as a trade-off.

Note: Butternut and other winter squash cook in the same way as above.

Spaghetti Squash

1. Cut lengthwise and remove seeds. Bake at 350° cut-side down, with a small amount of water, for 45 minutes; turn and bake until tender.
2. To steam, use a covered pot. Place cut squash in it with a cup of water, steam for 20 minutes.
3. To serve, release strands from the shell with a fork; season with "butter" and fresh ground pepper to taste.

Variation: Cover with hot spaghetti sauce just as you would a pasta.

Note: Grated cheese on the side is good for those not milk or lactose sensitive.

Salads

✖ ✖ ✖ ✖ ✖ ✖ ✖

TOSSED SALAD ✖ LARGE TOSSED VEGETABLE SALAD ✖ SALAD PLATE ✖ CHEF'S SALAD ✖ SPINACH SALAD ✖ STUFFED TOMATO SALAD ✖ STUFFED EGGS ✖ FRUIT PLATE ✖ SMALL FRUIT PLATE ✖ GELATIN VEGETABLE SALAD ✖ GELATIN FRUIT SALAD ✖ EASY FRUIT SALAD ✖ TRADITIONAL SUNSHINE SALAD ✖ CABBAGE SALAD ✖ BEAN SALAD ✖ PASTA AND BEAN SALAD ✖ TUNA EGG SALAD ✖ CREAMY POTATO SALAD ✖ COLESLAW ✖ COLESLAW WITH ALMONDS ✖ SALMON SALAD ✖ TUNA MACARONI SALAD ✖ CHICKEN CURRY SALAD ✖ CHICKEN AND NUT SALAD ✖ FRESH MUSHROOM SALAD ✖ MACARONI-AND-BEAN SALAD ✖ RICE SALAD ✖ CURRIED CHICKEN-AND-RICE SALAD ✖ AND MORE . . .

Tossed salads are the easiest and most versatile of salads. They go well with all sorts of dressings, or no dressing at all. Fresh lemon and fresh ground pepper add a nice spark, especially when a few peanuts are sprinkled on, also. There are many recipes for mayonnaise and French dressings, but with such an array of dressings available on the grocery shelf, this book will not include any. *Read labels* when purchasing any prepared dressings.

Dark green vegetables are sources of calcium for those of us who can not have milk or milk by-products. To make sure you get all the minerals and nutritional value from the produce, take your time with purchasing and with preparation. For head lettuce, try washing only as much as you will need at one time. This will avoid rusting the entire head if not used in a few days. Simply pull off what you need and refrigerate the rest. For leaf greens, spinach, leaf lettuce, beet greens, and so forth, swish around in a sink or pan full of cool water. If really sandy do this two or three times, then wash each leaf separately under running water and drain well. Removing as much water as possible will ensure that the greens will last well; refrigerate covered, or place in large plastic bags, then carefully squeeze out all the air and seal; they last very well this way.

When shopping for groceries buy stock, frozen, and nonperishables in quantity, but purchase fresh produce more often. If the kind of fruit or vegetable you want does not look good, try something different. Don't be afraid to examine the produce carefully, and be sure to check the pre-bagged produce. Be certain there are no questionable oranges, potatoes, onions, apples, grapefruit, or whatever at the bottom or in the middle of the bag. (See pg. 60 for selecting quality produce.)

At the checkout, don't be shy about telling the employees to be careful with the produce. Some clerks don't realize that pears, though hard, are still bruisable. If you don't like bruised fruit, keep holding them until the checker looks up, then ask to have them handled carefully, or handed back to you. It surprises them, but when the fruit ripens there will be fewer bruises on it.

Make a large salad and keep it in the refrigerator for several days. To do this, use a tightly sealed container or plastic wrap over glass or ceramic bowls. Tear the greens and do not add tomatoes or dressing—to avoid a limp salad. Tomatoes and strong-flavored vegetables can be prepared and kept in smaller bowls and added separately as the salad is used. Interesting flavors and texture can be added by using grated parsnip, fresh green peas, yellow or green beans, or various nuts. For vegetables that don't need to be peeled such as cucumbers, zucchini, and summer squash, wash thoroughly and dry; store, sealed as above, in refrigerator and slice as needed.

Vegetable Salads

Make by placing a bed of greens on individual salad plates or bowls. Use combinations of fresh and cooked vegetables. Green peas, green beans, lima beans, and asparagus tips are good in vegetable salads.

Also good with greens are crushed pineapple, orange sections, apples, raisins, nuts, and black olives.

Note: Green olives are preserved in lactic acid; it is not lactose but it is a milk by-product.

Try: Drained crushed pineapple and raisins combined with grated carrots.

Or overlap slices of unpeeled cucumber, tomato, and onion rings on lettuce or spinach leaves.

Note: Dark leaf vegetables, such as red or green lettuce, have more calcium than the lighter-colored heads of lettuce.

> ### SWITCH IT UP!
> *Experiment with various salad combinations—it's a great way to use your creative touch. You may also find that little ones are more interested in vegetables if they are allowed to create their own combinations.*
>
> **✗ ✗ ✗ ✗ ✗ ✗ ✗**

Tossed Salad

Head lettuce
Fresh spinach
Leaf lettuce
Green onion (or onion rings)

Zucchini, sliced thin
Summer squash, sliced thin
Fresh mushrooms, sliced

1. Tear greens in small pieces and toss with thinly sliced vegetables in a large bowl.
2. Serve dry and chilled with choice of dressing and toppings on the side.

Note: *Nuts or crunchy cereals are good toppings. If croutons are a favorite be sure to read the label.*

✖ ✖ ✖ ✖ ✖

Large Tossed Vegetable Salad

Lettuce, small pieces
Spinach, small pieces
Endive, small pieces
Celery, sliced
Cucumber, sliced
Cherry tomatoes, whole

Green pepper, cut into strips
Cauliflower florets
Broccoli florets
Onion, sliced in half rings
Carrots, sliced or shredded
Radish, thinly sliced

In a large bowl toss all ingredients lightly. Serve dry and chilled with dressings and toppings on the side.

Note: *This is fast if you have a food slicer to cut the vegetables into even slices. Begin with a base of torn greens and add any fresh vegetable that appeals to you.*

Salad Plate

Cauliflower florets   Onion rings
Radish, thinly sliced   Cherry tomatoes
Broccoli florets   Celery sticks
Carrot sticks

Serve with choice of dips, dressings, and toppings.

Note: *When serving raw vegetables, dips will make them more appealing to those who just aren't "into" fresh vegetables.*

Chef's Salad

Small leaf lettuce, torn   1   cup ham, julienne strips
½   bunch Romaine, torn   ¼   cup shredded carrots
½   cup chopped green onion   ¼   cup sliced ripe olives
½   cup sliced celery   Peanuts, optional

Toss greens with vegetables and ham; add olives and nuts if desired.

Spinach Salad

Fresh spinach, torn   1   medium carrot, shredded
1   onion, sliced   ¼   cup diced green bell pepper
1   stalk celery, sliced

Toss all ingredients. Serve with choice of dressings and toppings.

Stuffed Tomato Salad

1. For each serving use one medium to large tomato. Cut off top and a small slice from bottom so fruit will sit evenly. Scoop out interior and mix well with a tuna, chicken, or ham salad. Carefully stuff each tomato with mixture.
2. On individual salad plates arrange lettuce leaves and place stuffed tomato on each. Sprinkle with almonds or other nuts. Place a steak knife with each place setting to cut the tomato.

Stuffed Eggs

6 eggs, hard cooked	2 to 4 tablespoons mayonnaise
¼ cup minced onion	1 tablespoon prepared mustard
2 large fresh mushrooms, minced	Fresh ground pepper and salt to taste

1. Cut eggs in half lengthwise and cut a small piece from the base of each half to balance while on plate. Remove yolks and place in bowl with slivers of egg white and remaining ingredients. Mash and blend well; mound into egg-white shells.
2. Arrange on serving dish and sprinkle with paprika.

HEALTHY CHOICES PAY OFF

Fruits and vegetables are the original snack foods and should be enjoyed often. A bowl of several kinds of grapes, washed and snipped into small clusters, is both attractive and nutritious. Bananas, pears, oranges, peaches, and other fruits make a lovely fresh fruit bowl and are easy to pick up at snack time.

Over the years I've found that I feel best when I eat plenty of fresh fruits and vegetables. Perhaps it's possible that you will, also, if you are milk or lactose intolerant. And, of course, diabetics must always be aware of what they eat—fresh fruits and veggies are a smart choice.

✗ ✗ ✗ ✗ ✗ ✗ ✗ ✗

Fruit Salads

Fruit salads can be made ahead of time and refrigerated. Try to make what will be used at a particular time, or remove to serving dishes carefully, to avoid bruising the remaining fruit. To keep bananas or apple slices from turning dark, dip in lemon or grapefruit juice.

Fruit Salad Combinations

Serve on a bed of lettuce on individual salad plates or bowls. Combine fruit that appeals to you or try these combinations:

Slices of banana, pineapple chunks, and cranberry sauce. Pear halves topped with chopped walnuts.

Mandarin oranges and diced pineapple with toasted coconut. Fresh grapefruit half served chilled and plain—no sugar.

Note: *Do not put maraschino cherries on grapefruit halves if they are preserved in lactic acid and you are milk sensitive.*

Fruit Plate

Watermelon, cut from rind	*Seedless green grapes*
Cantaloupe and green melon,	*Strawberries*
cut from rind	*Apple slices, unpeeled*
Oranges, sliced and peeled	

1. Wash fruit, peel oranges, remove rind of watermelon, cantaloupe, and honey dew, or your choice of green melon. Build the salad on a dinner plate.
2. Start with a slice of watermelon, quartered if large, as a base. Then build an attractive tower with cantaloupe wedges, honeydew wedges, orange rounds, green grapes, strawberry halves, and red apple slices. This is a meal by itself, no dressing needed. Some like honey drizzled on it.

Small Fruit Plate

Cut a cantaloupe or honeydew melon into rings and peel. Place rings on individual serving plates, with or without lettuce leaves. Fill center of ring with seasonal fruit: bing cherries, green or red grapes, strawberries, raspberries, pear or apple slices, and so on.

Child's Salad

(as per her instructions)

On a "sauser" put some "lettus," just enough so it covers the plate and is flat. Next put a pineapple ring in the middle. Then, put half a banana in the ring and cut off a piece of the top so it's flat. Put some nondairy whipped topping* or salad dressing on the top of the banana so a little hangs down. On the whipped topping put half of a red gum drop (or half a maraschino cherry). Serve and eat—yummy!

Note: The appearance of this salad is a lighted candle. Children enjoy making this salad!

Gelatin Salads

Gelatin is great for make-ahead salads. The ingredients look and stay fresh longer than plain fruits and vegetables. They can be made in one large mold or in individual molds. Use water, juice, or your choice of liquid, and as a general rule, a 3-oz. package of gelatin for each 2 cups of ingredients. Be creative—gelatin can be plain, whipped, striped, cubed, or angled for eye appeal.

Spray molds with vegetable spray, then wipe with a paper towel to ensure the finished product will unmold. To unmold gelatin, dip mold in warm, not hot, water. Loosen edge with a spatula or knife, and place damp serving plate on top of mold. Turn mold and plate together, lift mold, and garnish your salad as you wish. (Dampening plate first will allow salad to slide if not centered. A little vegetable spray also works.) For molded vegetable salads, the gelatin bases usually preferred are lemon, lime, or unflavored. Follow package directions.

Gelatin Vegetable Salad

1　package gelatin, unflavored
½　cup cold water
1　teaspoon sugar
¼　teaspoon salt

2　tablespoons vinegar
1　tablespoon fresh lemon juice
1　cup water, bouillon, or juice
1½ to 2 cups salad ingredients

1. Place ½ cup cold water in saucepan; sprinkle in gelatin. Heat, stirring constantly, until dissolved, about 3 minutes. Remove from heat and stir in all but salad ingredients.
2. Chill, stirring occasionally, until thickened and syrupy. Add salad ingredients and pour into one large mold or into individual molds.
3. Chill until set.

Use your favorite combination of vegetables, or vegetables and meat, or fish:

Tuna ~ celery ~ minced onion ~ mushroom
~ shredded carrot ~ chicken cubes ~ black olives

Gelatin Fruit Salad

1　3-oz. package lime gelatin
1　cup boiling water
1　9-oz. can crushed
　　pineapple, drained (reserve
　　liquid)

½　cup finely chopped celery
1　cup mayonnaise (read the label)
½　cup chopped nuts
1　teaspoon horseradish

1. Dissolve gelatin in boiling water, then add the juice from the can of pineapple. Chill until it begins to thicken, then beat until frothy.
2. Combine remaining ingredients and fold in.
3. Chill until firm; garnish with additional ground nuts.

Easy Fruit Salad

1	6-oz. package gelatin	1	package frozen fruit

1. Dissolve gelatin in 2 cups boiling water; add 1 package frozen fruit and stir until gelatin begins to set. Refrigerate.
2. Serve plain or with nondairy whipped topping, or a mixture of mayonnaise and nondairy topping—*read the label*.

Simple combinations to try:
> Strawberry gelatin and frozen strawberries or mixed fruit
> Peach gelatin and frozen peaches or raspberries
> Raspberry gelatin and frozen raspberries or blueberries

Traditional Sunshine Salad

1	package lemon gelatin	1	8-oz. can crushed pineapple
1½	cups boiling water	1	cup shredded carrot
1	tablespoon fresh lemon juice	⅓	cup chopped pecans *

1. Dissolve gelatin in boiling water. Add undrained pineapple and lemon juice; chill until it begins to thicken.
2. Fold in carrots and nuts; pour into mold(s).

* Use walnuts or almonds if you prefer, or peanuts if you cannot ingest tree nuts.

Cabbage Salad

2 to 3 cups finely shredded cabbage		1	cup chopped red bell pepper
¼	cup thinly sliced celery	1	cup mayonnaise (read the label)
		1	teaspoon prepared mustard

½ cup minced green bell pepper
¼ cup shredded carrot
¼ cup minced green onion

1 teaspoon celery seed
¼ teaspoon fresh ground pepper

Toss all ingredients; chill and serve.

Bean Salad

1 can green beans, drained
1 can wax beans, drained
1 can kidney beans, drained
    and rinsed
1 small red onion, chopped

1 small green bell pepper, slivered
1 tablespoon olive or vegetable oil
¼ cup wine vinegar
½ teaspoon garlic powder

1. Combine all ingredients.
2. Refrigerate at least 2 hours before serving.

Pasta-and-Bean Salad

2 cups pasta, cooked and
    drained
1 16-oz. can red kidney
    beans, drained and rinsed
1 small onion, chopped
1 medium green bell pepper,
    chopped

1 stalk celery, minced
½ to ¾ cup mayonnaise (read the label)
1 clove garlic, crushed
½ teaspoon oregano
¼ teaspoon fresh ground pepper
½ teaspoon basil
¼ teaspoon salt

1. In a large bowl mix pasta and vegetables.
2. In small bowl combine mayonnaise and seasonings; mix well; add mixture to salad and blend thoroughly.
3. Place in serving bowl; cover and refrigerate several hours before serving.

Tuna-Egg Salad

1	6-oz. can tuna	18 to 20	ripe olives, sliced
1	11-oz. can mandarin oranges	2	tablespoons fresh lemon juice
4	eggs, hard cooked and sliced	1	tablespoon soy sauce
			Fresh ground pepper

1. Drain tuna, oranges, and olives. Flake tuna; slice olives and eggs.
2. Combine lemon juice, soy sauce, and pepper; toss all ingredients together.
3. Refrigerate 20 minutes or longer.
4. Serve chilled.

Creamy Potato Salad

4 to 5	medium potatoes, cubed, boiled, and cooled	1	tablespoon prepared mustard
1	medium onion, minced	$\frac{1}{2}$	teaspoon salt
2	stalks celery, minced	$\frac{1}{4}$	teaspoon fresh ground pepper
	Radishes, sliced for garnish	4	eggs, boiled: dice 3 and slice 1 for garnish
$\frac{3}{4}$	cup mayonnaise (read the label)	Paprika	

1. Combine all ingredients except egg and radish; mix lightly.
2. Add diced egg and mix in carefully; arrange in serving bowl. Garnish with egg and radish slices; sprinkle with paprika.

Note: It is not necessary to peel potatoes, but do so if you prefer. Keep it simple or be creative and add your own choice of ingredients. Try diced cucumber, grated carrot, diced green and red bell pepper, or pimiento for color.

Variation: Make it a complete meal by itself and add 2 cups of tuna, chicken, or ham. Increase mayonnaise if you like a moist salad.

Potato-Rice Salad: To the potato salad recipe, add 1½ cups rice, ¼ cup green bell pepper, ¼ cup additional mayonnaise.

Coleslaw

8 cups shredded cabbage	1 cup mayonnaise (read the label)
2 cups grated carrots	¼ cup wine vinegar
1 cup minced green bell pepper	1 teaspoon celery seed
½ cup sliced green onion	¼ teaspoon garlic powder

1. In a large bowl, combine the vegetables. Blend last 4 ingredients; mix thoroughly with the vegetables.
2. Chill to allow flavors to blend.

Coleslaw with Almonds

2½ cups shredded cabbage	¼ cup minced onion
½ cup minced celery	½ cup slivered almonds, toasted
¼ cup minced green bell pepper	½ cup mayonnaise (read the label)
1 tablespoon wine (or tarragon vinegar)	

1. Combine all ingredients and refrigerate.
2. Serve chilled.

Salmon Salad

1 can salmon	1 cup shredded carrots
2 cups cooked and drained pasta	¾ cup mayonnaise (read the label)
1 cup diced celery	1 tablespoon fresh lemon juice
1 cup peas *	¼ teaspoon fresh ground pepper
	¼ teaspoon salt, optional

1. Remove the skin of the salmon if you wish,** then flake salmon.
2. Add remaining ingredients and mix well.
3. Serve well chilled on crisp lettuce pieces.

The peas may be fresh or cooked, drained and cooled. Both ways are good.

** See pg. 255.

✖ ✖ *salads* ✖ ✖ 87

Tuna Macaroni Salad

1	cup macaroni shells	1	stalk celery, sliced
1	6-oz. can tuna, drained	½ to ¾ cup mayonnaise (read the label)	
1	small onion, diced	1	tablespoon prepared mustard

1. Cook and drain macaroni shells; rinse with cold water until cooled.
2. Mix all ingredients; season with salt and pepper to taste.
3. Serve chilled.

Note: *Cooked cubed chicken, ham, or turkey can be used in place of tuna for this salad. If using tuna, choose water-packed.*

✖   ✖   ✖   ✖   ✖

Chicken Curry Salad

4	cups diced chicken *	1	can pineapple chunks
1	cup diced celery	1	bunch green grapes
¼	cup minced onion	1	avocado, peeled and sliced
¼	cup minced pimiento	1	small cantaloupe, peeled and diced
1	cup mayonnaise (read the label)	1	pint fresh strawberries
3	tablespoons fresh lemon juice	½	cup slivered almonds
1	teaspoon curry powder	Salad greens **	

1. Blend first seven ingredients and chill.
2. Drain pineapple and prepare fruit. To serve, mound salad in center of platter and sprinkle with almonds.
3. Arrange salad greens around chicken and place fruit on the greens.

 * *Also a good use for leftover turkey.*
** *Fresh young spinach, leaf lettuce, red lettuce, etc.*

Chicken-and-Nut Salad

2 cups diced chicken	½ cup cashew nuts **
½ cup fresh green peas *	⅓ cup mayonnaise (read the label)
½ cup sliced fresh mushrooms	1 to 2 tablespoons wine vinegar
	Fresh ground pepper

Combine all ingredients; serve on crisp lettuce.

  * *Cooked and drained if you prefer.*
** *Walnuts, almonds, or peanuts are good, also.*

✖ ✖ ✖ ✖ ✖

Fresh Mushroom Salad

1 pound fresh mushrooms, whole	½ red bell pepper, minced
1 small onion, chopped	Fresh ground pepper to taste
½ cup sliced ripe olives	½ cup Italian dressing of
½ cup chopped green bell pepper	your choice (read the label)

1. Mix all ingredients.
2. Refrigerate several hours to blend flavors.
3. Serve chilled.

Macaroni-and-Bean Salad

2	cups cooked and drained macaroni	2	stalks celery, minced
1	10-oz. can red kidney beans, drained	¾	cup mayonnaise (read the label)
1	medium green bell pepper, minced	1	clove garlic, minced
1	medium onion, minced	½	teaspoon basil
		¼	teaspoon oregano
		¼	teaspoon fresh ground pepper
		¼	cup wine vinegar

1. Combine first 5 ingredients; mix well. In a separate bowl thoroughly mix remaining ingredients for dressing.
2. Combine salad and dressing; mix well and refrigerate in a covered bowl several hours before serving.

Rice Salad

3	cups cooked rice		
½	cup mayonnaise (read the label)		
1	small bell pepper, minced	¼	cup almond pieces
½	cup minced dill pickle	⅛	teaspoon cloves
2	scallions, thinly sliced	1	teaspoon curry powder
1	stalk celery, minced	½	teaspoon nutmeg

✗ ✗ ✗ ✗ ✗ ✗ ✗
Eating need never be dull—use ingredients that you like, but be willing to experiment, also.
✗ ✗ ✗ ✗ ✗ ✗ ✗

1. Combine all ingredients; chill well.
2. Serve plain or on lettuce leaves.

✗　✗　✗　✗　✗

Curried Chicken-and-Rice Salad

⅓	cup diced celery	½	teaspoon curry powder
⅓	cup diced onion	3	cups cooked and cooled rice
5	mushrooms, sliced	1	medium onion, diced *
1	tablespoon "butter"	1	tablespoon prepared mustard
1	5-oz. can chicken in broth	¼	cup mayonnaise (read the label)
		½	teaspoon salt, optional

1. Sauté diced onion, celery, and mushrooms in "butter" with a little water until tender-crisp.
2. Add chicken and curry powder; mix well.
3. Combine with all ingredients. Place in serving bowl, cover, and refrigerate until cooled.
4. Serve plain or on lettuce leaves.

* The diced onion can be replaced with sliced celery if preferred; slivered almonds are also good with this.

Soups

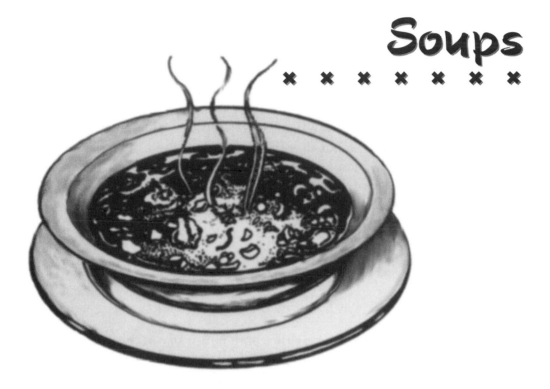

BASIC BEEF STOCK ✖ POULTRY STOCK ✖ BASIC THIN WHITE SAUCE ✖ "CREAM" OF

VEGETABLE SOUP ✖ "CREAM" OF MUSHROOM SOUP ✖ "CREAM" OF TOMATO SOUP ✖

CORNED BEEF "CREAM" SOUP ✖ VEGETABLE BEEF SOUP ✖ QUICK VEGETABLE SOUP ✖

FRENCH ONION SOUP ✖ VEGETABLE SOUP ✖ PSEUDO VICHYSSOISE ✖ CHICKEN EGG-DROP

SOUP ✖ LENTIL SOUP ✖ GREEK LENTIL SOUP ✖ SPLIT PEA SOUP ✖ AND MORE . . .

✖ ✖ ✖ ✖ ✖ ✖ ✖ ✖ ✖ ✖

Soups are an excellent source of nutrition and warmth on cold days. It's a food people the world over enjoy in any weather, however. Soups come in a huge variety, both homemade and prepared. There are some canned and some dry soups that do not have milk, lactose, or other milk by-products, in them, but many more that do. *Read the labels of soups* carefully if you are milk or lactose intolerant.

To make a can of soup a hearty meal in a hurry you can add your own extra ingredients. A couple of easy ideas:

> *Split pea soup with chunks of ham or browned sausage;*
>
> *A favorite soup served over hot rice;*
>
> *A rice soup with fresh lemon and a beaten egg.*

Dehydrated soups are good for a quick lunch, but *avoid* "cream of" soups if you are milk or lactose intolerant. What we call "cream" soups, require the milk alternative if you are milk or lactose intolerant. (See pg. 15. Be aware that some other alternatives may not taste right for a base.)

To make homemade soups you can begin with a bouillon base that you make (see the next recipes), or the stock from cooking vegetables, or par-boiling peppers. Or use bouillon cubes or canned bouillon (read the label). If you are watching your salt intake, bouillon cubes may be too salty. If you do use bouillon, do not salt the soup automatically; wait to see if the final product needs salt.

Create your own delicious soups by adding seasoning preferences or ingredient combinations to please your family's tastes or dietary needs.

Basic Beef Stock

(Bouillon)

4	pounds stew beef	1	tablespoon parsley flakes
2	pounds marrow bones, cracked*	2	bay leaves
3	quarts water	½	teaspoon fresh ground pepper
1	medium carrot, shredded	¼	teaspoon marjoram
1	medium onion, diced	¼	teaspoon thyme
2	stalks celery, diced with leaves		

1. Use a large kettle with a tight-fitting cover. Spray with vegetable spray and brown the meat. Add bones and water; bring to a boil, removing foam as it accumulates.
2. Add remaining ingredients and bring to a simmer. Cover and simmer for 4–5 hours, removing foam occasionally if necessary.
3. Strain and refrigerate immediately until needed. The stock will jell when it has cooled.

It is not absolutely necessary to use marrow bones; you will get very good stock with or without them.

Poultry Stock

(Consommé)

1	5-pound chicken, cut up	2	teaspoons parsley flakes
3	quarts water	1	bay leaf
1	small carrot, shredded	¼	teaspoon thyme
1	small onion, diced	¼	teaspoon fresh ground pepper
2	stalks celery, diced with leaves		

1. In a large kettle combine meat and water and bring to a boil, removing foam as necessary. Add remaining ingredients and bring to a simmer. Cover and simmer for 4–5 hours, removing foam occasionally if necessary.
2. Strain and refrigerate immediately until needed. Do not cool to room temperature before refrigerating; harmful bacteria will grow in any food.

To make a basic "cream" sauce for soups, use Basic Thin White Sauce below as the base. It is combined with chicken bouillon cubes or clarified poultry stock for part of the liquid. Add 1 cup cooked and diced chicken, fish, other meats, or vegetables to make 3 cups of cream soup.

Basic Thin White Sauce
(for soups)

2	cups "milk," cold	
1	tablespoon cornstarch	
1	tablespoon "butter"	

⅛	teaspoon fresh ground pepper
2	chicken bouillon cubes

1. Place cornstarch in a saucepan, add "milk," and stir thoroughly to combine.
2. Add remaining ingredients and bring to a boil over medium heat, stirring constantly; boil 1 minute.

> **✕ ✕ ✕ ✕ ✕ ✕ ✕ ✕**
> *Some bouillon cubes contain milk by-products—**read the label**.*
> **✕ ✕ ✕ ✕ ✕ ✕ ✕ ✕**

Variations:
***Instead** of bouillon cubes use 1 cup "milk" and 1 cup poultry stock.*
***Or** 1 cup "milk" and 1 cup chicken bouillon.*

"Cream" of Vegetable Soup

Double recipe of Basic Thin   1   tablespoon minced onion
    White Sauce (see facing pg.)   2   tablespoons "butter"
2   cups cooked vegetables

1. Use half "milk" and half chicken stock or bouillon for base.
2. Combine cornstarch with cold "milk" before beginning soup; mix thoroughly and mix again just before using—starch settles.
3. Sauté minced onion in "butter"; stir in vegetables and the sauce ingredients; bring to a boil, stirring constantly; boil 1 minute. Reduce heat and simmer 3–5 minutes until vegetables are heated through.
4. Serve hot.

Note: Use vegetables on hand: asparagus, peas, broccoli, carrots, spinach, etc. Use other spices in the sauce to add sparkle to individual soups, and add shredded or diced meat for more variations.

When adding spices, add with the fresh ground pepper to the basic sauce. If using carrots, peas, or zucchini, use basil also. If using cabbage, green bell pepper, or corned beef, add some garlic, minced or powdered. Use about ¼ teaspoon per cup of vegetable or meat.

"Cream" of Mushroom Soup

1   cup chopped fresh mushrooms   ¼   teaspoon onion powder
1   recipe Basic Thin White Sauce
    (see facing pg.)

1. Heat saucepan, spray with vegetable spray. Sauté mushrooms. Combine liquid, cornstarch, and onion powder; add to saucepan with remaining ingredients for making Basic Thin White Sauce.
2. Follow instructions for sauce; reduce heat and simmer 3–5 minutes.
3. Serve hot.

"Cream" of Tomato Soup

1	tablespoon minced onion	2	cups tomato juice
1	tablespoon "butter"	1	tablespoon fresh lemon juice
1	recipe Basic Thin White Sauce (see pg. 96)		

1. Spray saucepan with vegetable spray and sauté onion in "butter."
2. Combine "milk" and cornstarch before adding to saucepan with rest of ingredients for Thin White Sauce. Boil 1 minute.
3. Add remaining ingredients and bring to boil, reduce heat and simmer 3–5 minutes.
4. Serve hot.

> *"Cream" soups are a good way to use leftover diced meats or vegetables. Or if no leftovers are available, thaw and drain frozen chopped vegetables.*
>
> ✖ ✖ ✖ ✖ ✖ ✖ ✖ ✖

Corned Beef "Cream" Soup

2	tablespoons "butter"	2	cups chicken bouillon
3/4	cup thinly sliced celery	1/4	pound shredded corned beef
1/4	cup minced green bell pepper	2	cups shredded cabbage
1	cup minced green onion	1	cup shredded carrot
2	cloves garlic, minced	1	recipe Basic Thin White Sauce (see pg. 96)

1. Sauté celery, bell pepper, green onion, and garlic in "butter" for 5 minutes; add bouillon and cooked, shredded corned beef; simmer 10 minutes.
2. Add cabbage and carrot; return to simmer for an additional 10 minutes. Meanwhile, prepare Thin White Sauce; stir into soup and heat 2–3 minutes.
3. Serve hot.

Vegetable Beef Soup

1	pound beef stew beef	3	medium potatoes, diced
1	14-oz. can tomatoes	4	cups water + 4 beef bouillon cubes
2	carrots, sliced	½	teaspoon fresh ground pepper
3	stalks celery, sliced, leaves also	1	package frozen mixed vegetables, optional

1. Place beef, water, tomatoes, and bouillon in large kettle; cover and simmer until beef is tender.
2. Add fresh vegetables, return to simmer; simmer 10 minutes. Add frozen vegetables if used; bring to a simmer and simmer an additional 8–10 minutes.
3. Serve hot.

✸ ✸ ✸ ✸ ✸ ✸

Quick Vegetable Soup

3	envelopes vegetable soup mix (read the label)	6	cups water
		3	cups tomato juice

1. Place soup mix in large saucepan. Add water and tomato juice and stir in well; bring to boil.
2. Reduce heat; cover and simmer for 15 minutes.

French Onion Soup

6 large white onions, sliced	1½ teaspoons Worcestershire sauce
3 tablespoons "butter"	¼ teaspoon fresh ground pepper
6 cups beef bouillon*	

1. Spray a large deep skillet with vegetable spray; sauté onions in "butter" until tender.
2. Add bouillon and seasonings; heat thoroughly.

Or 6 cups water and 8 bouillon cubes.

Note: For those who can have it, serve with Parmesan cheese at the table.

French Onion Soup is usually served with a slice of French bread in the bottom of the bowl.

Vegetable Soup

1 pound stew beef	3 medium potatoes, cubed
6 cups water	1 tablespoon chopped parsley
1 large onion, chopped	½ teaspoon salt, optional
3 medium carrots, cubed	¼ teaspoon fresh ground pepper
2 stalks celery, sliced	2 bay leaves
3 medium tomatoes, chopped (or 1 16-oz. can)	½ teaspoon each: marjoram, thyme, garlic powder—all optional
1 small parsnip, cubed	

1. Heat a large kettle, then spray with vegetable spray. Brown the meat.
2. Add water and bring to a simmer; cover and simmer for 2½–3 hours, or until meat is tender.
3. Skim off any fat or foam; add remaining ingredients and simmer an additional 20–30 minutes, or until vegetables are tender-crisp.

Pseudo Vichyssoise

5 pounds potatoes, peeled and diced	1 large onion, minced
5 to 7 cups water	7 chicken bouillon cubes
3 stalks celery, minced	3 tablespoons "butter"

1. Use a large kettle with tight-fitting cover to keep water from evaporating. Place potatoes in pan, pour water in to half the depth of the potatoes; cook at a simmer until thoroughly done.
2. Drain water into a smaller saucepan. To the potato water, add the celery, onion, bouillon, and "butter"; cook until vegetables are tender. Meanwhile, mash the potatoes, adding nothing.
3. Combine the mashed potatoes and cooked vegetable mixture; if needed, add enough water to make a thick broth; heat thoroughly.
4. Serve hot, adding "butter" to soup in individual bowls to taste.

Chicken Egg-Drop Soup

4 cups chicken broth*	1/4 teaspoon fresh ground pepper
2 tablespoons cornstarch	1/4 teaspoon sugar
2 tablespoons water	2 eggs, lightly beaten
1 tablespoon soy sauce	2 green onions, chopped

1. In large saucepan heat broth to boiling. Meanwhile, in a small bowl blend cornstarch and cold water to make a smooth paste, stir in soy sauce, pepper, and sugar. Slowly stir mixture into broth. Bring to a boil and simmer until clear, stirring constantly.
2. Remove from heat, then gradually add beaten eggs, stirring until eggs separate into shreds. The hot broth cooks the egg. Add onions and serve.

The broth can be 4 cups water and 4–6 bouillon cubes.

Dried peas and beans should be looked over carefully to pick out any stones or hard soil. Rinse well, then:

> **Either:** *Soak overnight. (If quick-cooking product, omit this step.)*
> **Or:** *Place in pan and cover with water; bring to a boil and boil 2 minutes. Remove from heat and let soak 1 hour; drain and rinse; proceed with recipe. (Omit this step if using quick-cooking beans or peas.)*

This second process allows the gas that is in the beans to escape into the water. By draining and rinsing you are clearing your food of most of the gas that so many of us find uncomfortable when ingesting beans or peas.

Lentil Soup

1	package lentils (2 cups)	1	stalk celery, diced
½	pound hamburger, sausage, or combination of both	1	clove garlic, minced
1	small onion, diced	3	quarts water

1. Prepare lentils. Cook, crumble, and drain meat.
2. Place all ingredients in a large kettle; bring to a boil. Reduce heat, cover, and simmer until tender, 1–1½ hours.

Greek Lentil Soup

1	package lentils (2 cups)	1	stalk celery, diced
8	cups water	2	bay leaves
1	small onion, sliced	1	teaspoon salt, optional
1	small carrot, grated	2	tablespoons wine vinegar

1. Prepare lentils. In a large pan combine all ingredients except vinegar. Cook about 1 hour or until lentils are tender.
2. Remove bay leaves, stir in vinegar, and serve.

Split Pea Soup

1	package split peas (2 cups)	1	medium onion, minced
3	quarts water	2	stalks celery, minced
1	ham slice, diced	1	medium carrot, grated
1	sprig fresh parsley, minced	¼	teaspoon fresh ground pepper

1. Prepare peas. Place all ingredients in a large kettle; bring to boiling point and then reduce heat; cover and simmer 4-5 hours, until peas are tender.
2. Season to taste; serve hot.

Split Pea Soup can be put through a blender or a sieve to make it smoother, if you prefer it that way.

Or thin it with additional water or "milk." Find your own preferences.

Other dried legume soups (beans and peas) are made the same way as above.

✗ ✗ ✗ ✗ ✗ ✗ ✗
Have a cruet of wine or balsamic vinegar available with legume soups. A dash of vinegar in a bowl of soup adds a sparkle to the flavor.
✗ ✗ ✗ ✗ ✗ ✗ ✗

Note: When making soups with meat, dip a lettuce leaf, or leaves into the soup to pick up fat residue.

Sandwiches

✖ ✖ ✖ ✖ ✖ ✖ ✖ ✖ ✖ ✖

HOT SANDWICHES WITH GRAVY ✖ GRILLED PEANUT BUTTER AND JELLY ✖ GRILLED "REUBENS" ✖ CHICKEN-CUCUMBER POCKET SANDWICH ✖ HAM PITA POCKET ✖ CHICKEN (TURKEY) SALAD SANDWICH ✖ EGG SALAD SANDWICH ✖ TUNA SALAD SANDWICH ✖ QUICK TUNA SALAD ✖ HOT TUNA BUN ✖ HAMBURGERS ✖ MUSHROOM BURGER ✖ SLOPPY JOES ✖ RO'S SLOPPY JOES ✖ SPICY SLOPPY JOES ✖ SALMON BURGER ✖ HOT TUNA PASTY ✖ FRENCH-TOAST SANDWICHES ✖ BACON, LETTUCE, AND TOMATO ✖ AND MORE . . .

✖ ✖ ✖ ✖ ✖ ✖ ✖ ✖ ✖ ✖

Hot, cold, grilled, toasted; sliced bread, bagels, pockets, and baked in loaves; plain white, rye, whole wheat, sourdough, pumpernickel; meat, fish, vegetable, egg. *Sandwiches need never be boring.*

Remember though, always *read the labels*. Even for bread you buy regularly, scan the list of ingredients. Bakeries from one section of the country to another do change recipes for the same brand name. This may not happen often, but it does happen. Bakeries may even change ingredients when a good buy is available on a filler, such as whey solids. If margarine is listed, be wary, most are based on milk or milk by-products, lactose, whey, etc. Be careful also of bagels, there is no reason they can't be made with a milk product if they are not kosher. Bagels are not automatically kosher.

The majority of sliced lunchmeats have dried milk, whey solids, lactic acid, lactose, sodium caseinate, or some other form of milk in them. Read the labels carefully for all standard and low-fat cold cuts. Summer sausage is also a good place to find lactic acid or whey solids. When you find a summer sausage that is completely milk free it is very good with a little mustard on dill rye.

Be careful when buying deli meats, also. Take time to find out what's in each recipe and don't buy if the people behind the counter say they don't know. A good deli employee will know or will take the time to look up the ingredients list for you.

*A **word of caution:** Most delis, especially supermarket and fast food places, cut the meat **and** the cheeses on the same slicer. If you, or the person you buy for, is milk or lactose intolerant or sensitive, do not buy under those circumstances. If the deli does not use separate slicers, buy packaged meats (read the label). Many doctors will tell you that such a small amount of contamination will not cause distress. That's incorrect in many cases. **You** are the decision maker on what does or does not cause you, or your child, distress.*

Sandwiches are a traditional way to use leftover meats. Try:

Sliced roast beef with mustard or horseradish, onions, and lettuce

Sliced baked ham with pickle slices, mustard, onions, and lettuce

Sliced roast pork with onions, mayonnaise, lettuce, and tomato

Sliced turkey, dash of salt and pepper, with mayonnaise and lettuce

Sliced cold meat loaf with mustard or mayonnaise, onions, and lettuce

Pita Pockets with any of the above: chop finely and mix with a little mayonnaise, shredded lettuce, minced onion, and bell pepper. Add chopped tomato if you like, or avocado slices, or bean sprouts.

More suggestions:

Cold baked beans on whole wheat

Fried or scrambled eggs on toast with mayonnaise

Lettuce and tomato on fresh bread, or toast, with mayonnaise

Peanut butter and dill pickle on whole wheat—a college tradition

Peanut butter and jelly or jam

Don't forget that leftover cooked meats are good as hot sandwiches, also. Use a basic gravy and serve any time.

Hot Sandwiches with Gravy

2 cups broth or bouillon	1/4 teaspoon fresh ground pepper
1 to 1 1/2 cups cooked meat, diced	2 tablespoons cornstarch
1/2 teaspoon each: garlic and onion powder	1/4 cup cold water
	Bread

1. Heat the liquid, meat, and spices to the boiling point. Meanwhile, combine the cornstarch and cold water, mixing well.
2. Stir cornstarch mixture into boiling meat mixture, stirring constantly; boil 2 minutes.
3. Serve hot on toasted or fresh bread.

Or serve hot sandwiches with a mound of mashed potatoes. Pour gravy over bread and potatoes; serve with tossed salad.

These are favorites that don't have to be given up by people who are lactose or milk sensitive—just don't use cheese.

Grilled Peanut Butter and Jelly

Spread "butter" * on two slices of bread; on the other sides, spread one with peanut butter and the other with your favorite jam or jelly; put peanut butter and jelly sides together. Heat a griddle, spray with vegetable spray; place sandwich "butter"-side down on the heated surface and grill until crispy and golden brown. Turn and brown the other side—enjoy.

Other suggestions:

> *Ham and mustard on rye*
>
> *Turkey and mayonnaise on whole wheat*
>
> *Sliced corned beef and pastrami with mustard on dill rye (add*
> *drained sauerkraut, optional)*

* You may prefer to grill with olive oil instead of "butter."

Grilled "Reubens"

2 *4-oz. packages corned beef*	1 *loaf rye bread*
2 *4-oz. packages turkey slices*	*Slivered almonds, optional*
1 *recipe cole slaw,* **or**	
2 cups sauerkraut, drained	
and mixed with ½ cup	
mayo and 1 teaspoon paprika	

1. "Butter" 12 slices of rye and arrange corned beef and turkey slices on dry side of 6 slices.
2. Top with either the sauerkraut or cole slaw; sprinkle generously with

almonds if desired. Place a slice of bread on top with "buttered"-side up.

3. Heat grill or skillet, spray with vegetable spray; grill sandwiches until crisp and hot on both sides.

Chicken-Cucumber Pocket Sandwich

1	cup cooked and diced chicken	1	small clove garlic, minced
1	small cucumber, diced	1	medium tomato, diced, optional
2	small green onions, sliced	¼	teaspoon fresh ground pepper
¼	cup sliced ripe olives		Mayonnaise to moisten
½	cup shredded lettuce	2	pita bread pockets, halved

1. Combine all ingredients except pita bread and mix gently.
2. Serve in pita pockets.

Ham Pita Pocket

Ham, shredded	Green pepper, sliced thinly
Onion, diced	Mayonnaise and mustard
Lettuce, shredded	Pita bread pockets

1. Amounts depend on how many sandwiches you wish to make and how much you want in each sandwich.
2. Place ingredients in pita pockets and serve cold or warmed in 350° oven for 5-7 minutes.

Chicken (Turkey) Salad Sandwich

2	cups cooked and cubed poultry	½	cup chopped ripe olives
1	small onion, diced	1	tablespoon fresh lemon juice, opt.
1	stalk celery, diced	¼	teaspoon fresh ground pepper
			Mayonnaise to moisten

Mix all ingredients; serve on buns or toast.

Egg Salad Sandwich

5 to 6 eggs, hard cooked
1 small onion, minced
1 stalk celery, minced

1 tablespoon prepared mustard
Salt and pepper to taste
Mayonnaise to moisten*

Mix all ingredients; serve on bread or toast of choice.

Read the label on mayonnaise or any other packaged ingredient.

Tuna Salad Sandwich

1 12½-oz. can water-packed
    tuna, drained
1 stalk celery, chopped
1 medium onion, chopped
1 teaspoon prepared mustard

1 tablespoon wine vinegar
1 cardamom seed, crushed
    (or 1 teaspoon cardamom powder)
¼ teaspoon fresh ground pepper
Mayonnaise to moisten

Mix all ingredients; serve with lettuce, on bread or toast of choice.

Variations:
Add ¼-½ cup walnuts to mixture.
Or omit wine vinegar and cardamom seed; increase mustard to 2 tablespoons.

Quick Tuna Salad

1 can tuna
1 teaspoon garlic powder

1 teaspoon onion powder
Mayonnaise to moisten

Mix ingredients well; serve as above.

Hot Tuna Bun

Place tuna salad on hamburger buns;* heat in 375° oven for 5 minutes. This gives a crisp bun and a nice warm filling—very good.

Note: Any of these sandwiches are good heated. Simply place the ingredients on a sandwich bun and place in 375° oven for 5 minutes or so.

* *This is also very good on an onion bun, but be sure to read the label if milk or lactose intolerant.*

✗ ✗ ✗ ✗ ✗

Hamburgers

1 pound ground beef	1 large tomato, sliced
4 sandwich buns (read the label)	Leaf lettuce
1 large onion, sliced	Condiments of choice

1. Shape beef into 4 patties; broil to desired doneness.
2. Remove to buns, top each with a slice of onion, tomato, and lettuce.
3. Serve with choice of condiments.

Note: Broiling minimizes fat saturation.

Variations:
Serve with slices of crisp bacon in sandwich.
Or divide meat into 8 patties; flatten and place thick slices of onion on 4 patties; top with other patties and press edges together to enclose onion. Broil and serve as above.

Mushroom Burger

1	pound ground beef	1	cup chopped fresh mushrooms
¼	cup diced onions	1	teaspoon basil
Fresh ground pepper, to taste		1	teaspoon garlic powder

1. Combine all ingredients
2. Shape into patties; broil to desired doneness.
3. Serve on buns with choice of condiments.

Sloppy Joes

1	pound ground beef	1	small green bell pepper, minced
½	pound kielbasa, diced	1	8-oz. can tomato sauce
1	medium onion, chopped	1	teaspoon garlic powder
½	cup water	1	teaspoon fresh ground pepper

1. Brown beef and kielbasa; drain.
2. Cook onion and pepper with meat; or sauté in a small amount of water.
3. Combine all ingredients and simmer for 5 minutes.
4. Serve on toasted buns.

Ro's Sloppy Joes

4	pounds ground beef	2	large onions, diced
2	pounds ground sausage	1	large green bell pepper, diced
½	teaspoon garlic powder	3	8-oz. cans tomato sauce
Fresh ground pepper		2	small cans tomato paste
1	large garlic clove, minced	2	cups water

1. Heat a large kettle; spray with vegetable spray and sauté the garlic, onions, and bell pepper in a little water.

2. Add tomato sauce, tomato paste, and water and bring to a simmer. Simmer while browning meats.
3. In a large skillet brown meats with seasonings; drain and add to tomato mixture. Simmer until consistency desired, several hours at least.
4. Serve on buns or open-faced.

- Enough for a party -

Spicy Sloppy Joes

1½	pounds ground beef	2	8-oz. cans tomato sauce
1	large onion, minced	1	tablespoon Italian seasoning
2	stalks celery, minced	1	teaspoon basil
1	clove garlic, minced	1	teaspoon oregano
½	cup minced green bell pepper	¼	teaspoon fresh ground pepper
1	cup water	¼	teaspoon salt, optional

1. Brown beef, crumble, and drain well. Meanwhile, sauté onion, celery, bell pepper, and garlic in small saucepan with 2 tablespoons water.
2. Combine all ingredients and simmer for 15–20 minutes.
3. Serve on buns or choice of bread.

Salmon Burger

1	15½-oz. can salmon *	2	tablespoons fresh minced parsley
⅓	cup rolled oats	2	tablespoons fresh lemon juice
1	small onion, minced	1	tablespoon Worcestershire sauce
1	egg, lightly beaten		

1. Drain and flake salmon; mix all ingredients and shape into 4 patties.
2. Broil until golden brown; serve on hamburger or sandwich buns.

* Bones in canned salmon are soft and edible, making it an excellent source of calcium.

Hot Tuna Pasty

Tuna recipe (see pg. 54 or 110)   *Single-crust pie recipe*
                                                    (see pg. 220)

1. Mix dough for single-crust pie; divide into 4 balls and roll each to a 7"
   square.
2. Divide tuna recipe and place in center of each piece of dough; pull
   edges to meet in middle. Pinch dough together so it stays closed, leaving
   a small opening for steam to escape.
3. Place on ungreased baking sheet and bake at 425° about 20 minutes, or
   until crust is golden brown.
4. Serve hot.

Variations:
Use leftover meats and veggies. Chop or dice meat so it will heat through
and add your choice of vegetables, mayonnaise or gravy, and seasonings.
Mix ingredients, place on dough as above. Bake and enjoy.

leftover beef and gravy ~ diced potatoes (mince if not precooked)
minced onion ~ grated carrot

Or

ground beef (browned and drained) ~ minced onion ~
Fresh ground pepper ~ salt ~ minced parsley

Or

ground beef/sausage (browned and drained) ~ minced onion
~ green bell pepper, minced ~ ripe olives, minced ~ basil
~ Italian seasoning ~ tomato sauce

Note: *For those who **can** have it, add cheese.*

diced franks ~ drained sauerkraut ~ minced onion ~
~ mustard or chili ~

Or

diced ham ~ onion powder ~ celery seed ~
~ mustard ~ mayonnaise ~

Try chicken or turkey salad (see pg. 109).

Meals in a Bun

1. Make half of a favorite biscuit dough recipe; divide dough into 4 parts; roll out to 7" squares. Fill center with favorite meat or fish filling; bring ends together and seal.
2. Spray a baking sheet with vegetable spray; place buns on sheet; bake at 450° for 15–20 minutes, or until browned nicely.

Note: If you need only 2 or 3 buns, use remaining dough to make a cinnamon roll. Roll extra dough thinly; spread lightly with "butter" and sprinkle with a mixture of cinnamon and sugar. Roll and seal ends. Bake on a separate sheet until browned. Slice to serve.

French-Toast Sandwiches

Another way to enjoy hot sandwiches. Either brown in a skillet sprayed with vegetable spray, or bake at 400° on a baking sheet sprayed with vegetable spray, to brown and set egg.

1 egg   *¼ cup "milk"*

1. Beat egg with "milk" to combine thoroughly.
2. Make a ham sandwich, dip it in egg mixture, and brown on both sides.

Variations on next page.

Variations for French-Toast Sandwiches:
Do this for whatever filling you choose, but it is best to keep fillings simple.
*Try turkey slices and mayonnaise **or** thinly sliced beef with mustard or horse-*
radish and onion.

Bacon, Lettuce, and Tomato

Bacon, cooked crisp	*Mayonnaise (read the label)*
Lettuce, crisp and dry	*Salt to taste*
Tomato, sliced	*Bread of choice*

1. Cook bacon until crisp and drain on paper towel.
2. Wash lettuce and tomato, slice tomato fairly thick. Toast bread if desired. Spread with mayonnaise and layer with lettuce, bacon, and tomato; lightly salt if you wish. Top with second slice of toast.

Eggs

FRIED EGGS ✖ POACHED EGGS ✖ SCRAMBLED EGGS ✖ BAKED EGGS ✖ SIMPLE OMELET ✖ OLIVE OMELET ✖ "CREAMED" EGGS ✖ "CREAMED" EGGS WITH BEEF ✖ MEDIUM WHITE SAUCE ✖ "CREAMED" EGGS WITH HAM ✖ HEARTY SCRAMBLED EGGS ✖ CORNED BEEF HASH WITH EGGS ✖ DEVILED EGGS ✖ AND MORE . . .

✖ ✖ ✖ ✖ ✖ ✖ ✖ ✖ ✖ ✖

Many people think that eggs are the same as a milk by-product. They are not—all they have in common with milk is the dairy case at the grocery store and the fact that both come from farms. If you or someone you prepare meals for is milk/lactose intolerant, it does not follow that an egg allergy is present, also. If you suspect an egg intolerance, it is best to have a doctor check it out so you will know for certain.

Eggs are an excellent food when used in moderation. When fresh, they will have a dull shine on the shell. It's best to buy eggs from a refrigerated display; then keep them refrigerated at home. The shell color makes no difference in quality, unless you wish to color them for Easter or some other occasion.

When serving eggs hot—fried, poached, scrambled, etc.—serve them as soon as they are cooked. For the best results, have the people wait for the eggs, not vice versa.

Most of us call eggs that are cooked in the shell in hot water *boiled eggs*. **Do not** boil eggs if you want the best flavor and texture possible. If you have time, have the eggs at room temperature before cooking them. This helps to prevent cracks during cooking. Another way to prevent cracking is to add 2 tablespoons of vinegar for each quart of cooking water.

Choose a large enough container to have all the eggs in a single layer, and to cover completely with water. If doing a few eggs, particularly for soft cooked, begin with boiling water. Place eggs in the water with a spoon, being careful not to crack the shells, and immediately reduce the heat. Keep the water simmering for 3–7 minutes, find the time that suits your taste preference.

> *Soft cooked in shell* . . . . *3-7 minutes*
> *Hard cooked in shell* . . . . *17-20 minutes*

For hard-cooked eggs, cool eggs in cold water to stop the cooking process. Take time to crack the shell lightly just before cooling for easiest peeling. Tap each egg with the blade of a table knife while they are still in the hot water; then put the eggs into cold water. Peel, while eggs are cooling, under cold running water. Refrigerate if not using immediately.

Eggs that are fried or poached should be cooked at low to moderate temperatures. High heat will cause the egg protein to curdle or toughen.

Fried Eggs

Eggs   *Small amount of water*

1. Heat skillet over medium-low heat until pan is evenly heated; spray with vegetable spray.
2. Break eggs and slip them into skillet; add about 1 teaspoon of water for each egg.
3. Cover tightly and cook 5–6 minutes, depending on your preferences.
4. Serve eggs hot.

Note: If you have small children, season eggs before serving. For others, have seasonings at the table so everyone can choose their preference.

Poached Eggs

1. Spray skillet with vegetable spray. Add water to 1½" depth. Bring to a simmering point; keep at simmer. (If you use egg rings they will be sprayed with vegetable spray and placed in skillet with water.)
2. Break eggs into a saucer and slip one at a time into simmering water; slide egg to edge of pan to keep yolk in center of white. Simmer 3–5 minutes; lift with slotted spatula from water.
3. Serve hot and season to individual taste.

Scrambled Eggs

| 6 eggs | $\frac{1}{3}$ cup "milk" or water |
| Fresh ground pepper | |

1. Heat skillet evenly and spray thoroughly with vegetable spray.
2. Break eggs into bowl; add "milk" or water and fresh ground pepper; beat with fork or whisk until well mixed.
3. When skillet is heated, pour in egg mixture and turn heat to low.
4. When eggs start to set, lift portions and tilt the pan a little, or gently stir, to allow uncooked portion to get beneath cooked portion.
5. Serve when still moist and glossy but cooked through.

Baked Eggs

Spray individual baking dishes with vegetable spray; break one or two eggs in each. Bake at 350° for 15–20 minutes, until set; serve hot.

Note: A dot of "butter"; and 2 teaspoons "milk" may be added on top of each egg before baking.

Simple Omelet

| 3 eggs | $\frac{1}{8}$ teaspoon fresh ground pepper |
| 3 tablespoons "milk" | 1 teaspoon vegetable oil (if needed) * |

1. Heat skillet evenly; spray with vegetable spray.
2. Beat eggs until fluffy; add "milk" and pepper, continue beating until well mixed. Pour into heated skillet, over low heat, to cook slowly.
3. As eggs begin to set, lift with spatula to allow the uncooked portion to flow underneath and cook, also, tilting the pan slightly as necessary. While top is still moist and creamy, but all of mixture seems set, fold in half or roll with spatula. Serve immediately.

* Use oil if eggs stick in your pan. You will know after trying one without it. If it sticks, don't worry, it's scrambled eggs now.

Olive Omelet

6   eggs
½   cup sliced ripe olives
2   slices bacon, cooked and
        crumbled

⅓   cup water
Fresh ground pepper
Dill weed, optional

1. Cook, drain, and crumble bacon; combine bacon and olives, set aside.
2. Mix eggs, water, and pepper; beat thoroughly.
3. Heat skillet evenly; spray with vegetable spray. Pour in *half* the egg mixture; lift with spatula as eggs begin to set to allow uncooked portion to cook, also. While mixture is still moist and creamy looking, fill with half the olive mixture, fold in half or roll, turn out onto a plate with a quick flip of the wrist.
4. Sprinkle with dill weed if desired. Keep warm while preparing the other omelet.

- Serves 2 -

To make a French Omelet, *spread with your choice of jelly just before folding or rolling omelet. Serve hot.*

Add *herbs, tomato, meats, or fish; sprinkle 3-4 tablespoons of ingredients of choice on top of each omelet. Proceed as above.*

> ✗ ✗ ✗ ✗ ✗ ✗ ✗ ✗
> *Creamed eggs are versatile. Serve for breakfast, lunch, or dinner—an easy favorite for luncheon guests.*
> ✗ ✗ ✗ ✗ ✗ ✗ ✗ ✗

"Creamed" Eggs

4   eggs, hard cooked
1   cup Medium White Sauce
        (see pg. 122)

Toast, biscuits, or cooked rice

1. Quarter or dice eggs; fold into hot Medium White Sauce.
2. Serve on toast, biscuits, or hot rice.

Medium White Sauce

1	cup "milk," cold	2	tablespoons "butter"
1	tablespoon cornstarch	1/8	teaspoon fresh ground pepper

In a saucepan thoroughly combine "milk" and cornstarch; add "butter" and pepper; bring to boil over medium heat, stirring constantly. Boil 1 minute.

- 1 cup sauce -

"Creamed" Eggs with Beef

1	cup Medium White Sauce (see above)	1	4-oz. package dried beef
1	tablespoon minced onion	4	eggs, hard cooked, quartered or diced

1. Make Medium White Sauce, adding onion with seasonings.
2. Add shredded beef and quartered, or diced, eggs; heat through.
3. Serve hot on toast or biscuits.

"Creamed" Eggs with Ham

4	eggs hard cooked, quartered or diced	1	cup cooked, diced ham
1	cup Medium White Sauce	2	teaspoons minced onion
		1/8	teaspoon fresh ground pepper

1. Add onion with seasoning when making Medium White Sauce.
2. Add eggs and ham to hot white sauce; heat through.
3. Serve hot on fresh biscuits or toast.

Or omit ham; add tuna or salmon; turkey or chicken; crumbled bacon or bacon bits; or chopped steamed spinach.

Hearty Scrambled Eggs

6	eggs	¼	cup minced celery,
⅓	cup "milk"	2	fresh mushrooms, sliced
¼	cup minced onion	½	cup cooked and diced ham
¼	cup minced green bell pepper	1	cup salsa, mild or hot

1. Break eggs into a bowl, add "milk" and pepper; beat thoroughly.
2. Heat skillet; spray with vegetable spray. Sauté vegetables until onion is transparent (add water if needed).
3. Add ham and egg mixture; stir gently while cooking on low heat. Meanwhile, warm salsa in small saucepan.
4. When eggs are set, but still moist, place on individual serving plates; pour salsa on each and serve hot.

Corned Beef Hash with Eggs

1	can corned beef hash	Fresh ground pepper, optional
	Fresh eggs	

1. Spray shallow baking dish, or individual baking dishes, with vegetable spray. If baking dish, make desired number of hollows in hash with the bottom of a glass; break an egg into each. Sprinkle with fresh ground pepper if desired.
2. Bake at 350° for 18–20 minutes, or until eggs are set.
3. Serve hot.

✘ ✘ ✘ ✘ ✘ ✘

Deviled Eggs

1	dozen eggs, hard cooked	1/4	teaspoon fresh ground pepper
1/3	cup mayonnaise (read the label)	1/8	teaspoon salt
2	teaspoons prepared mustard	2	teaspoons lemon juice

1. Cut eggs in half lengthwise; remove sliver from bottom of each half so they will sit on plate evenly. *
2. Remove yolks with spoon; mash yolks and slivers of whites with a fork; add remaining ingredients and mix well. Refill egg whites with yolk mixture and sprinkle with paprika. *Or* replace lemon juice with rice or white wine vinegar.

* Not necessary if using an egg plate.

Variations:
Add *any of the following:*
    1 medium dill pickle, minced
    1/4 cup sweet pickle relish
    1 small can of tuna, drained and flaked
    6–8 slices of crisp cooked bacon, drained and crumbled

Sauces, Gravies, & Glazes

✖ ✖ ✖ ✖ ✖ ✖ ✖ ✖ ✖ ✖ ✖ ✖

BASIC WHITE SAUCE ✖ SAUCE FOR À LA KING ✖ HERB WHITE SAUCE ✖ CUCUMBER HERB SAUCE ✖ SPINACH SOUFFLÉ ✖ BASIC GRAVY ✖ QUICK GRAVY ✖ BASIC MUSHROOM GRAVY ✖ BASIC SWEET GRAVY ✖ TURKEY OR CHICKEN GRAVY ✖ QUICK CHICKEN GRAVY ✖ EASY SPAGHETTI SAUCE ✖ SPAGHETTI MEAT SAUCE ✖ EASY BARBECUE SAUCE ✖ AND MORE . . .

✖ ✖ ✖ ✖ ✖ ✖ ✖ ✖ ✖ ✖

I don't use sauces often, preferring the flavor of foods without them. However, I suspect I came to this preference because most sauces are made with butter, cream, or cheese. Therefore, the habit of leaving them off, or asking to have them left off, developed.

Second, sauces do add calories. However, excellent sauces can be made without milk or milk by-products. Those who wish to use them will find this chapter a good starting place.

The Basic White Sauce is our basis for many of the sauces. Flavorings and usage determine which consistency to use. Arrowroot is preferred by some—it is interchangeable with cornstarch in any recipe.

Basic Gravy is good with meat-and-potatoes meals, and for leftovers such as roast beef, pork and poultry, and meat loaf.

Fruit sauces are a nice accompaniment for meats served hot or cold. And though we may be milk or lactose intolerant, an occasional sweet sauce is always appreciated.

To most any of these sauces you can add your own touch if you wish. This is especially true for white sauces and gravies. For instance:

Add slivered almonds to gravies for chicken;
Or 1 tablespoon horseradish for beef gravies.

Be creative; try whatever strikes you, at least once.

Basic White Sauce – 3 consistencies

This **Medium Sauce** is the one used with the creamed eggs:

- *1 tablespoon cornstarch*
- *1 cup "milk"*
- *1 tablespoon "butter"*
- *1/8 teaspoon fresh ground pepper*
- *1/8 teaspoon salt*

This **Thick White Sauce** is used as a batter in croquettes:

2	tablespoons cornstarch	⅛	teaspoon fresh ground pepper
1	cup "milk"	⅛	teaspoon salt
1	tablespoon "butter"		

This **Thin White Sauce** is used for cream soups:

½	tablespoon cornstarch	⅛	teaspoon fresh ground pepper
1	cup "milk"	⅛	teaspoon salt
1	tablespoon "butter"		

Directions for all three consistencies:

In saucepan thoroughly combine "milk" with cornstarch; add "butter," salt, and pepper. Bring to boil over medium heat, stirring constantly. Boil 1 minute.

- 1 cup of sauce -

✖ ✖ ✖ ✖ ✖ ✖ ✖

Sauce for À la King

½	cup sliced mushrooms	1	cup cooked and cubed meat,
⅛	cup minced green bell peppers		(chicken, turkey, or ham)
2	tablespoons minced pimiento		Hot biscuits

1. Heat a skillet, spray with vegetable spray; sauté; vegetables in the "butter" normally used for the Medium White Sauce 4-5 minutes, add meat, and heat through.
2. Meanwhile, prepare the Medium White Sauce without the "butter"; add prepared vegetables and meat; heat 2 minutes.
3. Serve on hot biscuits.

Herb White Sauce

Prepare the Medium White Sauce (see pg. 126) and add:

$\frac{1}{2}$ teaspoon dill $\frac{1}{8}$ teaspoon nutmeg with seasonings

Variations:
Add $\frac{1}{2}$ teaspoon basil with seasonings.
Or add $\frac{1}{2}$ teaspoon curry powder for Curry Sauce.

Cucumber Herb Vegetables

Double recipe of Medium White   1 cup cherry tomatoes
    Sauce (see pg. 126)   2 cups grated carrots
1 teaspoon basil   3 cups sliced zucchini
1 cup minced or thinly sliced
    cucumber

1. Prepare double recipe of Medium White Sauce, adding basil.
2. Add cucumber after boiling 1 minute and heat through.
3. Spray a 2-qt. baking dish with vegetable spray. Toss Medium White Sauce
   with vegetables; place mixture in baking dish.
4. Bake at 350° for 20 minutes. Serve hot.

Spinach Soufflé

1 cup Thick White Sauce   3 eggs, separated
    (see pg. 127)   1 cup chopped and steamed spinach
1 tablespoon minced onion $\frac{1}{4}$ teaspoon cream of tartar
$\frac{1}{8}$ teaspoon nutmeg

1. Prepare Thick White Sauce, adding onion and nutmeg with seasonings.
   Add egg yolks one at a time, blending well; stir in spinach.

2. Beat egg whites with cream of tartar just until stiff.
3. Fold in sauce mixture; pour into unsprayed 1½-qt. baking dish. Set in pan with 1" of hot water. Bake at 350° for 50-60 minutes, until golden and puffed high. A table knife inserted into soufflé will come out clean when dish is done.
4. Serve immediately.

- Serves 4-6 -

✗ ✗ ✗ ✗ ✗ ✗ ✗

Gravy

When roasting or frying meats, gravy is usually included in the meal plan. However, the usual 2-3 tablespoons of fat is unnecessary, especially if you must watch fat intake. There is a way to get the divine flavor of gravy without the fat.

Drain the roasting or frying pan carefully of the fat only so that you retain the drippings and browned particles. Dip a lettuce leaf in the pan to absorb the remaining fat; discard the leaf/leaves. Stir the liquid (broth, bouillon, etc.) into the pan and heat, while stirring, to loosen the browned particles.

It is not necessary to make the gravy in an awkward-sized pan. Do so if you wish, of course. Otherwise, after the particles are loosened and all the flavor is mixed with the liquid, pour it into a skillet and proceed with the recipe.

For gravies, the liquid can be the water drained off after cooking potatoes or other vegetables. This liquid enhances gravy flavor and saves the vitamins and minerals that might otherwise be lost. Usually, vegetables should be cooked in minimal amounts of water to retain the vitamins and minerals. But, you could use an abundance of water if you're planning to make gravy.

Bouillon cubes are good flavor enhancers if needed. Simply dissolve them in the liquid while you are heating and dissolving the particles. Remember, they are salty, so keep that in mind when using them.

Basic Gravy – 3 consistencies

This **Medium Gravy** is used most often:

2 cups liquid: water, broth, bouillon, or "milk"	2 tablespoons cornstarch
Seasonings as desired*	¼ cup cold water

Thick Gravy:

2 cups liquid	3 tablespoons cornstarch
Seasonings as desired*	¼ cup cold water

This **Thin Gravy** is good for hot sandwiches:

2 cups liquid	1 tablespoon cornstarch
Seasonings as desired*	¼ cup cold water

Directions for all three consistencies:
1. Remove meat from pan and keep warm.
2. Drain fat from pan as directed on previous page.
3. Pour in liquid and heat while stirring to loosen particles (change pans if you wish). Meanwhile, mix cornstarch, cold water, and seasonings if used; blend thoroughly.
4. Stir the cornstarch mixture into the liquid in pan and bring to boil, stirring constantly; boil 2 minutes.

- About 2 cups -

* Seasonings: *salt, fresh ground pepper, garlic powder or onion powder, or other spices or herbs that suit your taste.*

For **Quick Gravies** make the Medium Basic Gravy using:

2	cups chicken bouillon for liquid	$\frac{1}{4}$	teaspoon poultry seasoning
1	teaspoon minced parsley		

Or

2	cups beef bouillon for liquid	$\frac{1}{4}$	teaspoon fresh ground pepper
1	small onion, minced	$\frac{1}{4}$ to $\frac{1}{2}$	teaspoon garlic powder

Sauté onion in roasting pan mixture for 5 minutes; then proceed with gravy making.

Basic Mushroom Gravy:

> *4-oz. can mushrooms ~ mushroom liquid*

Heat mushrooms in their own liquid before stirring in the cornstarch mixture.

Basic Sweet Gravy:

> *2 cups chicken bouillon to make basic gravy*

After gravy has boiled for 2 minutes, add $\frac{1}{4}$-$\frac{1}{2}$ cup fruit sauce or fruit preserves, stirring until smooth.

Note: Some frozen poultry comes with gravy packets for ease of preparation but most contain milk products.

✖ ✖ ✖ ✖ ✖

Turkey or Chicken Gravy

3 cups chicken stock (or bouillon)	¼ cup cold water
3 tablespoons cornstarch	¼ teaspoon poultry seasoning
	¼ teaspoon fresh ground pepper

1. Carefully pour fat from roasting pan, retaining juices and browned particles; remove fat residue with lettuce leaves.
2. Stir in bouillon and keep stirring to loosen the browned particles; transfer liquid to skillet and place over medium heat.
3. Mix cornstarch with cold water, stir into liquid and add seasonings. Bring to boil, stirring constantly; boil 2 minutes.

> ✗ ✗ ✗ ✗ ✗ ✗ ✗
> *By removing the fat before making gravy, there will be fewer calories than in traditional gravies. However, these recipes are not calorie free, so keep that in mind when planning meals.*
> ✗ ✗ ✗ ✗ ✗ ✗ ✗

Quick Chicken Gravy

2 cups chicken bouillon	1 teaspoon minced parsley
2 tablespoons cornstarch	¼ teaspoon poultry seasoning
¼ cup cold water	¼ teaspoon fresh ground pepper

1. Heat bouillon and seasonings over medium heat.
2. Mix cornstarch and water, add to bouillon, stirring constantly. Bring to boil; boil 2 minutes.
3. Gravies should be served immediately.

For a fruit flavor: Make recipe above; after 2 minutes of boiling, stir in ¼ cup apricot preserves; continuing stirring until smooth.

Note: These basic ingredients are also used for pork. You may wish to use "milk" to get a more traditional flavor.

Easy Spaghetti Sauces – 3 choices

1	can tomato paste	1	tablespoon Italian seasoning
1	cup water	1	teaspoon garlic powder
1	tablespoon onion powder	1/4	teaspoon brown sugar
1/8	teaspoon fresh ground pepper	1/4	teaspoon salt

Combine all ingredients in saucepan; bring to a simmer. Cover and simmer at least 15 minutes, stirring occasionally.

1	pound ground beef	2	teaspoons Italian seasoning
1	medium onion, chopped	1/2	teaspoon fresh ground pepper
1	large clove garlic, minced	1/2	teaspoon brown sugar
2	cups tomato juice	1/2	teaspoon basil

1. Brown beef and drain fat. Meanwhile, sauté onion and garlic in 2–4 tablespoons of water for about 5 minutes.
2. Combine all ingredients and bring to a simmer. Simmer 30 minutes, stirring occasionally.

1	pound ground beef	1/2	teaspoon salt
1	pound ground sausage	1	tablespoon oregano
2	medium onions, chopped	1	tablespoon basil
2	cloves garlic, minced	1/2	teaspoon fresh ground pepper
2	15-oz. cans tomato sauce	1	teaspoon Italian seasonings

1. Brown meat and drain the fat thoroughly. Meanwhile, in a small saucepan sauté onion and garlic in 2–4 tablespoons of water.
2. Add onion mixture to drained meat; add remaining ingredients; cover and cook at least 15 minutes.

Spaghetti Meat Sauce

1	pound ground beef	2	stalks celery, chopped
1	large onion, chopped	2	teaspoons oregano
2	cloves garlic, chopped	¼	teaspoon thyme
3 to 4	large tomatoes, chopped	½	teaspoon basil
2	6-oz. cans tomato paste	2	bay leaves

Brown meat and drain well. Place all ingredients in pan and stir well. Bring to a simmer; cover and simmer for 1–6 hours.

✖ ✖ ✖ ✖ ✖

Easy Barbeque Sauce – 2 choices

3	tablespoons brown sugar	¼	teaspoon salt
1	teaspoon paprika	¼	cup vinegar
2	tablespoons Worcestershire sauce	¼	cup catsup
½	cup water	½	cup tomato juice

1. Mix all ingredients in a saucepan; bring to boil and simmer 20 minutes.
2. Refrigerate if not using immediately. Use to brush on ribs while baking.

1	medium onion, minced	1	tablespoon Worcestershire sauce
1	cup tomato sauce	1	teaspoon brown sugar
¾	cup water	½	teaspoon fresh ground pepper
⅓	cup lemon juice	1	tablespoon paprika

1. Combine ingredients in saucepan; heat to boiling.
2. Refrigerate until needed. Use to baste chicken or other meat during cooking.

Oven Barbecue – 2 choices

3 tablespoons instant onion	1 tablespoon brown sugar
¾ cup catsup	1 tablespoon prepared mustard
¾ cup water	1 tablespoon Worcestershire sauce
½ cup vinegar*	1 teaspoon fresh ground pepper

Mix all ingredients in bowl; pour over round steak and bake as per Oven Barbecue Steaks recipe (see pg. 26), or pour over ribs when half done.

* If using on hamburgers use only ¼ cup vinegar.

⅓ cup orange juice concentrate	½ cup catsup
⅓ cup brown sugar	¾ cup steak sauce
¼ cup vinegar	

Combine all ingredients in saucepan; bring to boil; reduce heat and simmer 5 minutes. Use with chicken, beef, or pork.

Glazes for Meats

½ cup brown sugar	3 tablespoons vinegar
¼ cup prepared mustard	

Combine all ingredients. Spoon or brush over ham during last half hour of baking.

Orange Glaze

½ cup brown sugar	¼ cup orange juice
¼ teaspoon ginger	1 tablespoon prepared mustard

Combine all ingredients. Spoon or brush over ham, chicken, or turkey during last half hour of cooking.

Variations for other glazes:
> Brown sugar combined with crushed pineapple
> Cranberry sauce
> Currant jelly
> Orange marmalade ~ brown sugar ~ mustard ~ vinegar
> Apple jelly or mint jelly

Fruit Sauces

An occasional tangy fruit sauce, when there is no special reason, is a real treat. They are a nice addition to a simple meal and good served hot or cold. Fruit sauces are also easy to get along with. Put them on low heat and they will simmer away while you do other things. You can use fresh fully ripe fruit or frozen or canned fruit.

Applesauce

4	medium apples	1	tablespoon cinnamon
¼	cup water	2	tablespoons sugar

1. Wash and peel apples (or leave unpeeled); quarter and remove cores.
2. Place in saucepan and add remaining ingredients. Bring to a simmer; cover and simmer on low for 15–20 minutes.

Plum Sauce

1	30-oz. can purple plums	⅛	teaspoon allspice
3	tablespoons cornstarch	2	tablespoons fresh lemon juice
¼	teaspoon cinnamon	1	tablespoon "butter"

1. Reserving syrup, drain the plums and remove pits.
2. Combine syrup with cornstarch, cinnamon, and allspice; stir well.
3. Cook, stirring constantly until mixture thickens and clears; add remaining ingredients and heat through.

Nectarine Sauce

Wash fruit and remove pits; place in saucepan with 1/4 cup water. Bring to a simmer; cover and simmer until softened and somewhat transparent. If you choose to add sugar, use very little.

Rhubarb Sauce

1	30-oz. can purple plumbs	⅛	teaspoon allspice
3	tablespoons cornstarch	2	tablespoons fresh lemon juice
¼	teaspoon cinnamon	1	tablespoon "butter"

1. Reserving syrup, drain the plumbs and remove pits. Combine syrup with cornstarch, cinnamon, and allspice; stir well.
2. Cook, stirring constantly, until mixture thickens and clears; add remaining ingredients and heat through.

Sweet Sauces
(For the occasional sweet tooth)

Butterscotch Sauce

½	cup sugar	¼	cup "butter"
2	cups corn syrup	1	cup "cream"
⅒	teaspoon salt	½	teaspoon vanilla

In saucepan mix sugar, syrup, "butter," and half of the "cream." Cook over medium-low heat to soft ball stage, 234°. Stir in remaining "cream"; remove from heat; stir in vanilla. Use warm or cold.

Chocolate Sauce

8	ounces dark sweet chocolate	¼	cup sugar
¼	cup water	¼	cup "cream"

1. Melt chocolate, water, and sugar over hot water, or very low heat; stir until smooth.
2. Remove from heat and blend in "cream." Use warm or cold.

Quick Chocolate Mint Sauce

1	package semi-sweet chocolate pieces (read the label)	2	cups "cream"
		¼	cup hot water
		1	teaspoon peppermint flavoring

1. Combine ingredients in a saucepan; heat over low to medium heat, stirring constantly until smooth.
2. Use warm or cold; store covered in refrigerator.

Note: This is a thin sauce to be used as a topping or in "milk" as a chocolate drink for those who can not have regular milk. I thoroughly enjoy this as hot chocolate on cold days.

Caramel Sauce

1	cup brown sugar	1	teaspoon vanilla
¾	cup hot water	⅛	teaspoon salt

1. Melt sugar in heavy saucepan over low heat, stirring constantly until it forms a smooth syrup.
2. Remove from heat and slowly stir in hot water. Return to heat and simmer, stirring constantly until smooth; add vanilla and salt.
3. Store extra in refrigerator until needed.

Currant-Berry Sauce

³⁄₄   cup currant jelly   1   tablespoon cold water

2   cups raspberries,   2   teaspoons cornstarch
      fresh or frozen*

1. Combine currant jelly and berries in a saucepan; bring to a boil.
2. Blend cornstarch and water; stir into hot fruit mixture; boil 1 minute. Use warm or cold, store extra in refrigerator.

If berries are frozen, thaw them. Crush the berries before combining with jelly.

Strawberry Sauce

2   cups strawberries,   ¹⁄₄   cup sugar

      fresh or frozen   2   tablespoons water

Crush berries with sugar and place in saucepan with water; bring to a simmer; simmer on low 10–15 minutes. Use warm or cold; refrigerate extra.

> *The berry sauces are good on pancakes or waffles, and any are good for flavoring "milk" or milk, or as topping for nondairy frozen dessert, ice cream, or puddings. Refrigerate any unused sauce, of course.*
>
> ✖ ✖ ✖ ✖ ✖ ✖ ✖

Breads

✖ ✖ ✖ ✖ ✖ ✖ ✖ ✖

WHITE BREAD ✖ WHOLE WHEAT BREAD ✖ VERY DELICIOUS WHITE BREAD ✖ QUICK ROLL DOUGH—

"BUTTERMILK" ✖ QUICK ROLL DOUGH ✖ RAISIN BREAD ✖ QUICK ICING FOR WARM BREAD ✖ PIZZA

DOUGH ✖ EASY OATMEAL BREAD ✖ OATMEAL FRUIT BREAD ✖ PUMPERNICKEL CINNAMON ROLLS ✖ TEA

RING ✖ STOLLEN ✖ DATE-NUT BREAD ✖ BANANA BREAD ✖ CRANBERRY-NUT BREAD ✖ PINEAPPLE

BREAD ✖ PUMPKIN BREAD ✖ SPICY PUMPKIN BREAD ✖ ZUCCHINI BREAD ✖ FIBER-RICH FRUIT BREAD ✖

BASIC MUFFINS ✖ WHOLE WHEAT MUFFINS ✖ RAISIN MUFFINS ✖ BRAN MUFFINS ✖

OATMEAL MUFFINS ✖ PINEAPPLE MUFFINS ✖ CEREAL MUFFINS ✖ FRUIT MUFFINS ✖ BISCUITS ✖

"BUTTERMILK" BISCUITS ✖ PSEUDO BUTTERMILK ✖ DROP BISCUITS ✖ SOUR DOUGH DROP BISCUITS ✖

✖ YEAST PANCAKES ✖ WAFFLES ✖ "BUTTERMILK" WAFFLES ✖ AND MORE . . .

✖ ✖ ✖ ✖ ✖ ✖ ✖ ✖ ✖ ✖

This section has both standard recipes and some family favorites. For generations, bread was considered the staff of life. I can see why bread has always been considered a staple, especially fresh-baked breads. They taste good and smell wonderful. I suggest spraying baking pans with vegetable shortening rather than greasing the pans; it is a small savings in fats. For the most part the product you choose to prepare your baking pans is a matter of personal preference, since not many calories will be added by what's on a baking pan. However, the vegetable spray does seem to make clean-up easier and it will be recommended throughout this book.

We who cannot tolerate milk or lactose have to be cautious of restaurant-baked goods, and seldom can we enjoy fresh-baked bread when dining out. I really appreciate it when one of my children makes fresh bread; it's a real treat. Fresh breads make up a lot for all the things that we who are intolerant can't have. It is a nice thing we can do for ourselves or the people we cook for, whether milk/lactose intolerant or not.

Breads cover a wide range of textures, flavors, and methods of preparation. There are quick breads and yeast breads; plain, sweet, and tangy breads. This chapter will include at least a sampling of the major kinds, and you can expand and experiment from there. We will include yeast breads and rolls; doughnuts, biscuits, and muffins; coffee cakes, pancakes, and waffles; and dumplings and fritters. This book is meant to give you a good sampling, not to be all inclusive.

For additional tips, see About Yeast Breads (pg. 144).

White Bread

4 loaves		2 loaves	
2	*packages yeast*	2	*packages yeast*
1	*cup warm water*	½	*cup warm water*
3½	*cups warm "milk" **	1¾	*cups warm "milk" **
14 to 14½	*cups flour*	7 to 7½	*cups flour*
6	*tablespoons sugar*	3	*tablespoons sugar*
1	*teaspoon salt*	½	*teaspoon salt*
¼	*cup shortening*	2	*tablespoons shortening*

1. In a mixing bowl dissolve yeast in warm water. Add sugar, salt, shortening, "milk," and half the flour to dissolved yeast; beat until smooth. Mix in enough of the remaining flour until dough clears the bowl. Turn onto a lightly floured board; cover and let rest 15 minutes.
2. Knead until smooth, about 5–10 minutes. Place in a bowl sprayed with vegetable spray, cover with waxed paper and a kitchen towel/cloth. Let rise in warm place until doubled, 1–2 hours. (Shorter time if using fast-rise yeast.)
3. Punch down, cover, and let rise until about doubled again, 30–40 minutes.
4. Spray loaf pans with vegetable spray, then wipe with a paper towel to ensure even coating across the surface. Shape dough into loaves; place in prepared pans; cover with waxed paper and towel (the waxed paper keeps the towel from sticking to dough; you can grease the top of the loaf if you prefer); let rise 45 minutes to an hour. Don't allow it to rise too much. Preheat oven to 425°.
5. Place loaves into 425° oven and bake 25–30 minutes or until evenly browned. Loaves will sound hollow when done; tap loaves with fingers to test for sound. Immediately turn loaves out onto a wire rack to cool.

* You can use "milk," water, or potato water, to make these breads. The term "milk" is used throughout the book; however, be aware that you have a choice.

ABOUT YEAST BREADS

When a recipe calls for warm water to dissolve yeast, the water temperature should be 105°–115°. If the recipe calls for undissolved yeast mixed with the dry ingredients, the liquid temperature should be 120°–130°. Be sure to check the rate of rising when making yeast dough; the fast-rising yeasts take only half the time suggested in the recipes. These recipes call for active dry yeast, but work just as well with compressed yeast if that is what you prefer. Just follow the directions on the yeast package.

Warm dough rises best, so if the kitchen is a not warm (85°), heat your oven on low for a few minutes, turn it off, and place the dough in the warmed oven to rise. If you have a range and the oven is preheating, the top of the stove should be sufficient.

*One advantage of using "milk" is that in making yeast breads we **do not** scald the "milk," then cool to lukewarm to destroy the enzymes which milk contains, and which cause sticky bread dough. But do warm the "milk," for the sake of the yeast; it doesn't like to be cold.*

✖ ✖ ✖ ✖ ✖

When bread is baked, the crust will be crisp if left alone. If you want a soft crust, brush the top with vegetable oil or margarine after removing from pans and cover with a towel for a few minutes.

For a glazed crust, mix an egg yolk with 2 tablespoons of water; brush on the loaf *before* baking.

There are some hot roll mixes, some quick bread mixes, and some muffin mixes that are very good and do not use milk in the ingredients. However, most do have a milk by-product; *read the labels* to find which mixes you can use if milk or lactose sensitive. It doesn't matter if they ask to be

When allowing dough to rise, cover with waxed paper before covering with towel unless you grease the top. For the last rising, spray the baking pan with vegetable spray; cover with waxed paper, and then the towel. This is because the top will not be oily and the towel will stick to the dough without waxed paper.

✖ ✖ ✖ ✖ ✖ ✖ ✖ ✖

mixed with milk, we use the liquid nondairy creamer and they turn out nicely. But do *read the label*.

There are a few prepackaged mixes available for pancakes, also; read the ingredients list to find suitable ones. Frozen bread dough that does not contain milk or milk by-products may be available in some areas, but I have not found any.

Whole Wheat Bread

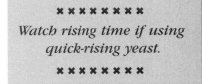

To make whole wheat bread, simply substitute whole wheat flour for one-third to one-half of the white flour called for in the recipe. You exchange only a portion, and you choose the amount of whole wheat flour you wish to use. (Don't use whole wheat flour exclusively—half at most.)

Very Delicious White Bread

5½ to 6 cups flour	2 packages yeast
3 tablespoons sugar	2 cups water
1 teaspoon salt	¼ cup oil (or shortening)

1. Stir together 2 cups flour, sugar, salt, and yeast.
2. Heat oil and water to 120–130°; add to flour mixture; blend on low speed of mixer or with a whisk, until mixed.
3. Stir in additional 3½–4 cups flour by hand, enough so dough pulls away from side of bowl. Turn onto floured surface; knead 1–1½ cups additional flour into dough. This will take about 10 minutes, or until blisters form on dough.
4. Spray a large bowl with vegetable spray. Place dough in bowl, cover with waxed paper, then a towel; let rise until doubled, about 1–1½ hours. Punch dough down; divide in half and allow to rest on the board, under cover, for 15 minutes.
5. Shape into 2 loaves or into rolls, working out any large air bubbles. Place in prepared pan(s) and cover; let rise about 45 minutes to 1 hour.
6. Bake in a preheated 375° oven for 45–55 minutes for loaves, or until hollow sounding. Remove immediately from pans.

Quick Roll Dough — "Buttermilk"

1	package yeast	1	tablespoon sugar
¼	cup warm water	¼	teaspoon salt
¾	cup warm "buttermilk"	3	tablespoons shortening
	(see pg. 15)	2½	cups flour
¼	teaspoon soda		

1. Dissolve yeast in warm water. Stir half the flour and the remaining ingredients into yeast. Add rest of flour and mix in well. Turn onto floured surface; knead until smooth.
2. Shape as desired, place in/on prepared pans, cover and let rise until doubled, about 1–1¼ hours.
3. Bake in a preheated 375° oven for 15–20 minutes.

Quick Roll Dough

2	packages yeast	½	teaspoon salt
2	cups water warm	2	eggs
⅓	cup sugar	⅓	cup shortening
6½	cups flour		

1. Combine water, sugar, and yeast; stir until dissolved.
2. Add salt and 2 cups flour; beat 2 minutes; add eggs and shortening; beat 1 minute. Work in remaining flour by hand. Let rest in bowl 20 minutes. Shape as desired. Half this recipe will make:

Type of Roll	Rise Time	Bake Temp. and Time
16 Pan Rolls	45 minutes	375° for 25–30 minutes
18 Fan Tans	45 minutes	375° for 18–20 minutes
18 Clover Leaves	45 minutes	375° for 18–20 minutes
20 Crescent Rolls	45 minutes	375° for 15–18 minutes
1 Easter Egg Bread	45 minutes	375° for 25–30 minutes

Raisin Bread

3 Loaves		1 Loaf	
½	cup warm water	¼	cup warm water
2	packages yeast	1	package yeast
1½	cups warm "milk"	½	cup warm "milk"
3	eggs	1	egg
¼	cup sugar	1	tablespoon sugar
½	teaspoon salt	¼	teaspoon salt
¼	cup shortening	2	tablespoons shortening
2	cups raisins	1	cup raisins
7 to 7½ cups flour		2¾ to 3 cups flour	

1. Dissolve yeast in warm water; stir in half the flour and the remaining ingredients, mixing until smooth. Add enough remaining flour to handle easily; turn out onto floured surface; knead. Let rise.
2. Shape into loaves, cover, and let rise again.*
3. Bake in a preheated 425° oven for 25–30 minutes. When done loaves will sound hollow; immediately turn out of pans to cool.
4. Shape into rolls if you wish and bake as for Quick Roll breads.

Cover all breads during the rising stages.

Alternatives:
Vary by substituting other fruit for raisins: chopped dates, prunes, or any dried fruit that you like.

Vegetable Bread: This is also a good place to use steamed and chopped vegetables. Spinach or cooked broccoli can be used in place of raisins, but reduce sugar to 2 tablespoons and 1 teaspoon respectively.

Quick Icing for Warm Bread

Stir powdered sugar with enough "milk" to get a spreading consistency. Add flavoring and spread or drizzle over still warm fruit breads, buns, or rolls.

Pizza Dough

2	packages yeast	¼	teaspoon salt
1	cup warm water	2½ to 3¾ cups flour
1	teaspoon sugar		

1. Dissolve yeast, sugar, and salt in warm water and allow to stand for 5 minutes.
2. Add flour, mixing only until blended. Spray a bowl with vegetable spray; place dough in it and cover. Let stand in warm place 20 minutes.
3. Preheat oven to 425°. Spray 2 baking sheets with vegetable spray; spread dough out on them. Spray your hands with vegetable spray to keep dough from sticking to you. Makes 2 thin crusts or 1 thick crust.
4. Add pizza toppings and bake at 425° for 8–18 minutes, depending on amount of toppings used and thickness of crust.

Easy Oatmeal Bread

¾	cup boiling water	¼	cup water warm
½	cup rolled oats	1	package yeast
3	tablespoons shortening	1	egg
¼	cup molasses	2¾ cups flour	
½	teaspoon salt		

1. In a large bowl blend the first 5 ingredients.
2. While cooling to lukewarm, dissolve yeast in warm water.
3. Add yeast, egg, and ½ cup flour to the lukewarm oats mixture; beat 2 minutes, scraping sides and bottom of bowl. Add rest of the flour, mixing until smooth.
4. Spray a loaf pan with vegetable spray, spread the bread mixture into it, and shape dough with floured hands.
5. Let rise in a warm place for 1½ hours. Preheat oven to 375°.
6. Bake at 375° for 50–55 minutes. Remove loaves from pans immediately.

Note: Most breads should not be in drafts when cooling.

Oatmeal Fruit Bread

Follow instructions for making **Easy Oatmeal Bread** (see opposite), but add ⅔ cup raisins or other dried fruit of choice. Serve warm with "butter"—excellent.

✗ ✗ ✗ ✗ ✗

Pumpernickel Bread

3 packages yeast	2 tablespoons shortening
1½ cups warm water	2 tablespoons caraway seed
½ cup molasses	2¾ cups rye flour
1½ teaspoons salt	3½ to 4 cups flour

1. Dissolve yeast in warm water; stir in the molasses, salt, shortening, and caraway seeds; beat until smooth.
2. Mix in rye flour until smooth; add enough white flour to make dough easy to handle.
3. Turn dough onto floured surface and knead about 5 minutes, or until smooth.
4. Spray a large bowl with vegetable spray; place dough in it; cover, and let rise in warm place until doubled, about 1 hour. Punch down, cover and let rise until doubled again, about 40 minutes.
5. Spray a baking sheet with vegetable spray and sprinkle with cornmeal; pinch dough in half; shape into round, slightly flat loaves; place on opposite corners of sheet and cover with waxed paper and towel. Let rise 1 hour.
6. Bake in a preheated 375° oven for 30–35 minutes.

Orange Bread

2	packages yeast	$\frac{1}{2}$	teaspoon salt
1	cup warm water	1	egg, room temperature
$5\frac{1}{2}$	cups flour	$\frac{2}{3}$	cup orange juice, room temperature
$\frac{1}{4}$	cup "butter"	3	tablespoons grated orange rind
$\frac{1}{2}$	cup sugar		

1. Dissolve yeast in water; mix in 2 cups flour and remaining ingredients; beat until smooth. Stir in enough flour to make a soft dough (pulls away from sides of bowl); turn onto a floured surface; knead until smooth, 8–10 minutes.
2. Spray a large bowl with vegetable spray; place dough in bowl and cover with waxed paper and towel. Let rise until doubled, about 1 hour. Punch down; divide in two and shape into loaves.
3. Spray loaf pans with vegetable spray, then place dough in pans; cover and let rise for 1 hour.
4. Bake in a preheated 400° oven for 30–35 minutes.

Russian Black Bread – San-Style

$2\frac{1}{2}$	cups flour	1	tablespoon cinnamon
2	cups bran cereal	4	tablespoons cocoa
2	packages yeast	$2\frac{1}{2}$	cups coffee, hot and fresh
1	tablespoon sugar	$\frac{1}{4}$	cup molasses
$\frac{1}{2}$	teaspoon salt	$\frac{1}{4}$	cup oil
1	tablespoon minced onion	3	cups rye flour
1	tablespoon cardamom	2 to 3	cups flour

1. Blend first 9 ingredients. In a separate bowl, blend hot coffee, molasses, and oil. Add hot liquid mixture (120–130°) to the dry ingredients; blend with a mixer on low speed, then beat on medium setting for 5 minutes. By hand, stir in the rye flour plus enough white flour to make a stiff dough. Knead in an additional 1–1½ cups flour.

2. Spray a large bowl with vegetable spray and place dough in it; cover and let rise about 1½ hours. Punch down; let sit 5 minutes; divide into 2 pieces; shape into circular loaves. Spray a baking pan with vegetable spray. Place loaves on sheet and cover. Let rise 1–1½ hours.
3. Bake in a preheated 375° oven for 45–55 minutes.

English Muffins

1 cup "milk"	3 tablespoons brown sugar
¼ cup water	¼ teaspoon salt
2 tablespoons butter-flvr. shortening *	1 package yeast
2 tablespoons "butter"	2 eggs
4 cups flour	¼ cup rye flour (or cornmeal)

1. In a saucepan heat "milk," water, shortening, and "butter" until very warm (120–130°).
2. Measure flour by sifting. Combine 2 cups flour, brown sugar, salt, yeast, and eggs; add the very warm liquid; beat for 2 minutes at medium speed.
3. Stir in remaining flour by hand; cover with plastic wrap and a towel and let rise until doubled, about 30–40 minutes, less if using fast-acting yeast.
4. On well-floured surface, knead dough until smooth, about 2 minutes; cover and let rest 10 minutes.
5. Roll dough on lightly floured surface to ½" thickness and cut into 3" rounds. Lightly cover each side with rye flour, or cornmeal, and place on ungreased baking sheets. Cover and let rise until doubled, about 30–40 minutes, less if using fast-acting yeast.
6. Bake in a preheated 375° oven for 7–8 minutes; turn each muffin over and bake 7–8 minutes longer.
7. To serve, split with fork (or just slice) and toast.

* If extremely sensitive to milk by-products, use plain shortening.

Raisin English Muffins: *Add 1 cup raisins with second addition of flour; proceed as directed.*
Cinnamon-Raisin English Muffins: *Add 1 tablespoon cinnamon with flour-sugar mixture; add 1 cup raisins with second half of flour; proceed as directed.*

Sweet Roll Dough

36 rolls or 2 loaves	18 rolls or 1 loaf
½ cup warm water	¼ cup warm water
2 packages yeast	1 package yeast
1½ cups warm "milk"	¾ cup warm "milk"
½ cup sugar	¼ cup sugar
1 teaspoon salt	½ teaspoon salt
2 eggs	1 egg
½ cup shortening	¼ cup shortening
7 to 7½ cups flour	3½ to 3¾ cups flour

1. Dissolve yeast in warm water; add next 5 ingredients and half of the flour to yeast; mix until smooth. Add remaining flour, turn onto floured surface, and knead until smooth, about 5 minutes.
2. Spray a bowl with vegetable spray, place dough in it and cover with waxed paper, then a towel; let rise until doubled, about 1½ hours (depending on type of yeast).
3. Punch down; let rise again until almost doubled, about 30 minutes.
4. Shape dough and let rise. Bake according to recipe chosen. For biscuits, crescents rolls, twists, buns, etc., bake in a preheated 400° oven for 12-15 minutes.

Cinnamon Rolls

1. Make a recipe for 1 loaf Sweet Roll Dough (above); after the last rising, roll into a 9 x 15" rectangle. Spread with "butter" and sprinkle with a mixture of ½ cup sugar and 1-2 tablespoons cinnamon.
2. Roll up tightly lengthwise and seal seam well. Cut roll into 1" slices; place on baking pan sprayed with vegetable spray; cover and let rise until doubled.
3. Bake in a preheated 375° oven for 25-30 minutes. It is optional to frost with Quick Icing for Warm Bread (see pg. 147), or with Orange Icing (see pg. 184).

Tea Ring

1. Make a recipe for 1 loaf of sweet roll dough; after last rising, shape into a 9 x 15" rectangle. Spread with "butter"; sprinkle with a mixture of:

   ½ cup sugar ~ 1–2 tablespoons cinnamon ~ ½ cup raisins

2. Roll up tightly lengthwise and seal seam well; place seam down on a baking sheet that has been sprayed with vegetable spray. Form dough into a circle, sealing the two ends together.
3. Use scissors to make cuts at 1" intervals and ⅔ of the way through the ring.
4. Lay each section flat by twisting and turning on its side. Cover and let rise until doubled. Bake in a preheated 375° oven for 25-30 minutes.
5. Frost, while still warm, with Quick Icing for Warm Bread (see pg. 147), sprinkle with ground nuts if you like.

Note: Don't worry about which way to lay the slices, just twist and place each on its side until you have formed a ring. It will turn out nicely.

Stollen

1. Make 1 loaf recipe of Sweet Roll Dough, with the first addition of flour add:

1	*cup raisins*	*1*	*tablespoon lemon rind*
½	*cup chopped almonds*	*¼*	*cup chopped citron*
¼	*cup candied cherries*		

2. After dough has risen, shape into an 8 x 12" oval. Spread with "butter" and fold in half lengthwise, forming a crescent. Press on the folded side so it will stay together.
3. Spray a baking sheet with vegetable spray; place stollen on sheet and spread top with "butter." Cover and let rise until doubled, 35-45 minutes.
4. Bake in a preheated 375° oven for 30-35 minutes, or until nicely browned. If you like, frost with Quick Icing for Warm Bread (see pg. 147), then decorate with green and red candied cherries and slivered almonds.

Variation for Stollen:
With first addition of flour ***add only****: 1 cup raisins, ½ cup slivered almonds, and 1 teaspoon fresh lemon juice. Proceed as above.*

✖ ✖ ✖ ✖ ✖

Quick Breads are breads that do not use yeast. With no yeast, they do not require rising time. There are a wide variety of quick breads and this book will try to include ideas for most of them. You can take it from there.

Date-Nut Bread

1	*cup chopped dates*	*2*	*teaspoons soda*
2	*cups hot water*	*2*	*teaspoons baking powder*
3	*cups flour*	*1*	*egg*
½	*cup sugar*	*1*	*tablespoon oil*
½	*teaspoon salt*	*½*	*cup chopped walnuts*

1. Place dates and hot water in large bowl; let set for 10 minutes.
2. Preheat oven to 400°. Add remaining ingredients and mix carefully.
3. Spray a loaf pan with vegetable spray; pour bread dough into pan. Bake at 400° until done, about 25–30 minutes for small loaves, 50 minutes to 1 hour for large loaf. Cool before slicing.

Variations:
Substitute *1 cup prunes for dates;*
Or *substitute 1 cup raisins for dates;*
Or *substitute 1 cup dried apricots for dates;*
Or *substitute any other nut for walnuts.*

Banana Bread

½	cup oil	2	cups flour
2	eggs, beaten	3	teaspoons baking powder
¼	cup sugar, optional	¼	teaspoon salt
1½	cups mashed bananas	1	cup chopped nuts
1	tablespoon lemon juice		

1. Preheat oven to 350°. Cream together oil and sugar if used; add eggs and beat well; stir in banana and lemon juice.
2. Combine flour, baking powder, and salt carefully; blend with banana mixture; fold in nuts.
3. Spray a loaf pan with vegetable spray; pour batter into it. Bake at 350° for 50–60 minutes.

�֍ ✖ ✖ ✖ ✖

Cranberry-Nut Bread

1	cup chopped cranberries	1½	teaspoons baking powder
½	cup chopped nuts	¼	teaspoon salt
1	tablespoon grated orange peel, optional	½	teaspoon soda
2	cups flour	2	tablespoons shortening
¾ to 1 cup sugar		1	egg, beaten
		¾	cup orange juice

1. Preheat oven to 350°. Mix together and set aside first 3 ingredients.
2. Combine flour, sugar, baking powder, salt, and soda; cut in shortening. Stir in egg and orange juice just until moistened. Add cranberry mixture, folding in carefully.
3. Spray a loaf pan with vegetable spray; pour batter into pan; bake at 350° for 50–60 minutes. Cool overnight before slicing to allow flavors to blend.

Pineapple Bread

½	cup sugar	2	teaspoons baking powder
3	tablespoons "butter"	¼	teaspoon each: soda and salt
2	eggs	1	9-oz. can crushed pineapple
2	cups flour	1	cup chopped nuts

1. Preheat oven to 350°. Cream sugar, "butter," and eggs until fluffy.
2. Combine the dry ingredients and carefully mix with pineapple and egg mixture, blending thoroughly; add nuts.
3. Spray loaf pan with vegetable spray; pour mixture into pan; bake at 350° 45-50 minutes. Cool before slicing.

Most modern flours are presifted. Sifting is a personal preference; sift if you like, or just spoon the flour lightly to measure.

✗ ✗ ✗ ✗ ✗ ✗ ✗

Pumpkin Bread

2	cups pumpkin	1½ to 2 cups sugar	
4	eggs	2	teaspoons soda
1	cup oil	1	tablespoon pumpkin pie spice
⅓	cup water	½	teaspoon salt
3½	cups flour		

1. Preheat oven to 350°. Combine pumpkin, egg, oil, and water; mix well. In a separate mixing bowl mix the dry ingredients; add pumpkin mixture; blend carefully.
2. Spray 2 loaf pans with vegetable spray; pour batter into pans. Bake at 350° for 50-60 minutes. Cool before slicing.

✗ ✗ ✗ ✗ ✗

Spicy Pumpkin Bread

3½ cups flour	½ teaspoon allspice
2 to 2½ cups sugar	½ teaspoon cloves
½ teaspoon salt	2 cups pumpkin
2 teaspoons soda	4 eggs
½ teaspoon baking powder	1 cup oil
1 teaspoon cinnamon	⅓ cup water
½ teaspoon nutmeg	⅔ cup raisins, optional

1. Preheat oven to 350°. In a mixing bowl mix the dry ingredients together.
2. Combine pumpkin, eggs, oil, and water thoroughly; add to dry ingredients; mix carefully and add raisins.
3. Spray two 9 x 5 x 3" loaf pans with vegetable spray and pour batter into them. Bake at 350° for 50–60 minutes.
4. Cool before slicing.

Variation with nuts: *Make Spicy Pumpkin Bread, omitting the nutmeg and allspice; increase cloves to 1 teaspoon and add ⅔ cups chopped nuts with the raisins. Proceed as above.*

Zucchini Bread

3 eggs	½ teaspoon salt
1 cup oil	1 teaspoon soda
1½ to 2 cups sugar	3 teaspoons cinnamon
2 cups grated zucchini	¼ teaspoon baking powder
1 teaspoon vanilla	½ cup chopped nuts
3 cups flour	½ cup coconut

1. Preheat oven to 350°. Beat eggs until foamy; add oil, sugar, zucchini, and vanilla; mix thoroughly. Add remaining ingredients. Pour into 2 prepared loaf pans.
2. Bake at 350° for 50–60 minutes.
3. Cool before slicing.

Fiber-Rich Fruit Bread

1½ cups chopped prunes
½ cup raisins
2 cups boiling water
3 eggs, lightly beaten
¾ cup brown sugar
2 cups whole wheat flour
2 teaspoons baking powder
1 teaspoon soda
1 teaspoon cinnamon
½ teaspoon cloves
2 cups bran cereal
1 cup chopped nuts

1. Preheat oven to 350°. Combine prunes and raisins; pour boiling water over them and mix well; set aside.
2. Beat eggs until light; add sugar and beat until creamy. Fold in 1 cup whole wheat flour, baking powder, soda, cinnamon, and cloves. Stir in half the fruit mixture, bran cereal, and an additional cup of whole wheat flour. Add remaining fruit mixtures and nuts; mix well. The mixture will be thick.
3. Spray 2 loaf pans with vegetable spray; place half the mixture into each. Bake at 350° for about 45 minutes.
4. Cool before slicing.

Alternative: *Use dates instead of prunes, or a 2-cup combination of all three.*

Note: *This bread keeps well in the freezer and is very good toasted.*

✖ ✖ ✖ ✖ ✖

Muffins should never be overmixed; the batter should appear lumpy in order to bake up light. If batter is overmixed, muffins will turn out solid and heavy.

As a general rule, mix the dry ingredients and set aside. Combine and thoroughly mix the wet ingredients in a mixing bowl. Add the dry ingredients and mix gently. If adding fruit or additional ingredients, add before the flour is combined with wet ingredients. You will avoid overmixing. The exception to the rule is brown sugar. Granulated sugar will mix thoroughly with the flour, etc., but brown sugar is mixed with the eggs, shortening, and "milk." This will ensure an even assimilation of the brown sugar.

To prepare the muffin pans, either line the individual cups with paper, or spray the pans with vegetable spray then wipe with a paper towel to ensure all areas are covered. Fill the muffin cups about two-thirds full and bake as per the recipe.

> *Muffins, coffee cake, corn bread, and nut breads are spoonable batters. The batters should be treated carefully. Don't overmix or the finished product will not be light and tender. Stir the batter just until moistened and you will be pleased with your breads.*
>
> ✗ ✗ ✗ ✗ ✗ ✗ ✗

Basic Muffins

2 cups flour	1 egg
2 to 4 tablespoons sugar	1 cup "milk"
3 teaspoons baking powder	$\frac{1}{4}$ cup oil
$\frac{1}{4}$ teaspoon salt	

1. Preheat oven to 400°. Line muffin pans with paper or spray with vegetable spray.
2. Combine dry ingredients and set aside.
3. In a large bowl beat egg; stir in "milk" and oil. Combine all ingredients just until moistened; don't overmix, muffin batter should be lumpy.
4. Fill muffin cups two-thirds full and bake at 400° for 20–25 minutes, until nicely browned.

- 12 muffins -

Whole Wheat Muffins: *Make Basic Muffins, except use 1 cup flour and 1 cup whole wheat flour; proceed as per instructions.*

Raisin Muffins: *Make Basic Muffins, except use brown sugar instead of white, and add $\frac{1}{2}$ teaspoon cinnamon. Proceed as per instructions, and fold in $\frac{3}{4}$ cup raisins with egg mixture.*

Bran Muffins

1¼ cups flour	1 cup bran cereal
1 tablespoon baking powder	1 cup "milk"
¼ teaspoon salt	1 egg
2 to 4 tablespoons sugar	3 tablespoons oil (or shortening)

1. Preheat oven to 400°. Prepare the muffin pans.
2. Combine dry ingredients and set aside.
3. Place cereal and "milk" in mixing bowl and let stand 1–2 minutes, until cereal is softened. Then add eggs and oil, or shortening; beat well. Add flour mixture; mix only until combined.
4. Fill prepared muffin cups two-thirds full. Bake at 400° for 20–25 minutes, until nicely browned.

- 12 muffins -

✖ ✖ ✖ ✖ ✖

Oatmeal Muffins

2 cups flour	⅔ cup shortening
2 cups rolled oats	2 cups "soured milk" (see pg. 16)
1½ teaspoons baking powder	2 eggs
1 teaspoon soda	⅔ cup brown sugar
½ teaspoon salt	

1. Preheat oven to 400°. Prepare muffin pans.
2. Combine dry ingredients except brown sugar; set aside.
3. In a mixing bowl mix shortening, "milk," eggs, and brown sugar thoroughly. Add remaining ingredients and mix just until moistened.
4. Fill muffin cups two-thirds full. Bake at 400° for 20–25 minutes.
5. Good served warm or cooled.

- 24 muffins -

Pineapple Muffins

2 cups flour	¼ cup shortening
1 to 2 tablespoons sugar	2 eggs
3 teaspoons baking powder	1 9-oz. can crushed pineapple
¼ teaspoon salt	

1. Preheat oven to 400°. Prepare muffin pans.
2. Combine dry ingredients in mixing bowl; cut in shortening.
3. In a small bowl, beat egg lightly, then add pineapple. Stir egg-pineapple mixture into dry ingredients, just until moistened.
4. Fill prepared muffin pans two-thirds full. Bake at 400° for 20–25 minutes.

- 18 muffins -

Cereal Muffins

1¼ cups flour	1¼ cups "milk"
3 teaspoons baking powder	1 egg
¼ teaspoon salt	⅓ cup shortening (or oil)
¼ to ⅓ cup sugar	
3 cups cereal, raisin bran, or plain bran	

1. Preheat oven to 400°. Combine first 4 ingredients and set aside. In mixing bowl mix cereal and "milk" and let stand 1–2 minutes. Add egg and shortening; beat well. Add dry ingredients to liquid mixture and stir only until combined.
2. Fill prepared muffin cups two-thirds full. Bake at 400° 20–25 minutes, until nicely browned.

- 12 muffins -

Fruit Muffins

1½	cups flour	1	egg
¼ to ⅓ cup sugar		½	cup "milk"
2	teaspoons baking powder	⅓	cup oil
¼	teaspoon salt	1	cup chopped fruit

1. Preheat oven to 400°. Prepare muffin pans.
2. Combine dry ingredients; set aside.
3. Combine egg, oil, and "milk" thoroughly; blend in 1 cup fruit of your choice. Stir in dry ingredients just until moistened.
4. Fill muffin pans two-thirds full. Bake at 400° for 20–25 minutes.

- 12 muffins -

✖ ✖ ✖ ✖ ✖

Biscuits are most like yeast breads in that they are a soft dough, which is usually kneaded lightly. Baking powder or soda creates the leavening for most quick breads.

Biscuits

2	cups flour	¼	cup shortening
3	teaspoons baking powder	¾	cup "milk"
¼	teaspoon salt		

1. Preheat oven to 450°. Mix dry ingredients; cut in shortening; add "milk" and stir just enough to hold dough together.
2. Place on lightly floured surface; knead lightly; roll about ½" thick.
3. Cut with floured cutter and bake on ungreased baking sheet at 450° for 12–15 minutes.

"Buttermilk" Biscuits: *Use 2 tablespoons fresh lemon juice plus enough "milk" to equal ¾ cup liquid. Use 2 teaspoons baking powder and ¼ teaspoon soda.*

Pseudo Buttermilk Biscuits

2	cups flour	$\frac{1}{4}$	teaspoon soda
2	teaspoons baking powder	$\frac{1}{4}$	cup oil
$\frac{1}{4}$	teaspoon salt	$\frac{2}{3}$	cup "buttermilk" *

1. Preheat oven to 475°. In a medium bowl mix dry ingredients. Pour both "buttermilk" and oil into dry ingredients and stir until mixture forms a ball.
2. Use waxed paper rather than flour to knead and roll the dough. Knead by placing dough on waxed paper and lifting the ends to press the ball of dough with. Proceed until the dough is smooth. Place dough between 2 sheets of waxed paper to roll out to desired thickness. (Barely dampening the surface under the first layer of paper will help keep it from sliding when rolling out the dough.)
3. Cut biscuits with unfloured cutter and bake on ungreased baking sheet at 475° for 10–12 minutes.

* 2 tablespoons fresh lemon juice plus "milk" to make $\frac{2}{3}$ cups liquid.

For Plain Biscuits: *simply use $\frac{2}{3}$ cup "milk" and omit the lemon juice. Also omit soda and use 3 teaspoons baking powder instead. Proceed with recipe.*

Drop Biscuits

2	cups flour	$\frac{1}{4}$	cup shortening
3	teaspoons baking powder	1	cup "milk"
$\frac{1}{4}$	teaspoon salt		

1. Preheat oven to 450°. Mix dry ingredients; cut in shortening. Stir in "milk" until dough is mixed.
2. Spray a baking sheet with vegetable spray; drop dough by teaspoonfuls onto sheet.
3. Bake at 450° for 8–10 minutes, or until browned.

Sour Dough Drop Biscuits: *Follow Drop Biscuit recipe except use only 2 teaspoons baking powder and add $\frac{1}{2}$ teaspoon soda. Add 1 tablespoon vinegar to "milk" to make it sour.*

Poppy Seed Twists

1	cup flour	1/3	cup "milk"
1½	teaspoons baking powder	2	tablespoons "butter"
¼	teaspoon salt	2	tablespoons poppy seeds
¼	cup shortening		

1. Preheat oven to 450°. Mix dry ingredients except seeds; cut in shortening. Stir in "milk" just until moistened.
2. Turn onto lightly floured surface; knead briefly. Roll to a 6 x 12" rectangle. Spread with 2 tablespoons "butter." Sprinkle with seeds and press them into dough.
3. Cut dough into twenty-four 6" strips, then twist the strips and place on ungreased baking sheet. Bake at 450° for 10–12 minutes, or until lightly browned.

✖ ✖ ✖ ✖ ✖

Be sure griddle is at the right temperature when cooking **pancakes** or **griddle cakes**. If a drop of water sizzles when sprinkled on the griddle, the griddle is ready for the pancake batter.

Any pancake recipe can be modified to meet your particular needs. If you wish to, you can add finely chopped ham, mashed banana, or bran cereal for extra flavor or fiber.

Pancakes– "Griddle Cakes"

1	egg	1	tablespoon sugar
1¼	cups "milk"	1	teaspoon baking powder
2	tablespoons oil	½	teaspoon soda
1¼	cups flour	¼	teaspoon salt

1. Blend egg, "milk," and oil.

2. In a separate bowl, combine dry ingredients; add to "milk" mixture and beat until moistened. Batter will be slightly lumpy.
3. Heat griddle and spray with vegetable spray. Pour batter on griddle; turn cakes when they are puffed and bubbly, but before bubbles break. Brown both sides.
4. Keep warm between folds of a warm towel in a warm oven.

"Buttermilk" Pancakes: Substitute "buttermilk" for regular "milk" in Pancakes recipe (see pg. 15). Use only 1 teaspoon baking powder + ½ teaspoon soda.

Fruit Pancakes: Make pancakes and add ½–¾ cup fresh or frozen fruit, cut into small pieces, folded in after batter is made. Drain frozen and canned fruits. Cook as above and enjoy.

Yeast Pancakes

1 package yeast	⅓ cup butter-flavored shortening, softened (read the label)
½ cup warm water	
2 cups cold water	1 tablespoon molasses
2 cups whole wheat flour	1 teaspoon soda dissolved in
1 cup flour	½ cup hot water
½ teaspoon salt	

1. Dissolve yeast in warm water; add cold water.
2. Combine flours and salt; add to yeast water and beat until smooth.
3. Cover and refrigerate several hours or overnight. When ready to use, stir in shortening, molasses, and dissolved soda. Leave at room temperature for 30 minutes.
4. Bake on griddle by same method as for pancakes.

For Plain Cakes: Use 4 cups flour, omit whole wheat flour.

Waffles

2	eggs	2	teaspoons baking powder
2	cups "milk" (or "buttermilk"*)	1	teaspoon soda
2	cups flour	¼	teaspoon salt
6	tablespoons shortening		

1. Preheat waffle iron.
2. Beat eggs thoroughly; beat in remaining ingredients until smooth. Pour into center of hot waffle iron, spreading to cover surface. Close cover and bake until no longer steaming; lift off with fork.
3. Serve hot and enjoy.

- 8 waffles -

Waffles are a favorite but I have yet to find any toaster waffles that are milk-free and lactose-free. So, if we want them, we have to make them.

Neither waffles nor pancakes require syrup in order to be good. They are excellent with a hot fruit sauce (pgs. 136–137), or with "creamed" egg or beef, or plain with a touch of "butter."

✖ ✖ ✖ ✖ ✖ ✖ ✖ ✖ ✖ ✖ ✖ ✖ ✖ ✖ ✖

"Buttermilk" Waffles

3	eggs	½	cup shortening
1½	cups "buttermilk"	2	teaspoons baking powder
	(see pg. 15)	1	teaspoon soda
1¾	cups flour	¼	teaspoon salt

Proceed as for Waffles recipe above for richer waffles.

Yeast Waffles

¼ cup warm water	3 eggs
1 package yeast	¼ cup butter-flavored shortening
1¾ cups warm "milk"	(read the label)
1 tablespoon sugar	2 cups flour
¼ teaspoon salt	

1. Dissolve yeast in warm water in mixing bowl; add "milk," sugar, and salt.
2. Beat in remaining ingredients; cover and let rise for 1½ hours.
3. Stir down, cover, and refrigerate until ready to use. Can be refrigerated overnight for breakfast use.
4. Stir down again when ready to make waffles. Pour into heated waffle iron; bake until browned and crisp.

Note: Waffle mixture may be baked as pancakes.

Cinnamon Coffee Cake

1½ cups flour	1 egg
2 teaspoons baking powder	¼ cup shortening
¼ teaspoon salt	½ cup "milk"
½ to ¾ cup sugar	

Topping

2 teaspoons cinnamon	½ cup brown sugar

1. Preheat oven to 375°. Spray a square baking pan with vegetable spray. Blend dry ingredients; set aside.
2. In a separate bowl combine egg and shortening thoroughly; stir in "milk." Add dry ingredients and stir to blend.
3. Spread batter in pan; sprinkle on topping; bake at 375° for 25–30 minutes, or until toothpick tests clean.
4. Good served warm with fresh coffee, tea, or "hot chocolate."

Use above recipe without the topping to make a variety of coffee cakes.

Variations for Coffee Cake:
Orange Coffee Cake: *Substitute orange juice for "milk." Combine ½ cup sugar, ⅓ cup flour, 1 teaspoon cinnamon, and 3 tablespoons "butter" for topping. Mix until crumbly, sprinkle on cake; proceed with directions for Cinnamon Coffee Cake on previous page.*

Raspberry Coffee Cake: *Make Cinnamon Coffee Cake on previous page except combine ½ cup flour with ½-¾ cup raspberry jelly or preserves. Spread on top of cake batter; it will melt down into cake while baking. Use any favorite jelly or preserves.*

Streusel Coffee Cake

1½	cups flour	1	egg
2	teaspoons baking powder	¼	cup shortening
¼	teaspoon salt	½	cup "milk"
½	cup sugar		

Streusel

½	cup brown sugar	2	tablespoons "butter"
2	tablespoons flour	½	cup chopped nuts
1	tablespoon cinnamon	¼	cup rolled oats

1. Preheat oven to 375°. Combine all ingredients for streusel; set aside.
2. Spray a square pan with vegetable spray. Blend dry ingredients for coffee cake; set aside. Combine egg and shortening thoroughly; stir in "milk." Add dry ingredients, stir well.
3. Spread half the batter in pan; sprinkle with half the streusel mix; add rest of batter, sprinkle on rest of streusel.
4. Bake at 375° for 25-30 minutes.

> ### Suggestions for Fresh Fruit
> Use ¾ cup of any of the following for coffee cakes or pancakes: **Blueberries; strawberries; minced peach or nectarine; chopped apple or pear; raspberries or chopped bing cherries.** These should be washed and well drained.
>
> If using frozen or canned fruit, use only ½ cup per recipe because they will be more moist. If you use banana, use 1 cup mashed banana and reduce the amount of sugar.

Crunchy-Top Coffee Cake

2	cups flour	1/3	cup butter-flavored shortening
1/2	cup sugar		(read the label)
3	teaspoons baking powder	1	egg
1/4	teaspoon salt	2/3	cup "milk"

Topping

2 to 4 tablespoons "butter"		1/4	cup brown sugar
2	tablespoons flour	1	teaspoon cinnamon
1/4	cup coconut	1/4	cup chopped nuts

1. Preheat oven to 350°. Spray square pan with vegetable spray. Blend dry ingredients. Add shortening, "milk," and egg; beat thoroughly. Pour into pan.
2. Mix topping ingredients with fork and sprinkle on top of coffee cake. Bake at 350° for 35–40 minutes.
3. Serve warm.

Pineapple Upside-Down Cake

1/3	cup "butter"	1/4	teaspoon salt
1/2	cup brown sugar	1/3	cup shortening
1	can pineapple slices, drained	2/3	cup "milk"
1 1/2	cups flour	1	egg
3/4 to 1 cup sugar		1	teaspoon vanilla
2	teaspoons baking powder		

1. Preheat oven to 350°. Melt "butter" in square baking pan or heavy 10" skillet; sprinkle brown sugar over the melted "butter." Arrange pineapple slices in a pattern.
2. In a mixing bowl combine dry ingredients; add remaining ingredients and mix thoroughly; beat 4–5 minutes with mixer.
3. Pour batter over fruit; bake at 350° for 40–50 minutes.
4. Remove from oven and immediately turn upside down on a serving plate; leave pan over cake briefly.
5. Serve warm.

Corn Bread

1	cup flour	4	teaspoons baking powder
1	cup cornmeal	2	eggs
¼	teaspoon salt	¼	cup melted margarine
4 to 6 tablespoons sugar		1	cup "milk"

1. Preheat oven to 425°. In a mixing bowl combine the first 5 ingredients.
2. In a small bowl beat remaining ingredients until blended. Pour liquid ingredients into dry and mix, just until moistened; do not overmix.
3. Spray an 8" square pan with vegetable spray. Pour the batter into the pan and bake at 425° for 25–30 minutes.
4. Serve warm.

✖ ✖ ✖ ✖ ✖ ✖ ✖

Popovers

1	cup flour	1	cup "milk"
¼	teaspoon salt	2	eggs

1. Preheat oven to 425°. Spray popovers pan or custard cups with vegetable spray thoroughly.
2. Combine all ingredients; beat just until smooth.
3. Fill cups half full and bake at 425° for 40-45 minutes.
4. Serve immediately.

> ### POPOVERS
> Popovers will be high, crusty, and hollow. Serve as hot bread, or fill with creamed fish, egg, or meat for the main course. Experiment and have fun.
>
> ✖ ✖ ✖ ✖ ✖ ✖ ✖ ✖

Parsley Dumplings

1½ cups flour	¼ teaspoon salt
2 teaspoons baking powder	3 tablespoons shortening
3 tablespoons minced parsley	¾ cup "milk"

1. Blend dry ingredients; cut in shortening; mix in "milk."
2. Have meat and stock at boiling point. Slide spoonfuls* of batter into the boiling stock; cook on medium heat uncovered for 10 minutes, then 10 additional minutes covered. A domed cover will prevent soggy dumplings by directing moisture droplets from them.
3. Serve hot.

- 10 dumplings -

* *Dip spoon into hot liquid before dipping into dumpling mixture. Do this for each dumpling to ensure easy sliding from spoon.*

> *Dumplings are a quick bread cooked by steam.*
>
> **x x x x x x x x**

Plain Dumplings: *omit parsley.*
Chive Dumplings: *substitute minced chives for parsley.*
Herb Dumplings: *substitute 1 teaspoons sage or other herb.*

Cornmeal Dumplings

¾ cup flour	¼ cup shortening
½ cup cornmeal	1 egg
2 teaspoons baking powder	6 tablespoons "milk"
¼ teaspoon salt	

1. Combine dry ingredients; cut in shortening.
2. Beat egg with "milk"; add to dry ingredients and mix thoroughly.
3. Have stock at boiling point; drop batter onto the stock; cook uncovered 10 minutes, then covered 10 minutes longer.
4. Serve hot.

- 12 dumplings -

Fritter Batter – 2 choices

1	cup flour	2	eggs
1	teaspoon baking powder	½	cup "milk"
¼	teaspoon salt	1	teaspoon oil

1. Combine dry ingredients in mixing bowl.
2. In separate bowl combine eggs, "milk," and oil; add to dry ingredients and beat until smooth. *For a thinner batter, use only 1 egg; increase "milk" to 1 cup and increase oil to ¼ cup.*
3. Heat vegetable oil to 375°. Coat dry food with flour and dip into batter; allow excess to drip off and transfer to hot oil. Fry until nicely browned; drain on absorbent towel. Newspaper under paper towel works very well for absorbing oils.

Note: Use dry or moist foods that will be dipped individually. You can use many foods to make fritters. Use your imagination and experiment. Try these:

Shrimp
Fish fillets
Boneless chicken strips
Potato slices
Onion rings

Bananas
Pineapple slices

Fritters and doughnuts are also quick breads. However since they are usually deep fried, frequent indulgence is not recommended.

✗ ✗ ✗ ✗ ✗ ✗ ✗ ✗

Corn Fritters

1. Make fritter batter and add 1 cup corn, cooked and drained. Cook by spoonfuls in hot oil; serve with "butter."
2. Make fruit fritters with chopped fruit of choice and roll in powdered sugar after frying if you like.

- 15 fritters -

Note: Use thick fritter batter for corn, fruit, or other ingredients that are very moist. You want it thick enough to hold together. The thin batter is good for shrimp, fish, etc.

Doughnuts

3½	cups flour	¼	teaspoon salt
2	teaspoons baking powder	2	eggs
1	teaspoon soda	¾ to 1 cup sugar	
¼	teaspoon nutmeg	2	tablespoons shortening
½	teaspoon cinnamon	¾	cup "buttermilk"

1. Blend dry ingredients; set aside.
2. Beat eggs; add sugar and shortening, beat thoroughly; stir in "buttermilk." Add dry ingredients; mix well.
3. Heat oil to 375°.* Roll out on flour-covered surface to ⅓" thick. Cut with doughnut cutter. Carefully slip doughnuts into hot oil with a spatula, turn as doughnuts rise to surface, to brown evenly, about 2–3 minutes total; drain.
4. Serve plain, sugared, or glazed.

At 375° oil will brown a cube of bread in about 60 seconds.

Chocolate Glaze for Doughnuts

1	square unsweetened chocolate, melted	2½	cups confectioner's sugar
½	teaspoon vanilla	¼	cup "milk"

1. Mix chocolate, vanilla, and sugar.
2. Stir in "milk" just until smooth and of glaze consistency.

Potato Doughnuts

2¾	cups flour	3	eggs
4	teaspoons baking powder	1	cup mashed potato, plain
¼	teaspoon salt	¾	cup sugar
¼	teaspoon nutmeg	3	tablespoons shortening
¼	teaspoon mace		

1. Combine first 5 ingredients; set aside. In a mixing bowl beat eggs; add potato, sugar, and shortening; beat well. Add dry ingredients to egg mixture and blend thoroughly.
2. Heat oil, 3–4" depth, to 375°.* Roll dough out on lightly floured surface to about ⅓" thickness; cut with floured cutter and then *carefully* slip into hot oil. Turn doughnuts, and holes, as they rise, to brown evenly. They will cook in 2–3 minutes.
3. Drain; dust with sugar and cinnamon, or powdered sugar if desired.

Orange Doughnuts

2	cups flour	½ to ¾ cup sugar	
2	teaspoons baking powder	2	tablespoons butter-flavored
½	teaspoon cinnamon		shortening (read the label)
¼	teaspoon nutmeg	½	cup orange juice
¼	teaspoon salt	2	tablespoons grated orange rind
2	eggs		

1. Combine first 5 ingredients; set aside.
2. Mix orange juice and orange rind; set aside.
3. In a mixing bowl beat eggs; add and beat in sugar and shortening. Stir the dry ingredients into egg mixture alternately with orange mixture. Mix thoroughly; cover and chill for 1 hour.
4. Roll out on flour-covered surface to ½" thickness; cut with floured cutter.
5. Heat oil to 375°.* Carefully slip doughnuts into heated oil. When doughnuts rise, turn to brown evenly; drain.
6. Dust with sugar and cinnamon, or powdered sugar if you like.

At 375° oil will brown a cube of bread in about 60 seconds.

Desserts

✖ ✖ ✖ ✖ ✖ ✖ ✖ ✖ ✖ ✖

DELICATE PUFFS ✖ SPRITZ COOKIES ✖ CHOCOLATE COOKIES ✖ SNACKERWHATSITS ✖ PEANUT BUTTER
ICING FOR LEMON COOKIES ✖ COOKIE WREATHS ✖ SUGAR COOKIES ✖ PEPPERMINT SUGAR COOKIES
✖ CHRISTMAS COOKIES ✖ GINGERBREAD PEOPLE ✖ FAVORITE GINGERBREAD PEOPLE ✖ DECORATING
ICING ✖ MARSHMALLOW TREATS ✖ BROWNIES ✖ COCONUT-CHERRY BARS ✖ POPCORN BALLS ✖
MUMSY'S LEMONY COCONUT BARS ✖ ORANGE-COCONUT BARS ✖ APPLESAUCE CAKE ✖ MAPLE-
WALNUT CAKE ✖ BASIC YELLOW CAKE ✖ BASIC WHITE ✖ CHOCOLATE-ALMOND FLUFFY "BUTTER"
FROSTING ✖ CHOCOLATE FROSTING ✖ FLUFFY COCOA FROSTING ✖ ORANGE FROSTING ✖ MAPLE
RHUBARB CUSTARD PIE ✖ CHERRY PIE ✖ PEACH PIE ✖ GELATIN PEACH PIE ✖ AND MORE . .

✖ ✖ ✖ ✖ ✖ ✖ ✖ ✖ ✖ ✖

Almost everyone has a favorite cookie or dessert. Most families have several cookie traditions, ours does and they will be included here. Be aware that sugars other than lactose sometimes cause intestinal distress also. Eat sweets sparingly to feel your best. Some recipes give you a choice on the amount of sugar to use. *You* decide how sweet you want your food; it will be great either way.

Be aware of how your system reacts to foods. A small amount of sugar may be acceptable, but in larger amounts one can feel uncomfortable, then tired. That's because with sugar intake, blood sugar levels rise quickly, then drop just as quickly, with a resulting tired feeling.

The dessert section is included for people who cannot ingest milk, but it is a good section for anyone who wants to create tasty desserts. It is great for milk- or lactose-intolerant children who expend lots of energy. You can make treats and desserts for them that their friends will enjoy, also.

Delicate Puffs

2½ cups flour	½ to ¾ cup sugar
1 teaspoon baking powder	¾ cup shortening + "butter"
1 3-oz. package fruit gelatin	2 eggs
¼ teaspoon salt	1 teaspoon vanilla

1. Combine dry ingredients; set aside.
2. Cream shortening, "butter," and sugar; beat in eggs and vanilla; blend in dry ingredients. Chill.
3. Preheat oven to 400°. Shape into ¾" balls and place about 3" apart on ungreased baking sheets. Flatten with bottom of a glass dipped in granulated sugar to keep it from sticking to cookies.
4. Bake at 400° for 5–6 minutes.

- 3 dozen cookies -

COOKIES

When making cookies don't overbake them. When cookies are done, remove them from the baking sheet immediately, unless instructed otherwise. Cookies continue baking as long as they are on the hot surface. Also remember, **do not** *use too much flour. Measure lightly, don't pack flour, and don't add more than necessary when rolling. Excess flour makes cookies dry.*

Remember, brown sugar is beaten with eggs and shortening to ensure even assimilation. In this section the recipes will simply ask to have the sugars mixed or creamed, whether brown or granulated (white) sugar is used.

Shortening + "butter": *Use butter-flavored shortening and "butter." If severely milk intolerant, do not use butter-flavored shortening; use plain shortening or margarine with same fat content as butter. If only shortening is used, cookies are very firm. If only "butter" is used, cookies are very soft. Use approximately ⅔ shortening to ⅓ "butter," or half and half. You decide how you prefer them. This replaces butter and margarine in recipes.*

Spritz Cookies

2½ cups flour	*½ to ⅔ cup sugar*
¼ teaspoon baking powder	*1 egg*
¼ teaspoon salt	*1 teaspoon vanilla*
1 cup shortening + "butter"	*½ teaspoon almond flavoring*

1. Combine dry ingredients; set aside.
2. Cream shortening/ "butter" and sugar; add eggs and flavorings, mix well.
3. Add dry ingredients to egg mixture and combine thoroughly.
4. Chill at least 1 hour. Preheat oven to 375°. Press through cookie press onto ungreased baking sheets.
5. Bake at 375° about 8–10 minutes.

- Enough for 1 or 2 spritz lovers, or
6 dozen medium cookies –

Variations: *Add ¼ cup finely chopped almonds*
Or *blend 2 squares unsweetened chocolate, melted, into the shortening mix.*

Chocolate Cookies

2½ cups flour	⅔ to ¾ cup sugar
¼ teaspoon soda	1 egg
¼ teaspoon salt	1 teaspoon vanilla
¼ cup "milk"	2 squares unsweetened chocolate,
1 cup shortening + "butter"	melted

1. Combine the dry ingredients; set aside.
2. Cream shortening + "butter" with sugar; add egg, vanilla, and melted chocolate, beat well.
3. Add dry ingredients to egg mixture, alternately with "milk"; beat after each addition. Chill at least 1 hour.
4. Preheat oven to 400°. Press dough through cookie press onto ungreased baking sheets.
5. Bake at 400° for about 8 minutes.

- 6 dozen cookies -

Snackerwhatsits

> When rolling cookies, use a cloth-covered board if possible. By covering the cloth with flour, less flour is taken up into the dough.

1⅓ cups flour	
⅔ to ¾ cup sugar	
½ teaspoon soda	½ teaspoon baking powder
⅛ teaspoon salt	1 egg
¼ cup cereal nuggets	1 teaspoon vanilla
½ cup shortening	Sugar and cinnamon for rolling cookies in before baking, optional

1. Preheat oven to 400°. Combine dry ingredients; set aside.
2. Cream shortening and sugar; beat in egg and vanilla, blend in dry ingredients.
3. Roll rounded tablespoonfuls of dough into cinnamon mix, and drop dough onto an ungreased baking sheet. Bake at 400° for about 8 minutes.

- 3-4 dozen cookies -

Peanut Butter Cookies

1¼ cups flour	½ cup shortening + "butter"
½ teaspoon baking powder	½ cup peanut butter
¾ teaspoon soda	⅓ cup brown sugar
⅓ cup sugar	1 egg
⅛ teaspoon salt	

1. Combine dry ingredients; set aside. Combine remaining ingredients and mix thoroughly; stir in dry ingredients; chill.
2. Preheat oven to 375°. Roll into 1½" balls and place 3" apart on baking sheets sprayed with vegetable spray. Flatten with the bottom of a glass dipped in flour; or with a fork in crisscross fashion.
3. Bake at 375° for 10-12 minutes. (Less time if smaller size.)

- 3 dozen cookies -

***Vary** by adding 1 teaspoon cinnamon with the dry ingredients.*

Peanut Butter-Oatmeal Cookies

3 cups rolled oats	1 cup peanut butter
1½ cups flour	¾ to 1 cup brown sugar
½ teaspoon soda	⅓ cup water
¼ teaspoon salt	1 egg
¾ cup shortening + "butter"	1 to 2 teaspoons vanilla

1. Combine dry ingredients; set aside.
2. Mix shortening, "butter," peanut butter, and sugar until fluffy; add egg, water, and vanilla; mix thoroughly.
3. Add dry ingredients; mix well; chill dough for at least 1 hour.
4. Preheat oven to 375°. On ungreased cookie sheets place 1" balls of dough; flatten with the bottom of glass dipped in flour, or use a fork dipped in flour for the traditional crisscross design. Keep sizes uniform.
5. Bake at 375° for 8-10 minutes.

- 5-6 dozen small cookies -

Applesauce Cookies

2¼ cups flour	¾ to 1 cup brown sugar
½ teaspoon soda	1 egg
¼ teaspoon salt	½ cup applesauce
1 teaspoon cinnamon	1 cup raisins
¼ teaspoon cloves	½ cup chopped nuts
¾ cup shortening	

1. Preheat oven to 375°. Combine dry ingredients; set aside.
2. Beat shortening, sugar, and egg thoroughly; add applesauce; stir in dry ingredients. Mix in raisins and nuts.
3. Drop by teaspoonfuls onto baking sheets sprayed with vegetable spray. Bake at 375° for 10–12 minutes.

- 4 dozen cookies -

Oatmeal Cookies

3 cups rolled oats	1 egg
1 cup flour	¾ to 1 cup brown sugar
¼ teaspoon salt	½ cup sugar
½ teaspoon soda	¾ cup shortening + "butter"
1 to 2 teaspoons vanilla	¼ cup water

1. Preheat oven to 350°. Combine dry ingredients; set aside.
2. Beat remaining ingredients together until creamy; add dry ingredients and mix well.
3. Spray baking sheets with vegetable spray; place dough by teaspoonfuls onto sheets.
4. Bake at 350° for 10–12 minutes.

- 5 dozen cookies -

Variations:
Add up to 1 cup of raisins;
Or 1 cup of chocolate chips, read the label;
Or 1 cup coconut to egg mixture;
Or 1 teaspoon cinnamon to dry ingredients.

Raisin Cookies

2¾ cups flour
½ teaspoon soda
¼ teaspoon salt
1 cup chopped nuts
1 cup chopped raisins
½ cup shortening

1 cup brown sugar
2 eggs
1 cup "buttermilk"
    (see pg. 15)
1 to 2 teaspoons vanilla

1. Preheat oven to 375°. Combine dry ingredients; set aside.
2. Cream shortening, sugar, and eggs; stir in "buttermilk" and vanilla. Add dry ingredients to egg mixture; combine well.
3. Spray baking sheets with vegetable spray. Drop teaspoonfuls of dough 2" apart. Bake at 375° about 10 minutes.

- 4 dozen cookies -

Variations: *With raisins* **add** *1 cup coconut*
Or *1 6-oz. package chocolate chips, read the label.*

Jumbo Banana Cookies

3 cups flour
1½ teaspoons soda
¼ teaspoon salt
1 cup chopped nuts
1 to 2 teaspoons vanilla

1 cup shortening
¾ to 1 cup sugar
2 eggs
2 bananas, mashed (1 cup)
½ cup "buttermilk"
    (see pg.15)

1. Combine dry ingredients; set aside.
2. Mix shortening, sugar, and eggs thoroughly; stir in "buttermilk," vanilla, and banana. Add dry ingredients to banana mixture and chill for 1 hour.
3. Preheat oven to 375°. Spray a baking sheet with vegetable spray; place dough by tablespoonfuls about 2" apart on sheet. Bake at 375° about 10 minutes.

- 3 dozen cookies -

Pumpkin Cookies

4	cups flour	1½ to 2 cups brown sugar	
2	cups rolled oats	¾ to 1 cup sugar	
2	teaspoons baking powder	1	egg
2	teaspoons cinnamon	1 to 2 teaspoons vanilla	
¼	teaspoon salt	1½	cups pumpkin
1½	cups shortening + "butter"	1	cup raisins

1. Preheat oven to 350°. Combine dry ingredients; set aside.
2. Cream shortenings and sugars until fluffy; add eggs and vanilla; mix thoroughly. Add dry ingredients and pumpkin alternately, mixing well; stir in raisins.
3. Spray baking sheet with vegetable spray and drop dough by ¼ cups, separating cookies slightly. Bake at 350º for 20–25 minutes, until firm and lightly browned. Remove cookies from baking sheets. Cool and decorate if desired. (Bake shorter time if smaller size.)

- 32 large cookies -

Vary *by adding ½ cup semi-sweet chocolate pieces (read the label) with the raisins;* **Or** *omit raisins and add 1 cup chopped nuts and ½ cup chocolate pieces (read the label).*

Pineapple Cookies

3½ cups flour		1	cup shortening
1	teaspoon soda	1 to 1½ cups sugar	
¼	teaspoon salt	1	egg
¼	teaspoon nutmeg	1	9-oz. can crushed
½	cup chopped nuts		pineapple, undrained

1. Combine dry ingredients; set aside.
2. Mix shortening, sugar, and egg; stir in pineapple. Add dry ingredients; chill about 1 hour.

MARGARINE AND BUTTER

If severely milk or lactose intolerant, most brands of margarine and all butter will cause digestive problems. Butter, the "normal" baking ingredient, contains at least 80 percent fat. The rest is milk solids and water.

When choosing a substitute, use shortening or a combination of shortening (butter-flavored may be best, but do not use if severely lactose intolerant) and margarine. The margarine you use as a spread may not be a good choice for baking or other cooking. Do not use soft spreads (not even soft butter), they do not contain enough fat. Make your choice for spreads and if it's a soft spread, or a stick margarine that is not at least 80 percent fat, find another alternative for baking. A combination of shortening and "butter," or margarine works well. Reduced calorie margarine is not for baking.

✗ ✗ ✗ ✗ ✗ ✗ ✗ ✗ ✗ ✗ ✗ ✗ ✗ ✗ ✗

3. Preheat oven to 400°. Spray baking sheets with vegetable spray. Place dough by teaspoonfuls 2" apart on sheets. Bake at 400° for 8–10 minutes.

- 4 dozen cookies -

Chocolate Chip Cookies

1½ cups flour	⅔ cup shortening
¼ teaspoon salt	⅔ cup brown sugar
½ teaspoon soda	⅓ cup sugar
1 6-oz. package chocolate chips (read the label)	1 egg
½ cup chopped nuts	1½ teaspoons vanilla

1. Preheat oven to 375°. Combine dry ingredients; set aside.
2. Cream shortening, sugar, egg, and vanilla. Add dry ingredients and mix well.
3. Drop dough by teaspoonfuls about 2" apart on ungreased baking sheets. Bake at 375° for 8–10 minutes.

- 2-3 dozen cookies -

Toll House Cookies

2¼ cups flour	1 cup shortening
1 teaspoon soda	½ to ¾ cup brown sugar
¼ teaspoon salt	½ to ¾ cup sugar
1 12-oz. package chocolate chips (read the label)	1 teaspoon vanilla
	1 egg
1 cup chopped nuts	

1. Preheat oven to 375°. Combine dry ingredients; set aside.
2. Cream shortening, sugar, vanilla, and egg. Mix dry ingredients in well.
3. Stir in chocolate and nuts. Place by spoonfuls onto ungreased baking sheets. Bake at 375° for 8–10 minutes.

- 4 dozen cookies -

Orange Cookies

2 cups flour	¾ cup sugar
½ teaspoon baking powder	1 egg
½ teaspoon soda	½ cup orange juice
¼ teaspoon salt	2 tablespoons grated orange rind
⅔ cup shortening	

1. Preheat oven to 400°. Combine dry ingredients; set aside.
2. Mix shortening, sugar, and eggs; stir in orange juice and orange rind. Add dry ingredients.
3. Place by teaspoonfuls about 2" apart on ungreased baking sheets. Bake at 400° for 8–10 minutes.
4. Frost with Orange Icing if desired.

- 2 dozen cookies -

Orange Icing

2 cups powdered sugar	½ teaspoon vanilla
2 tablespoons "butter"	2 tablespoons orange juice

Blend sugar, "butter," and vanilla with enough orange juice to make a smooth frosting. Add 1 teaspoon of orange rind if you like.

Vary by replacing orange juice and rind with lemon in cookies.

Scotch Shortbread

½ cup butter-flavored	¼ cup sugar
shortening (read the label)	2 cups flour
¼ cup "butter"	¼ teaspoon salt

1. Preheat oven to 350°. These cookies are usually best if mixed by hand; a mixer will create a tough dough. Blend the shortening and "butter" with the sugar in a mixing bowl; add combined flour and salt; work it in thoroughly, this may take up to 5 minutes.
2. On a lightly floured board, roll dough to ⅓–½" thickness; cut into desired shapes.
3. Place on ungreased baking sheets and bake at 350° for 20–25 minutes.

- 2 dozen cookies -

Note: These cookies do not change shape and they do not brown. This is a good cookie to decorate.

Lemon Slice Cookies

1 cup shortening + "butter"	2 tablespoons lemon rind
1 cup powdered sugar	2½ cups flour
¼ teaspoon salt	1 egg white
¼ teaspoon yellow food coloring	Yellow-tinted sugar

1. Preheat oven to 375°. Combine all ingredients, except flour, and mix well; blend in flour.
2. On floured board roll dough to ¼" thickness. Cut into 2" circles—then cut in half.
3. Place on ungreased baking sheets and bake at 375° for 6–8 minutes.

4. Beat 1 egg white together with 1 teaspoon water. Roll round edge of baked and cooled cookies in egg mixture, then in yellow-tinted sugar.

Icing for Lemon Cookies

    1 cup powdered sugar $\frac{1}{8}$ teaspoon salt
    Lemon juice to blend,
        about 1–2 tablespoons

1. Blend powdered sugar with lemon juice and salt until mixture can be forced through an icing tube or funnel, yet is thick enough to hold its shape.
2. Use icing tube or waxed paper funnel, squeeze a thin line of icing to resemble white line of lemon slice along rounded edge of cookie.

Cookie Wreaths

    1 cup shortening + "butter" $\frac{1}{2}$ teaspoon almond extract
    $\frac{3}{4}$ cup powdered sugar   1 cup rolled oats
    2 cups flour   Green food coloring and
    $\frac{1}{4}$ teaspoon salt   red and green candied
                            cherries for decorations

1. Preheat oven to 350°. Cream shortening and sugar until fluffy. Add flour, salt, and almond extract; mix thoroughly. Stir in oats and tint dough with green food coloring. Shape teaspoonfuls of dough into 6" lengths; form the lengths into wreaths.
2. Place cherries on overlap to represent holly berries and leaves. Bake at 350° for 10 minutes; cool for 1 minute *before removing* from baking sheets, then cool on wire racks.

- 3 dozen cookies -

Sugar Cookies

$2\frac{1}{2}$ cups flour
$\frac{3}{4}$ to 1 cup sugar
1   teaspoon baking powder
$\frac{1}{4}$ teaspoon salt
$\frac{1}{2}$ cup butter-flavored shortening
     (read the label)

$\frac{1}{4}$ cup "butter"
2   eggs
1   teaspoon vanilla (or $\frac{1}{2}$ teaspoon
     lemon flavoring)

1. Combine dry ingredients; set aside. Combine remaining ingredients thoroughly; stir in dry ingredients. Chill at least 1 hour.
2. Preheat oven to 400°. Turn onto floured board; roll to $\frac{1}{8}$" thickness. Cut with cookie cutters. Place on ungreased baking sheets and bake at 400° for 6-8 minutes.

- 4 dozen cookies -

Peppermint Sugar Cookies

5   cups flour
$1\frac{3}{4}$ to 2 cups sugar
2   teaspoons baking powder
$\frac{1}{2}$ teaspoon salt

$1\frac{1}{2}$ cups shortening
4   eggs
1   teaspoon peppermint flavoring
$\frac{1}{2}$ teaspoon vanilla

1. Combine dry ingredients; set aside. Mix remaining ingredients; blend dry ingredients into egg mixture and mix well. Chill at least 1 hour.
2. Preheat oven to 400°. Drop by teaspoonfuls onto greased baking sheets; flatten with bottom of glass dipped in sugar or flour. Bake at 400° for 6-8 minutes.

- 9 dozen cookies -

Christmas Cookies

2¾	cups flour	⅓	cup shortening
⅓	cup sugar	1	egg
1	teaspoon soda	1	teaspoon lemon flavoring
¼	teaspoon salt	⅔	cup honey

1. Combine dry ingredients; set aside. Mix remaining ingredients thoroughly; blend in dry ingredients. Chill.
2. Preheat oven to 375°. Roll on lightly floured board to ¼" thickness; cut into desired shapes.
3. Spray cookie sheets with vegetable spray and place cookies 1" apart on sheets. Bake at 375° for 8–10 minutes.
4. Cool and decorate.

- 3 dozen cookies -

Gingerbread People

3½	cups flour	¼	teaspoon salt
1	teaspoon baking powder	1	cup shortening + "butter"
1	teaspoon ginger	½ to ⅔ cup brown sugar	
1	teaspoon allspice	½	cup molasses
1	teaspoon cinnamon	1	egg
1	teaspoon cloves	Icing (see opposite page)	

1. Combine dry ingredients; set aside. Cream shortening, sugar, molasses, and egg; stir in dry ingredients. Chill until dough is firm enough to handle.
2. Preheat oven to 350°. On lightly floured surface roll half the dough into ¼" thickness (keep the rest chilled); cut out figures with person-shaped cookie cutter.
3. Spray baking sheets with vegetable spray; place cookies on sheets without letting them touch. Bake at 350° for 10–12 minutes, or until lightly browned.
4. Cool on wire racks.

- 2 dozen cookies -

Favorite Gingerbread People

4½ cups flour	½ teaspoon salt
1 teaspoon soda	1 cup shortening
1 teaspoon baking powder	¾ to 1 cup sugar
1 teaspoon ginger	1 cup dark molasses
½ teaspoon cinnamon	

1. Combine dry ingredients; set aside. Cream shortening and sugar, stir in molasses; add dry ingredients, mix well. Chill until dough is firm enough to handle.
2. Preheat oven to 375°. On lightly floured surface roll dough to ¼" thickness; cut into desired shapes and place on ungreased baking sheets. Bake at 375° for 8–10 minutes.
3. Cool and decorate.

- 3 dozen cookies -

Decorating Icing

4 cups powdered sugar	¼ cup "milk"
1 tablespoon flavoring	Food coloring

1. Blend powdered sugar with flavoring of your choice (vanilla, almond, peppermint, lemon, etc.) Add about ¼ cup "milk," or just enough to easily force icing through a pastry tube or waxed paper funnel, yet thick enough to hold its shape.
2. Divide into small bowls and tint as desired with food coloring.

Marshmallow Treats

¼ cup "butter"	3 cups crisped rice cereal
1 10-oz. package marshmallows	2 cups rolled oats

1. Melt "butter" in large saucepan on low heat; add the marshmallows; stir until melted; remove from heat. Add cereal, stir until well coated.

2. Spray a 13 x 9" pan with vegetable spray. Press the mixture evenly into the prepared pan; cool.

- 2 dozen squares -

Variations:
Add *1 cup raisins with cereal*
Or *1 cup peanuts*
Or *stir ½ cup peanut butter in with the melting marshmallows*

Brownies

9″ square pan	13 x 9″ pan
¾ cup flour	1½ cups flour
⅓ to ½ cup cocoa	⅔ to 1 cup cocoa
¼ teaspoon baking powder	½ teaspoon baking powder
¼ teaspoon salt	¼ teaspoon salt
½ cup chopped nuts	1 cup chopped nuts
½ cup vegetable oil	1 cup vegetable oil
1 cup sugar	2 cups sugar
1 teaspoon vanilla	2 teaspoons vanilla
2 eggs	4 eggs

1. Preheat oven to 350°. Combine the dry ingredients; set aside. In a mixing bowl blend the oil, sugar, vanilla, and eggs; beat well. Add the dry ingredients gradually to the oil mixture until well blended.
2. Spray baking pan with vegetable spray and spread batter into pan. Bake at 350º for 20–25 minutes, until brownies begin to pull away from pan.
3. Cool in pan and cut.

Variations: Use *coconut instead of nuts;*
Or *use a variety of nuts;*
Or *flavor with 1 teaspoon peppermint and ½ teaspoon vanilla.*

✖ ✖ ✖ ✖ ✖

Oatmeal-Chocolate Chip Bars

$3\frac{1}{2}$ cups rolled oats
$1\frac{1}{2}$ cups flour
$\frac{1}{4}$ teaspoon salt
1 teaspoon soda
1 teaspoon vanilla
1 cup shortening + "butter"

2 to $2\frac{1}{2}$ cups brown sugar
2 eggs
1 12-oz. package chocolate chips
   (read the label)
$\frac{1}{2}$ to $\frac{3}{4}$ cup walnut pieces

1. Preheat oven to 350°. Combine dry ingredients; set aside. Cream shortening and sugars; add eggs, vanilla, and water; beat until creamy. Add the dry ingredients to the creamed mixture; mix well; add the chocolate chips and nuts.
2. Spray a 13 x 9" pan with vegetable spray; put batter into pan. Bake at 350° for 25–30 minutes, or until browned. Do not overbake.
3. Cool and cut into bars.

Coconut-Cherry Bars

$2\frac{1}{2}$ cups flour
$1\frac{1}{2}$ teaspoons baking powder
$\frac{1}{4}$ teaspoon salt
$\frac{1}{2}$ cup chopped nuts
$\frac{2}{3}$ cup coconut
1 6-oz. package chocolate chips,
   (read the label)

1 cup shortening + "butter"
$\frac{3}{4}$ cup sugar
1 egg
1 teaspoon vanilla
$\frac{1}{2}$ cup cherries, red or pitted bing

1. Preheat oven to 375°. Combine the dry ingredients; set aside. Cream shortening and sugar; add eggs and vanilla; mix well. Add the dry ingredients and cherries; combine thoroughly.
2. Spray a 9 x 13" pan with vegetable spray; spread dough into the pan. Bake at 375° for about 25 minutes.
3. Cool slightly in pan; cut into bars.

- 40 bars -

Popcorn Balls

12 cups popped corn	1 cup corn syrup
1 cup sugar	2 teaspoons vanilla

1. Spray a large bowl or pan with vegetable spray and place the popped corn in it; place in a 250° oven. Stir the sugar and corn syrup together in a saucepan and bring to boil over medium heat.
2. Cook without stirring. When mixture reaches 290° on a candy thermometer, remove from heat and stir in the vanilla. Carefully pour over warmed popcorn and stir well.
3. Cool just until you can handle it. Spray your hands with vegetable spray and quickly shape popcorn into balls.

- 8-10 balls -

✖ ✖ ✖ ✖ ✖

Mumsy's Lemony Coconut Bars

1¼ cups flour	⅔ cup brown sugar
½ teaspoon soda	1 egg
¼ teaspoon salt	1 to 2 teaspoons fresh lemon juice
½ teaspoon cinnamon	1½ teaspoons lemon rind
¼ teaspoon nutmeg	1 cup rolled oats
¼ teaspoon mace	1 cup coconut
½ cup shortening	½ cup chopped nuts

1. Preheat oven to 350°. Combine dry ingredients; set aside. Cream shortening and sugar, add egg, and beat well. Add remaining ingredients, mixing thoroughly.
2. Spray an 8" square pan with vegetable spray; spread batter into pan.
3. Bake at 350° for 18 minutes. Cool and cut into bars.

Optional topping: *¾ cup chocolate chips (read the label) + ¼ cup finely chopped nuts. Bake bars for about 12 minutes. Spread with topping. Return to oven for about 5 minutes. Spread topping with a knife if necessary; cool in pan.*

Orange-Coconut Bars: *Substitute orange juice and orange rind for the lemon and lemon rind.*

Walnut Bars

½	cup flour	1	cup brown sugar
⅛	teaspoon salt	1	teaspoon vanilla
¼	teaspoon soda	1	cup chopped walnuts
1	egg		

1. Preheat oven to 350°. Combine the flour, salt, and soda; set aside.
2. Cream the egg, sugar, and vanilla. Stir in dry ingredients and add nuts.
3. Spray an 8" square pan with vegetable spray; spread dough in pan. Bake at 350° for 18–20 minutes.

- 16 bars -

Note: *These bars will be soft in the middle when ready to be removed from oven. Do not overbake. Cool and cut.*

✖   ✖   ✖   ✖   ✖

✖ ✖ ✖ ✖ ✖ ✖ ✖ ✖ ✖ ✖

Cakes, pies, and desserts are usually made with milk, or cream, and butter. These recipes are milk and lactose-free, and low in salt. Some allow you to choose how much sugar to use. Remember, if you decide to use less sugar, the textures may be a little different than you are used to, that is to be expected. When cooking desserts for diabetics I suggest using a sugar substitute.

As for box cake mixes, other than angel food cakes I have yet to find any that are lactose- and milk-free. I will admit that I haven't looked very hard, preferring to make scratch cakes. Manufacturers are not required to include small or trace amounts of lactose/milk in the list of ingredients. By baking from scratch *you* control what goes into your food.

These recipes are all made by using an electric mixer and by mixing for a total time of 3–5 minutes. Additional mixing may result in a tough- or firm-textured cake that does not rise as it should. For any cake, sift to measure the flour, or put the flour into the measuring cup lightly, then combine all the dry ingredients and blend well, unless instructed otherwise. Remember, brown sugar is not a dry ingredient, and always pack brown sugar when measuring.

I suggest lining the cake pan or pans with waxed paper (see pg. 15). If you prefer to grease and flour them do so, of course. Just remember do not use the wrappers from margarine if they contain a milk-based product. What you put on the pans will be a part of the finished product. If greasing the pans, dust sides and bottoms with flour for most cakes, but for choco-late cakes dust with cocoa.

After the cakes are baked, remove from the oven and allow to cool in the pans 8–10 minutes. Then remove from pans and cool completely on wire racks before decorating or frosting.

To make cupcakes, use paper cups to line muffin pans. Fill the cups about half full with regular cake recipe, and about seven-eighths full with chiffon recipe. Bake at 400° for 18–20 minutes.

Essentially icing is sugar. There is no way to get around that, except to use it sparingly. However, if you are going to use it, use enough to make your efforts worthwhile. That is, when you make a cake, make it attractive, use enough icing to show off your creation.

To get an attractively frosted cake, rub the edges, tops, and bottoms of each layer to remove as many crumbs as possible. This way you can use less icing to make the cake attractive because you needn't hide the crumbs that get caught in the frosting.

To decorate a cake, frost it with your choice of icing/frosting, then add the decorations of your choice. Cakes and other desserts can be made special with decorations other than icings. Use fresh flowers and leaves, or fresh evergreen and berries. Wash and dry the chosen items and put plastic wrap under them if you wish. *Do not* allow them to be ingested unless safe. I think most children have a Christmas cactus, grown from the leaves and flowers used to decorate one birthday cake or another. Use the items you have at hand for decorating cakes, like nuts and fresh fruits such as grapes, cherries, and strawberries. These make lovely decorations when used imaginatively. Also, birthdays don't have to be celebrated with cakes; pies or fancy gelatins are very nice, also.

Cake Decorating Ideas

Make a Cherry Chiffon Cake (see pg. 208) and frost it with a thinned version of Maraschino Cherry Frosting (see pg. 215). The thinned frosting will settle down the edges of the cake and form a "hat brim" on the plate. The frosting will glaze. After it has set up, or glazed, place a ribbon of tissue paper, or other ribbon, around the cake and allow a long trailing portion to hang free. Place a colorful feather or flowers in the ribbon, and with additional decorations on the top you have a very nice spring or Easter bonnet.

Make a flower by placing whole blanched almonds around a candied cherry center. Then roll green gum drops flat and cut into strips for stems and leaves.

Make balloons by placing jelly beans or other milk-free round candies on the cake. Or make and use peppermint wafers (see pg. 240). Draw strings on the frosting with food coloring and a toothpick or fine brush, or with frosting tinted a different color. **Or** cut round gumdrops and use the circles for the balloon shapes.

Make a flower with large marshmallows. Make 3–4 cuts about two-thirds of the way through the marshmallow. Twist and flatten the cut pieces to resemble petals. Place a yellow gum drop or jelly bean in the center; add flat green gum drop strips for leaves.

Chocolate leaves on a fluffy white frosting are impressive. Gather and wash an assortment of leaves. Melt semisweet chocolate and spread it on the leaves; place the leaves in refrigerator to cool and firm. Peel the leaves off the chocolate and use the chocolate leaves to decorate the cake sides and top. See page 212 for more chocolate ideas.

Coconut is an all-time favorite for decorating cakes. Plain white coconut on a white icing is an elegant way to make a cake special for any occasion.

To tint coconut, fill a jar about half full with coconut and sprinkle the desired coloring over the top. Cover the jar and shake vigorously, until the coloring is evenly distributed. Use a few drops at a time and repeat until you get the intensity of color you want.

To toast coconut, spread it evenly in a shallow baking pan and place in a 350° oven for 8–12 minutes. Stir the coconut often to toast it evenly.

To flavor coconut, toss with the desired flavoring in a small bowl or covered jar. For ½ cup coconut use ¼–½ teaspoon cinnamon; use it to top the frosting of spice cake, or sprinkle on cereal or puddings. Or use 1 tablespoon grated orange or lemon rind for 1½ cups coconut.

Fruitcake

3	cups flour	1	cup orange juice
1	teaspoon baking powder	2	cups candied fruit mix
½	teaspoon salt	1	cup raisins
2	teaspoons each: allspice and cinnamon	½	cup candied pineapple
1	teaspoon cloves	½	cup candied cherries
1	cup shortening	½	cup citron
1½	cups brown sugar	½	cup candied lemon peel
4	eggs	1 to 1½ cups nuts	

1. Preheat oven to 300°. Prepare two loaf pans by cutting heavy wrapping paper or brown paper bag to fit; line pans with the paper and oil the paper well. (It keeps the sides from browning too much.)
2. Combine the dry ingredients; set aside. Mix the shortening, sugar, and eggs until fluffy. Combine orange juice and flavoring; mix the orange juice and dry ingredients alternately to shortening mixture. Blend in fruit and nuts; fill the pans.
3. Bake at 300° for 2½–3 hours, or until toothpick tests clean.

Variations:
Omit orange juice and use ¾ cup of any other fruit juice.

Or use 1 cup "milk" and any 5- to 6-cup combination of fruits and nuts to suit your taste. Proceed as above.

✖ ✖ ✖ ✖ ✖

Victory Cake

1	cup water	1	teaspoon cloves
⅔	cup brown sugar	2	cups flour
1	cup raisins	1	teaspoon soda
½	cup shortening	⅛	teaspoon salt
1	teaspoon cinnamon	1½	cups chopped walnuts
1	teaspoon nutmeg		

1. Line a 9" square pan with waxed paper (see pg. 15).
2. Combine the first 7 ingredients in a saucepan; bring to boiling point; simmer 2 minutes; cool at least 1 hour. Combine remaining ingredients and stir into cooled raisin mixture.
3. Preheat oven to 300°. Pour batter into prepared pan and bake at 300° for 50-60 minutes, or until cake tests done.
4. Cool in pan, dust top with powdered sugar, or sprinkle the sugar through a paper doily to create a design.

Dee's Carrot Cake

2½	cups flour	⅛	teaspoon nutmeg
½	cup rye flour	3	eggs
1½	cups sugar	¾	cup oil
2	teaspoons soda	¼	cup water
2	teaspoons baking powder	1	teaspoon vanilla
¼	teaspoon salt	4 to 5 carrots, shredded *	
1½	teaspoons cinnamon	1	cup chopped walnuts
⅛	teaspoon ginger	1	8-oz. can crushed pineapple, undrained

1. Preheat oven to 350°. Line a 9 x 13" pan with waxed paper (see pg. 15).
2. Measure flours by sifting or spooning lightly; combine dry ingredients; set aside. In large bowl beat eggs, oil, water, and vanilla until fluffy; add

dry ingredients and mix well. Fold in remaining ingredients. Pour into pans. Bake at 350° for 40-45 minutes, or until cake tests done.

3. Frost, if desired, with Fluffy Spice Frosting (see pg. 215).

I use large carrots, but the recipe asks for medium—your preference.

Vary *by using 3-4 carrots and adding 1 cup coconut;*
Or *add ¾ cup chocolate chips; read the label if milk or lactose sensitive.*

✗ ✗ ✗ ✗ ✗

Ginger Cake

2⅓	cups flour	½	teaspoon cinnamon
1	cup sugar	¼	teaspoon cloves
1	teaspoon soda	½	cup butter-flavored shortening
1	teaspoon baking powder		(read the label)
⅛	teaspoon salt	1	egg
½	teaspoon ginger	¼	cup molasses
		1	cup "sour milk" (see pg. 16)

1. Preheat oven to 350°. Line 9 x 13" pan(s) with waxed paper (see pg. 15).
2. Measure flour carefully. Combine dry ingredients; set aside. Combine shortening, egg, and molasses until fluffy; scrape sides and bottom of bowl. Add dry ingredients and "milk" alternately and beat only until batter is smooth, remembering to scrape sides and bottom of bowl.
3. Pour into pan(s). Bake at 350° for 35-40 minutes.
4. Cool in pans(s) for 8-10 minutes; remove to wire racks to finish cooling.

Banana-Nut Cake

2½ cups flour
1 to 1⅔ cups sugar
1¼ teaspoons baking powder
1¼ teaspoons soda
¼ teaspoon salt
⅔ cup shortening

3 eggs
1 teaspoon vanilla, optional
⅔ cup "soured milk" (see pg. 16)
1¼ cups mashed bananas *
⅔ cup chopped nuts

1. Preheat oven to 350°. Line two 9" layer pans, or a rectangle pan, with waxed paper (see pg. 15), or spray with vegetable spray and dust with flour.
2. Measure flour carefully; combine dry ingredients; set aside. Beat shortening, eggs, vanilla, and "milk" until combined thoroughly; add bananas and nuts and mix well. Blend in dry ingredients and beat until batter is smooth. Remember to scrape bottom and sides of bowl and do not over beat.
3. Pour into pans. Bake at 350° for 30-35 minutes for layers, 40-45 minutes for rectangle, or until cake tests done.

Banana-Spice Cake

3 cups flour
1½ cups sugar
2 teaspoons baking powder
1¾ teaspoons soda
¼ teaspoon salt
½ teaspoon cinnamon
½ teaspoon cloves

½ teaspoon allspice
⅔ cup shortening
⅔ cup "milk" +
    1 tablespoon lemon juice
2 cups mashed bananas *
3 eggs

1. Preheat oven to 350°. Line a 9 x 13" pan with waxed paper (see pg. 15).
2. Measure flour carefully. Combine the dry ingredients and mix well. Add shortening, "milk," lemon juice, and bananas. Beat about 2 minutes, remembering to scrape the bowl.

3. Add eggs and beat 1 minute more; scrape bowl and beat another ½ minute.

4. Pour batter into pan and bake at 350° for 40-45 minutes, or until cake tests done.

To make this a layer cake, *cut in half and frost with Fluffy "Butter" Frosting or variation (see pg. 214) as for layer cake, except leave cut edge unfrosted, or allow extra frosting to drip down the cut edge.*

*If bananas are thoroughly ripe, use less sugar.

Applesauce Cake

2¾ cups flour	½ teaspoon allspice
2 cups sugar	½ cup shortening
¼ teaspoon baking powder	½ cup water
1½ teaspoons soda	1½ cups unsweetened applesauce
¼ teaspoon salt	2 eggs
1 teaspoon cinnamon	½ cup ground walnuts
½ teaspoon cloves	1 cup raisins

1. Preheat oven to 350°. Line two 9" square pans or one 9 x 13" pan with waxed paper (see pg. 15), or spray with vegetable spray and dust with flour.

2. Measure flour carefully; combine dry ingredients; blend well. Add shortening, water, and applesauce; beat thoroughly. Scrape bowl, add eggs, and beat 1 minute; scrape bowl, beat an additional ½ minute.

3. Fold in the nuts and raisins.

4. Pour into pan(s). Bake at 350° for 35-40 minutes for layers, 45-50 minutes for rectangles.

5. Cool in pan(s) for 8-10 minutes; remove to wire racks and cool completely.

6. Frost with Fluffy Spice Frosting or Penuche Frosting (see pgs. 215-216) if desired.

✖ ✖ ✖ ✖ ✖

Maple-Walnut Cake

2½ cups flour

1⅓ to 1⅔ cups sugar

3½ teaspoons baking powder

¼ teaspoon salt

⅔ cup shortening

1¼ cups "milk"

2 eggs

½ teaspoon vanilla

1 teaspoon maple flavoring

1 cup walnuts

1. Preheat oven to 350°. Line two 9" square pans or one 9 x 13" pan with waxed paper (see pg. 15), or spray with vegetable spray and dust with flour.
2. Measure flour carefully and combine the dry ingredients; mix well. Add the shortening and "milk"; beat 1½–2 minutes; scrape sides and bottom of bowl. Add eggs, flavorings, and walnuts, beat 1½–2 minutes; scrape bowl, beat additional ½ minute. Pour batter into pan(s) and bake at 350° for 30–35 minutes for layers, 40–45 minutes for rectangle.
3. Cool in the pan(s) for 8–10 minutes; remove to wire racks and cool completely.
4. Frost with Fluffy Maple Frosting (see pg. 215), and decorate.

How To "Fold In"

Fold in means to blend ingredients carefully so that it remains light and airy. To do that:

Cut through the center of the bowl and bring the spatula or spoon back up at the side of the bowl, turning the spoon as you proceed. Use a turning motion of the hand as you bring the spoon up the side of the bowl and move back to the center for the downward stroke. Use a gentle motion, scraping sides and bottom and turning the bowl as you proceed. Continue until the ingredients are blended well.

✖ ✖ ✖ ✖ ✖ ✖ ✖ ✖

Basic Yellow Cake

2¼ cups flour	½ cup shortening
1½ cups sugar	1 cup "milk"
3 teaspoons baking powder	2 eggs
¼ teaspoon salt	2 teaspoons vanilla

1. Preheat oven to 350°. Line two 9" square pans or one 9 x 13" pan with waxed paper (see pg. 15), or spray with vegetable spray and dust with flour.
2. Measure flour carefully and combine the dry ingredients; mix well. Add the shortening and "milk"; beat for 1 minute. Scrape sides and bottom of bowl and beat 1 minute more. Add the eggs and vanilla and beat about 1½ minutes, scraping the bowl. Beat an additional ½ minute.
3. Pour batter into pan(s). Bake at 350° for 30-35 minutes for layers, 40-45 minutes for rectangle.
4. Cool in pan(s) 8-10 minutes; remove from pans and cool completely on wire racks; frost as desired.

Butterscotch Cake: *Replace sugar with brown sugar and use a butter-flavored shortening (read the label). Cream the sugar with the shortening before adding "milk." Very nice with Penuche Frosting (see pg. 216).*

Chocolate Chip Layer Cake: *Make Basic Yellow Cake then fold in 1 cup mint chocolate chips (read the label). After cooling, put bottoms of cakes together when frosting with a mint icing (see pg. 215). The chips settle to bottoms of layers and will be a middle layer when served.*

Peanut Butter Cake: *Make Basic Yellow Cake except use ½ cup peanut butter and only ⅓ cup shortening. Frost with Peanut Butter Frosting (see pg. 216) and sprinkle ground peanuts between layers.*

Spice Cake: *Make Basic Yellow Cake and add 2 teaspoons cinnamon, ¾ teaspoon allspice, and 1 teaspoon cloves. Proceed with recipe.*

Replace *the "milk" in any of the above cakes with "buttermilk."*

Basic White Cake

2¼ cups flour	½ cup shortening
1½ cups sugar	1 cup "milk"
3½ teaspoons baking powder	1 teaspoon vanilla
¼ teaspoon salt	4 egg whites

1. Preheat oven to 350°. Line pan(s) with waxed paper (see pg. 15), or spray with vegetable spray and dust with flour.
2. Measure flour carefully and combine the dry ingredients; blend well. Add shortening and "milk"; beat for about 1 minute, scraping the sides and bottom of bowl; add vanilla and egg whites. Beat 1½ minutes. Scrape bowl and beat ½ minute more.
3. Pour the batter into pan(s) and bake at 350° for 30-35 minutes for layers, 35-40 minutes for rectangle.

Note: This is a very elegant cake when frosted and covered with coconut.

Cherry Cake: Make Basic White Cake. Add sugar-free cherry gelatin and use only ⅔ cup sugar. Fold in 1 cup diced cherries, optional. (If using maraschino cherries do not use the ones preserved in lactic acid if you are milk/lactose sensitive; read the label.)

Chocolate Chip Cake: Make Basic White Cake. Carefully fold in ¾ cup minced semi-sweet chocolate chips; read the label.

"Buttermilk" Cake: When making Basic White Cake, mix 2 tablespoons lemon juice with enough "milk" to make 1 cup.

Devil's Food Cake

2¼ cups flour	½ cup shortening
1 cup sugar	1 cup "milk"
1¾ teaspoons soda	2 eggs
1 teaspoon baking powder	1 teaspoon vanilla
⅔ cup cocoa	

1. Preheat oven to 350°. Line two 9" square pans or a 9 x 13" pan with waxed paper (see pg. 15).
2. Measure flour carefully and combine dry ingredients; blend well. Add the shortening and "milk," and beat for 1 minute. Scrape the bowl and beat 1½ minutes more. Add eggs and vanilla; beat about 2 minutes; scrape bowl and beat an additional ½ minute. Pour batter into pan(s).
3. Bake at 350° for 30–35 minutes for layers, 40–45 minutes for rectangle.

Vary by substituting "buttermilk" for "milk";
Or by using ½ teaspoon each of vanilla and peppermint;
Or add 1 teaspoon cloves with the dry ingredients and frost with a Spice Frosting (see pg. 215).

Chocolate-Cherry Cake: *To Devil's Food Cake add ½ teaspoon almond flavoring and ¼–½ cup drained chopped maraschino cherries; read the label.*

Chocolate-Nut Cake: *Make Devil's Food Cake and fold in ¾ to 1 cup nuts.*

Cupcakes: *Make one of the preceding recipes. Use paper liners in muffin pans or spray the pan or muffin cups with vegetable spray. Fill pans/cups about half full; bake at 400" for 18–20 minutes. Frost or decorate if desired.*

Chocolate Cake

2¼ cups flour	1⅔ cups sugar
⅔ to 1 cup cocoa	⅔ cup shortening
¼ teaspoon baking powder	3 eggs
1¼ teaspoons soda	1⅓ cups water
¼ teaspoon salt	1 teaspoon vanilla

1. Preheat oven to 350°. Line two 9" square pans or a 9 x 13" pan with waxed paper (see pg. 15).
2. Measure flour carefully and combine with dry ingredients; blend well and set aside.
3. Beat the shortening and eggs until fluffy, remembering to scrape the bowl. Combine water and vanilla. Add dry ingredients and water alternately to shortening mixture; scrape the bowl. Mix well.
4. Pour batter into pan(s). Bake at 350° for 30–35 minutes for layers, 40–45 minutes for rectangle. Orange Frosting (see pg. 215) is good with this.

Cocoa Cake

2 cups flour	⅓ cup shortening
¾ to 1 cup cocoa	3 tablespoons "butter"
1½ to 1¾ cups sugar	2 teaspoons vanilla
1 teaspoon baking powder	3 eggs
1 teaspoon soda	1 cup "milk"
¼ teaspoon salt	

1. Preheat oven to 350°. Line pan(s) with waxed paper (see pg. 15).
2. Combine the dry ingredients; blend well and set aside.
3. Beat the shortening, "butter," and vanilla until fluffy; add the eggs and blend well, remembering to scrape the bowl. Add the dry ingredients alternately with "milk" to egg mixture; blend well.
4. Pour into pan(s). Bake at 350° for 30–35 minutes for layers, or 40–45 minutes for rectangle.

Variations: Fold in *1 cup ground nuts after mixing cake.*
Or use ½ *teaspoon vanilla and* 1½ *teaspoons peppermint flavoring. Frost with a peppermint or plain frosting, sprinkle with crushed peppermint candy.*
Or use Coconut-Almond (below) or Pecan Frosting between layers and on top.

German Chocolate Cake

2 cups flour	½ cup "butter"
2 cups sugar	1 cup "buttermilk" (see pg. 16)
1½ teaspoons soda	2 eggs
1 teaspoon baking powder	1 4-oz. package dark sweet
¼ teaspoon salt	chocolate, melted (read the label)
½ cup butter-flavored shortening	
(read the label)	

1. Preheat oven to 350°. Line pan(s) with waxed paper (see pg. 15).
2. Measure flour carefully and combine with dry ingredients; blend well and set aside. Beat shortening and "butter" until mixed well and softened; add remaining ingredients and blend together, beating about 2 minutes; scrape bowl and beat 1 minute longer.
3. Pour into pan(s). Bake at 350° for 30–35 minutes for layers, 40–45 minutes for rectangle, or until cake tests done.
4. Cool in pan(s) for 8–12 minutes; remove to wire racks and cool completely.
5. Spread Coconut-Almond Frosting (below) between layers and over top.

Coconut-Almond Frosting

1 cup "cream"	¼ cup butter-flavored shortening
1 cup sugar	(read the label)
3 egg yolks, lightly beaten	1 teaspoon vanilla
¼ cup "butter"	1⅓ cups coconut
	1 cup slivered almonds

1. Combine first 6 ingredients in saucepan. Cook and stir over medium heat until thickened—be patient, it will take 12 minutes or longer. Remove from heat; add remaining ingredients.

2. Cool, beating occasionally, until thick enough to spread. Spread between layers and over top for traditional German Chocolate Cake.

Coconut-Pecan Frosting

Make above Coconut Almond Frosting except use pecans rather than almonds. (Try peanuts if you can't ingest tree nuts.)

Vary the frosting by using orange juice instead of "cream" for an orange filling and topping.

Cherry Chiffon Cake

MERINGUE

2 egg whites	½ cup sugar

Beat room-temperature egg whites until frothy; continue beating while adding sugar a little at a time. Beat until stiff and glossy; set aside.

CAKE BATTER

2¼ cups flour	¼ cup maraschino cherry juice, (read the label)
1½ cups sugar	
1 teaspoon baking powder	2 egg yolks
¾ teaspoon soda	1 teaspoon vanilla
¼ teaspoon salt	½ cup finely chopped maraschino
½ cup oil	cherries (read the label)
¾ cup "milk"	½ cup ground nuts

1. Preheat oven to 350°. Line pan(s) with waxed paper (see pg. 15), or spray with vegetable spray and dust with flour.
2. In mixing bowl measure flour carefully, combine dry ingredients, and blend well. Add oil and "milk," beat 2 minutes; scrape sides and bottom of bowl. Add egg yolks, cherry juice, and vanilla; beat 2 minutes; scrape bowl; beat 1 minute more.

3. Fold in meringue. Sprinkle nuts and cherries on top and fold in carefully.
4. Pour into pan(s). Bake at 350° for 30–35 minutes for layers, 40–45 minutes for rectangle.
5. Cool in pan(s) for 8–12 minutes, then remove to wire racks to cool completely.
6. Frost as desired.

Vary by using ¾ cup maraschino cherries and omit the nuts. Frost with a Maraschino Cherry Frosting (see pg. 215).

Chocolate Chiffon Cake

MERINGUE

2 egg whites	½ cup sugar

Beat room-temperature egg whites until frothy; continue beating and add sugar a little at a time. Beat until stiff and glossy; set aside.

CAKE BATTER

1¾ cups flour	⅓ cup oil
1 cup sugar	1 cup "milk"
¾ teaspoon soda	2 egg yolks
½ teaspoon baking powder	2 squares (2 oz.) unsweetened
¼ teaspoon salt	chocolate, melted

1. Preheat oven to 350°. Line pan(s) with waxed paper (see pg. 15).
2. Measure flour carefully and combine the dry ingredients; blend well. Add oil and "milk." Beat for 2 minutes and scrape the bowl. Add egg yolks and melted chocolate, beat 2 minutes, scrape bowl; beat additional 1 minute.
3. Carefully fold in meringue.
4. Pour into pan(s). Bake at 350° for 30–35 minutes for layers, 40–45 minutes for rectangle.
5. Cool in pan(s) for 8–12 minutes, then remove to wire racks to cool completely.
6. Frost as desired.

Spice Chiffon Cake

MERINGUE

2 egg whites $^1\!/_2$ cup sugar

Beat egg whites until frothy; continue beating and add sugar gradually. Beat until stiff and glossy; set aside.

CAKE BATTER

$2^1\!/_4$ cups flour   1 teaspoon cinnamon
1 teaspoon baking powder   1 cup packed brown sugar
$^3\!/_4$ teaspoon soda $^1\!/_3$ cup oil
$^1\!/_4$ teaspoon salt   1 cup "buttermilk"
$^3\!/_4$ teaspoon nutmeg   2 egg yolks
$^3\!/_4$ teaspoon cloves

1. Preheat oven to 350°. Line pan(s) with waxed paper (see pg. 15), or spray with vegetable spray and dust with flour.
2. Measure the flour carefully. Combine the dry ingredients; blend well. Add the brown sugar, oil, and "buttermilk," beat for 2 minutes; scrape bowl. Add egg yolks and beat 1 minute; scrape bowl and beat 2 minutes more.
3. Carefully fold in meringue.
4. Pour into pan(s). Bake at 350° for 30-35 minutes for layers, 40-45 minutes for rectangle.
5. Cool in pan(s) for 8-12 minutes, then remove to wire racks to cool completely.
6. Frost as desired.

✖ ✖ ✖ ✖ ✖

Angel Food Cake

	Normal		Supreme
1	cup flour	1	cup flour
⅞	cup (14 tablespoons) sugar	¾	cup sifted confectioner's sugar
12	egg whites	12	egg whites
1½	teaspoons cream of tartar	1½	teaspoons cream of tartar
¼	teaspoon salt	¼	teaspoon salt
¾	cup sugar	1	cup sugar (granulated)
1½	teaspoons vanilla	1½	teaspoons vanilla
¼	teaspoon almond flavoring	½	teaspoon almond flavoring

1. Preheat oven to 375°. Use an *ungreased* 10 x 14" tube (angel food cake) pan.
2. Measure flour carefully; combine with first amount of sugar; set aside.
3. In a large bowl place egg whites, cream of tartar, and salt; beat until foamy. Add second amount of sugar gradually, beating until meringue holds stiff peaks; add flavorings.
4. Sprinkle flour mixture by 2-3 tablespoonfuls at a time onto the meringue and fold in until flour is taken up each time. Continue folding in flour until it is all taken into the cake batter.
5. Place the batter into the ungreased tube pan and cut through carefully to prevent air bubbles and to level. Bake at 375° for 30-35 minutes; remove from oven and invert in pan—allowing to hang upside down until completely cooled.
6. Frost if you wish, or use as a base for strawberry (or other fruit) short-cake, sweetened or unsweetened.

✖ ✖ ✖ ✖ ✖ ✖ ✖ ✖ ✖ ✖

When preparing icings or frosting, there is a "fudge" factor. Add the liquid a little at a time until you get the consistency you want. Add more liquid if you wish to drizzle, less if you want a thick frosting. Be sure to make plenty if you prefer a thick frosting; it rarely goes as far as you think it will.

Note about chocolate: You have to be careful when melting chocolate. If you are not, you can end up with a solid mass. Break chocolate into pieces, or use chips, and melt them in a double boiler over hot, not boiling, water. If you use a heavy pot over direct *low* heat, be sure to watch carefully and remove from heat as soon as the outer surface of the chocolate has melted. Remove from heat and stir to finish melting. You can melt a solid square of chocolate without breaking it, but do be careful not to overheat it. As soon as the chocolate has melted, use as desired. Burned chocolate does not taste, nor smell, good.

Chocolate can also be melted in a warm oven, or in hot water in a heavy-gauge plastic bag. Remember to use hot, not boiling, water. If you use a microwave oven, follow manufacturer's directions or; place 1 square of unwrapped chocolate in microwave on a dish. Heat on high for 1–2 minutes, stirring once. Remove when almost melted and stir until smooth. For each additional square of chocolate add 10 seconds.

Whichever way you melt chocolate, do not overheat it and you will get good results. After melting the chocolate, spread it very thinly on a baking sheet and chill until firm. Then push a sturdy turner, or spatula, against it to force it up into curls. Place the curls on waxed paper and chill again until hard, then use as decorations. Or drizzle melted chocolate over a white frosting, then draw a knife though it to form ripples. Or drizzle in circles and draw a knife through in straight lines to get a web pattern. (See pg. 196 for directions for making chocolate leaves and other decorations.)

When you make frostings, refrigerate any extra and use it to make Graham Cracker Cookie Treats; they are a good occasional treat for children and adults.

If you have young children, baking is a good way to get them involved in the kitchen. Supervising children while they cut raisins or dates may take longer than using a food processor, but the food processor gets no satisfied feeling from having helped create a homemade goodie. Older children can run the processor, or assemble and measure ingredients, and you can enjoy creative time together.

Basic Chocolate Icing

4½ cups powdered sugar	½ cup margarine (*read the label*)
⅔ cup cocoa	2 tablespoons "milk"
⅛ teaspoon salt	2 teaspoons vanilla

Combine sugar, cocoa, and salt. Add 2 cups of the sugar mixture to the softened margarine. Add remaining mixture alternately with the combined "milk" and vanilla. Beat until of spreading consistency; use more "milk" if needed.

Chocolate-Almond Frosting

½ cup margarine (*read the label*)	2 pounds powdered sugar
¼ teaspoon salt	¾ cup cocoa
2 teaspoons vanilla	⅓ cup "milk"
1 teaspoon almond flavoring	

Place the margarine in a large bowl and soften in a warm oven; add salt and flavorings and blend thoroughly. Combine the sugar and cocoa; add alternately with "milk" to margarine mixture. Use enough "milk" to obtain desired spreading consistency.

Note: *This is a large amount of frosting; keep any extra in refrigerator and use to make Graham Cracker Cookie Treats.*

Vary *by using thawed orange juice concentrate for liquid, for a chocolate-orange frosting.*

Fluffy Frosting—Porcelain Icing

2 egg whites	¼ cup sugar
¼ teaspoon cream of tartar	¾ cup light corn syrup
⅛ teaspoon salt	1 teaspoon vanilla

1. In a medium bowl beat egg whites, cream of tartar, and salt together until soft peaks form. Add sugar a little at a time, beating until smooth and glossy. Add syrup and vanilla gradually while beating, until stiff peaks form.
2. Add color if desired.

- Frosts 9″ layers or 9 x 13″ rectangle cake -

Note: *This frosting uses uncooked egg whites so refrigerate cake after frosting.*

Fluffy "Butter" Frosting

⅓ cup "butter" (read the label)	¼ to ⅓ cup "milk"
⅛ teaspoon salt	3 cups powdered sugar
2 teaspoons vanilla	

Place "butter" in a large bowl, soften in a warm oven or microwave. Add salt and vanilla; mix well. Add powdered sugar, 1 cup at a time, alternating with the "milk." Beat thoroughly until blended smooth and of desired consistency. Add more "milk" a little at a time if needed.

- Fills and frosts 9″ layers or 9 x 13″ rectangle cake -

Chocolate Frosting: *Make basic frosting, then blend in 3-4 squares of melted, unsweetened chocolate.*

Fluffy Cocoa Frosting: *Make basic frosting, but blend 3-4 tablespoons cocoa with sugar; use "milk" as needed.*

Lemon Frosting: *Make basic frosting except use only ½ teaspoon vanilla and replace the "milk" with fresh lemon juice, or, if too intense a flavor, thawed lemonade concentrate. Color with yellow food coloring for a bright, sunny creation.*

Orange Frosting: *See Lemon Frosting, but use orange juice concentrate. Use grated rind with either lemon or orange frosting for extra flavor if desired. Colored orange and with a few candy decorations this makes a great pumpkin.*

Maple Frosting: *Make basic frosting except use only ½ teaspoon vanilla and 1½ teaspoon maple flavoring. Do this for any flavor you like:* **peppermint, rum, almond, etc.**

Experiment to find your own favorite spicy icings.

✗ ✗ ✗ ✗ ✗ ✗ ✗

Spice Frosting: *Make basic frosting and add ¼ teaspoon cloves; Or ½ teaspoon cinnamon and ¼ teaspoon allspice.*

✗ ✗ ✗ ✗ ✗ ✗ ✗

Maraschino Cherry Frosting

½ cup margarine, softened	2 tablespoons cherry juice
⅛ teaspoon salt	¼ cup drained and chopped
4 cups powdered sugar	maraschino cherries

Mix the margarine with salt; blend in 2 cups powdered sugar. Add remaining sugar and cherry juice alternately until blended smooth; add chopped fruit if desired.

Note: *Be certain to read the label for maraschino cherries, most have lactic acid in them as a preservative.*

Penuche Frosting

½ cup "butter"	¼ cup "milk"
1 cup brown sugar	2 cups powdered sugar

1. Melt "butter" in saucepan; stir in brown sugar; bring to boil and continue to boil for 2 minutes, stirring continuously.
2. Stir in "milk" and return to boil while stirring. Cool to lukewarm; gradually stir in powdered sugar; cool and stir until thick enough to spread. (To speed things up, place bowl in ice water and stir until thick.)

- Frosts 2 layers or 1 rectangle -

Peanut Butter Frosting

Make **Penuche Frosting** except use 1 tablespoon shortening and 4 tablespoons peanut butter. Melt peanut butter and shortening in saucepan and continue with recipe.

Very good with Spice Cake or Peanut Butter Cake (see pg. 203).

Note: *If your frosting turns out too thick, add more liquid. If too thin, add more powdered sugar.*

Fudge Frosting

1½ cups sugar	2 squares unsweetened
½ cup water	chocolate, shaved or cut
1 tablespoon corn syrup	1 teaspoon vanilla
1 tablespoon "butter"	

1. Mix all ingredients, except the vanilla, in a saucepan; cover and cook slowly until mixture reaches boiling point.
2. Remove cover and continue cooking, but don't stir, to 234° on candy

thermometer, or to soft ball stage. A little dropped into cold water will form a soft ball.

3. Remove from heat and let stand until cool. Add vanilla and beat until desired consistency is reached.

Caramel Frosting

3 tablespoons "butter"	$\frac{1}{3}$ cup "milk"
1 cup brown sugar	1 teaspoon vanilla
$\frac{1}{8}$ teaspoon salt	$1\frac{1}{2}$ cups powdered sugar

1. Melt "butter" in saucepan; add brown sugar and salt, stir until sugar dissolves. Add "milk," cook 3 minutes, stirring constantly. Remove from heat and cool.
2. In a mixing bowl combine the brown sugar mixture, vanilla, and powdered sugar; blend together, then beat until desired consistency is reached.

- Frosts two 8″ layers -

Almond Whip Icing

3 cups nondairy whipped topping (read the label)	$\frac{1}{2}$ teaspoon almond flavoring
$\frac{3}{4}$ cup slivered almonds	

1. Thaw the nondairy topping and blend all ingredients well.
2. Use to cover Angel Food or Spice Cake just before serving.

Note: This is also a good pie topping, especially for pumpkin.

✖ ✖ ✖ ✖ ✖ ✖ ✖ ✖ ✖ ✖

Pie crust is a simple and useful pastry. It complements fruits, eggs, meats, or vegetables. Leftover bits of dough need not go to waste. Spread them with "butter," and sprinkle with sugar and cinnamon and baked.

Work pastry dough lightly. Use a minimum of flour when rolling out. Roll out to a size that will allow the crust to be fitted into the pan. Avoid pulling the pastry to fit, or it may shrink back while baking. For long baking periods, protect the crust with a ring cut from aluminum foil or from a brown paper bag.

To roll dough on a cloth-covered board or surface, rub flour into the cloth, and use a stockinet on the rolling pin. Rub the pin with flour, also, whether you use a stockinet or not. Place a ball of dough in the flour and flatten with your hand into a circle; turn over to lightly flour other side. With rolling pin, work the dough outward into a circle about ⅛" thick, being careful not to take up excessive flour, but don't let the crust stick, either. Fit into pan as directed; don't pull the dough.

To roll dough on a counter top, sprinkle the surface with flour and rub flour into the pin. Follow rolling procedure, being careful not to take up too much flour. Excess flour makes finished pastry tough and less flaky.

Or roll between two pieces of waxed paper. Slightly moisten the counter top to hold the bottom sheet in place; sprinkle with flour and place ball of dough on it. Flatten and turn, then place the second sheet of waxed paper on the dough in a crosswise manner. Roll the dough to fill the overlap of paper and it will be about a 12" circle, a good size to fit into a 9" pie pan.

To bake an empty pie shell, fit the crust into the pan; trim the pastry to about a half inch larger than the pan; fold pastry under and flute the edges. That is, put a finger on the rim of the crust in an outward position, pinch the crust around the finger to form a ruffle; do this all around the edge of the crust. Hook a point of each ruffle under the pan edge, where possible, to help prevent shrinkage. Prick the bottom and sides of the shell with a fork; bake at 475° for 8–10 minutes. Cool and fill as desired. Use the same procedure for a filled single-crust pie, except *do not* prick the shell before filling.

For a double-crust pie divide dough with a larger half for the bottom crust. Put pastry into pan and trim overhang evenly. Fill the pastry shell and cover with a top crust that is at least an inch larger than the pie pan. Lightly moisten the edge of the bottom crust with water; fit the top crust on and fold it under the edge of the bottom crust. Then either flute the crust, or press a floured fork around the edge of the pie pan, *or* simply pinch the pastry between thumb and finger and twist slightly. Make your own design, but remember that however you finish your edges, be certain to cut several decorative slits in the top crust to allow steam to escape.

For custard pies, you can bake the filling in the crust or you can bake the filling and crust separately, then slide the filling into the baked shell. Use the same size pan for both the shell and the filling.

To freshen the crust of leftover pie, place in a preheated 350° oven for about 5 minutes.

If you like a well-filled pie as I do, catch the bubble-over with either foil or a cookie sheet under the pie while it is baking. Keep in mind that aluminum foil can be discarded, but the baked-on filling can be very difficult to remove from a cookie sheet.

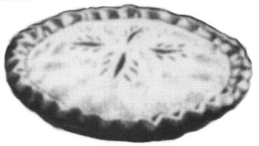

Pie Crusts

Double Crust	Single Crust
2 cups flour	1⅓ cups flour
½ teaspoon salt	¼ teaspoon salt
⅔ cup shortening	⅓ cup shortening
¼ to ⅓ cup water	2 to 3 tablespoons water

1. Preheat oven to 425°. Measure flour by sifting. Combine flour and salt; cut in shortening until the flour resembles course meal. Add water and mix until flour is moistened and mixture clears sides of bowl. Press into a ball and proceed to roll out as per previous instructions.
2. For double-crust pie, divide dough in half with one half larger for the bottom crust. Bake as recipe asks.
3. Bake single crust at 425° for 10–15 minutes, until browned.

Note: A favorite spice or herb can be added to this recipe: 1 teaspoon for double crust; ½ teaspoon single. Cinnamon or nutmeg for fruit pies; onion powder, garlic powder, or oregano for meat pies.

✖ ✖ ✖ ✖ ✖

Graham Cracker Crust

1 to 3 tablespoons sugar   ⅓ cup softened "butter"
1½ cups graham
    cracker crumbs

1. Preheat oven to 350°. Mix sugar with crumbs in bowl; add "butter" and mix thoroughly. Press firmly and evenly against bottom and sides of 9" pie pan; bake at 350° for 8–10 minutes.
2. Cool; pour in desired filling.

Coconut Crust

1½ to 2 cups coconut	*2 tablespoons softened "butter"*

1. Preheat oven to 325°. Mix the "butter" into the coconut, using fingers to help disperse evenly. Press the mixture evenly and firmly around sides and bottom of pie pan with fingertips.
2. Bake at 325° for 15–20 minutes, or until lightly browned.
3. Cool and fill as desired.

✖ ✖ ✖ ✖ ✖ ✖ ✖

Apple Pie

½ to ¾ cup sugar	*7 to 8 cups apple slices ***
2 tablespoons flour *	*1 teaspoon "butter"*
2 teaspoons cinnamon	*1 teaspoon lemon juice, optional*
	Pastry for double-crust pie

1. Preheat oven to 425°. Peel apples and remove cores; slice. Mix dry ingredients; combine with apple slices and lemon juice if used.
2. Pour into pastry-lined pie pan and dot with "butter." Place top crust over filling, seal and flute edges. Remember to cut slits in top crust.
3. Bake at 425° for 50–60 minutes.

* 1 tablespoon cornstarch can replace the flour if preferred.

** This will make a full pie, use only 6 cups apples if you prefer. Use less sugar with sweet apples; 1 cup if you want a sweeter pie. If you wish, cook the apples before pouring into shell, then bake for shorter time or until shell is browned.

Raspberry Pie

¾ to 1 cup sugar

2½ tablespoons cornstarch *

½ to 1 teaspoon cinnamon

6 cups raspberries

1 teaspoon "butter"

Pastry for a double-crust pie

1. Preheat oven to 425°. Wash berries and drain well. Remove stems and hulls and any foreign objects. Mix dry ingredients; combine carefully with berries. Pour into pastry-lined pie pan, dot with "butter"; place top crust over filling; seal and flute edge; cut slits in top.
2. Bake at 425° for 40–45 minutes, or until crust is brown and juice bubbles through slits.
3. Cool to just warm to serve, or serve completely cooled.

Replace cornstarch with arrowroot, or ⅓ cup flour can replace cornstarch if preferred.

Berry Pies

Follow the recipe for raspberry pie, except use the berries of your choice, either fresh or frozen. If fruit is large, as strawberries may be, cut them in half. Use blueberries, black and red raspberries, boysenberries, loganberries, strawberries, or mulberries. All are good.

Mincemeat Pie

1 jar mincemeat pie filling (read the label)

Pastry for double-crust pie

Preheat oven to 425°. Pour mincemeat mixture into a pastry-lined pie pan, Place top crust over filling, seal and flute edges, cut slits. Bake at 425° for 40–45 minutes, or until crust is browned nicely.

Vary *by adding 1½ cups chopped apples. Proceed as directed.*

Rhubarb Pie

1½ to 2 cups sugar	2 teaspoons "butter"
4 tablespoons cornstarch *	Pastry for double-crust pie
6 cups rhubarb, cut in 1″ pieces	

1. Preheat oven to 425°. Wash and cut rhubarb into 1" pieces (never use the toxic leaves). Mix dry ingredients and combine with fruit; pour into pastry-lined pie pan, dot with "butter," and place top crust over filling; slit top and flute edges.
2. Bake at 425° for 45–55 minutes, until browned.

* ½ cup flour can replace cornstarch or use arrowroot.

✗ ✗ ✗ ✗ ✗

Rhubarb Custard Pie

3 eggs, lightly beaten **	¾ teaspoon nutmeg, optional
3 tablespoons "milk"	5 cups rhubarb, cut into 1″ pieces
1½ to 2 cups sugar	1 tablespoon "butter"
¼ cup flour	Pastry for double-crust pie

1. Preheat oven to 400°. Beat eggs lightly then combine eggs with the "milk." In a separate bowl combine the sugar, nutmeg if used, and flour; stir into the egg mixture. Mix in the rhubarb and pour into pastry-lined pie pan. Dot with "butter" and cover with top crust; seal, flute, and cut slits in top.
2. Bake at 400° for 40–50 minutes, until browned.

Note: *Always preheat oven when doing **any** baking.*

** For custard pies, it is best to beat the eggs before adding or combining with "milk."

Cherry Pie

¾ to 1 cup sugar *
3   tablespoons cornstarch **
6   cups red tart cherries, pitted

¼   teaspoon almond or vanilla flavoring
1   teaspoon lemon juice, optional
1   teaspoon "butter"
Pastry for double-crust pie

1. Preheat oven to 425°. Combine the sugar and cornstarch; mix with cherries, flavorings, and lemon juice; pour into pastry-lined pie pan; dot with "butter." Place the top crust over filling, seal, flute, and cut slits in top crust.
2. Bake at 425° for 40–50 minutes.

The amount of sugar depends on tartness of the cherries.
*** ⅓ cup flour can replace cornstarch if preferred.*

Peach Pie

¾ to 1 cup sugar
2   tablespoons cornstarch

½   teaspoon cinnamon
6 to 7 cups sliced peaches

1. Preheat oven to 425°. Combine all ingredients; place in pastry-lined pie pan; place top crust over filling. Seal, flute, and cut slits in top crust.
2. Bake at 425° for 40–45 minutes, until crust is browned and juice bubbles through slits.
3. Cool to just warm, or serve completely cooled.

Note: *When baking pies for long periods remember to protect the crust edges with foil or brown paper.*

Gelatin Peach Pie

1   3-oz. package peach gelatin,
       sugar free
1   20-oz. package frozen peaches,
       unsweetened

1   single-crust pie shell,
       baked and cooled

1. In a mixing bowl dissolve gelatin in 1 cup boiling water. Add 1 cup cold water and frozen peaches; mix well.
2. When gelatin begins to thicken, pour into baked pie shell; refrigerate until completely set.

Gelatin Fruit Pies

Follow instructions for Gelatin Peach Pie. Use favorite combinations of fruit and gelatin. Strawberry gelatin and strawberries—fresh or frozen—is popular. Raspberry gelatin with fresh or frozen raspberries is very also good. Or mix flavors to suit your own taste.

Top with nondairy whipped topping if allowed. *

Vary by using coconut or graham cracker crusts.

Light After-Dinner Pie

> 1   package gelatin, lemon, orange, or lime
> 3½ cups nondairy whipped topping *
> Graham cracker or coconut crust

1. Dissolve gelatin in one cup boiling water; add 1½–2 cups ice cubes. Stir until gelatin thickens and remove unmelted ice. Beat the thickened gelatin until it is foamy, then fold, or beat in nondairy whipped topping mixing until smooth.
2. Mound into pie shell and chill about 3 hours.

* I'm not aware of any nondairy toppings that are altogether free of milk by-products. Nondairy topping is not suggested for the severely milk-intolerant; use your own discretion.

Vary by adding 1 cup fruit—fresh, canned, or frozen. Be certain to drain canned fruit and use the juice as part of the boiling liquid if desired.

Cran-Apple Pie

3 eggs
1¾ to 2 cups sugar
2 cups cranberries

3 cups sliced apples
2 teaspoons softened "butter"
1½ teaspoons vanilla
Pastry for double-crust pie

1. Preheat oven to 325°. Clean and chop cranberries; mix berries and apples. Beat eggs and sugar until fluffy. Add softened "butter," vanilla, and prepared fruit.
2. Pour into pastry-lined pie pan; cover with top crust; seal, flute, and cut slits in top. Bake at 325° for 55–60 minutes.

Pumpkin Pie

2 eggs, lightly beaten
1¾ cups pumpkin *
½ to ¾ cup sugar
¼ teaspoon salt
1½ teaspoons cinnamon

½ teaspoon ginger
¼ teaspoon cloves
½ teaspoon nutmeg
1½ cups "cream" (see pg. 15)
Pastry for single-crust pie

1. Preheat oven to 425°. Mix pie ingredients; pour into pastry-lined pie pan.
2. Bake at 425° for 45–50 minutes, or until knife inserted near edge of filling comes out clean.

* Use this recipe for making pies of mashed yams or mashed squash—very tasty.

Pumpkin Chiffon Pie

1½ cups pumpkin
½ cup corn syrup
1 teaspoon cinnamon

¼ teaspoon cloves
⅛ teaspoon nutmeg
½ cup ground nuts, optional

¼ teaspoon ginger	½ cup nondairy whipped topping *
	Graham cracker pie crust

1. Combine all pie ingredients, except nondairy topping, and mix thoroughly. Fold in topping and pour into crust. Freeze until firm, 3-4 hours.
2. To serve, allow to stand at room temperature for 20-25 minutes.

Cherry Chiffon Pie

1 can cherry pie filling	3½ cups nondairy topping *

Make as for pumpkin chiffon pie; no spices necessary.

Any canned or prepared pie filling can be used in this manner to make a chiffon pie. Use meringue (below) if seriously milk sensitive.

* Be sure to read the labels! (See pg. 16.)

Note: *Ready pie crusts are available without milk by-products, but be certain to read the label since many do have whey solids in them. I find most too salty.*

Pie Meringue

3 egg whites	¼ cup to 6 tablespoons sugar
1 teaspoon lemon juice **	

1. Preheat oven to 350°. In a small bowl, beat the whites and lemon juice on high speed until foamy. Add sugar gradually, beating until stiff peaks form and all the sugar is dissolved. Spread meringue on hot pie filling, touching pie crust all around.
2. Bake at 350° for 12-15 minutes, or until lightly browned. Do not over-bake or you may get a weepiness in the finished meringue.

** Or ¼ teaspoon cream of tarter; lemon juice and cream of tartar are interchangeable. I often use egg whites and sugar only.

Lemon Meringue Pie

⅔ to ¾ cup sugar
5 tablespoons cornstarch
1½ cups water
3 egg yolks, lightly beaten
5 to 6 tablespoons fresh lemon juice

Rind of 1 lemon, grated
Pastry for single-crust pie, baked
and cooled
2 tablespoons "butter," optional

1. In saucepan, combine sugar and cornstarch thoroughly. Add cold water and stir until mixed; add egg yolks; bring to boil over medium heat, stirring constantly; boil 1 minute and remove from heat.
2. Stir in lemon rind and fresh lemon juice; (add 2 tablespoons "butter" at this time if you like). Pour into pie shell and top with meringue. Follow directions for pie meringue on previous page.

Orange Meringue Pie

½ cup sugar
5 tablespoons cornstarch
3 egg yolks, lightly beaten

1¾ cups orange juice (or
diluted concentrate)
Pastry for single-crust pie, baked
and cooled

1. In a saucepan, combine sugar and cornstarch thoroughly. Add orange juice and stir until mixed; add egg yolks and bring to boil over medium heat, stirring constantly; boil 1 minute and remove from heat.
2. Pour into pie shell and top with meringue. Proceed as with Lemon Meringue Pie above.

Lemon Chiffon Pie

⅔ to ¾ cup sugar
5 tablespoons cornstarch
1½ cups water
3 egg yolks, lightly beaten

6 tablespoons fresh lemon juice
Rind of 1 lemon, grated
1 pie crust of choice, baked
and cooled

1. In a saucepan combine sugar and cornstarch thoroughly. Add cold water and stir until mixed; add egg yolk. Bring to boil over medium heat, stirring constantly; boil 1 minute and remove from heat. Stir in lemon rind and fresh lemon juice; cool, stirring occasionally.
2. Make Pie Meringue (see pg. 227), then fold meringue carefully into the cooled lemon mixture and combine well. Pour mixture into pie shell and refrigerate until set, at least 3 hours.

Orange Chiffon Pie

Prepare using Orange Meringue Pie recipe and following Lemon Chiffon Pie directions. These are light and lively pies for any occasion, but are especially nice if a dessert is wanted after a fairly heavy meal.

> ### CHIFFON PUDDINGS
> *are made by folding the meringue into the cooled pudding, then spooning into dessert dishes.*
> ✱ ✱ ✱ ✱ ✱ ✱ ✱ ✱

Blueberry Chiffon Pie

1   can blueberry pie filling
1   recipe Pie Meringue
     (see pg. 227)

1   pie crust of choice, baked
     and cooled

Open blueberry or other prepared pie filling of choice. Follow directions for Lemon Chiffon Pie, except use prepared filling, no cooking is necessary. Simply combine filling with meringue and fill pie shell. Chill until set.

Cran-Meringue Chiffon Pie

Follow directions for Orange Meringue Pie, except use one of the "cran" juices for the liquid. Try this with any of your favorite juices; it makes unusual pies that have a very nice flavor. Whether it is meringue or chiffon depends on how you use the meringue.

"Cream" Pie

½ to ⅔ cup sugar
3 tablespoons cornstarch
¼ teaspoon salt
3 cups "cream" *
3 egg yolks, lightly beaten

2 teaspoons vanilla
1 tablespoon "butter," optional
Pastry for single-crust pie with high-
fluted sides, baked and cooled

1. Preheat oven to 350°. Mix the dry ingredients in saucepan; add cold "cream" and mix thoroughly. Stir the egg yolks into the mixture in the saucepan and bring to boil over medium heat, stirring constantly. When the mixture reaches full rolling boil, boil 2 minutes; remove from heat and stir in vanilla. Add "butter" if using it.
2. Pour into pie shell and top with meringue while hot. Bake at 350° for 12–15 minutes. Or cover with a circle of waxed paper and then plastic wrap; cool in refrigerator to set.

Note: The waxed paper will absorb the moisture as the pie cools.

* "Cream" is the original liquid nondairy creamer, but the fat-free creamers work as well, with fewer calories—your choice.

Banana "Cream" Pie

2 to 3 bananas, sliced
Cream Pie Filling (above)

Pastry for single-crust pie,
baked and cooled

Place slices from 2–3 bananas into pie shell and pour filling on top. Top with meringue or nondairy topping—read the label.

Note: Top any of the cream pies with nondairy whipped topping, if ingestible for you, but be sure to chill the filling first, and read the label. These are all nice with meringue, also.

Coconut "Cream" Pie: Add 1 cup coconut to finished cream filling before pouring into shell.

Chocolate "Cream" Pie: Add ½-⅓ cup cocoa and full amount of sugar or 3-4 ounces melted semi-sweet chocolate to filling before cooking. Finish and pour into shell.

Orange-Coconut "Cream" Pie: Make Cream Pie, except replace "cream" with orange juice. Mix 2 cups coconut in with the vanilla. Top with, or fold in, meringue made with lemon juice.

Simple Custard Pie

4	eggs	2⅔ cups "cream," warmed	
⅔	cup sugar	½ teaspoon vanilla	
¼	teaspoon salt	Pastry for a single-crust pie	
¼	teaspoon nutmeg		

1. Preheat oven to 425°. Beat eggs slightly; add remaining ingredients and mix well.
2. Pour into pastry-lined pie pan. Bake at 425° for 25–30 minutes, or until knife inserted near edge of pie comes out clean.

Note: The center may appear soft but it will set. Baking too long will ruin custard. Warm "milk" reduces total baking time.

Chocolate Custard Pie: Make Simple Custard Pie except mix ½ cup cocoa with the sugar, or 3-4 squares melted unsweetened chocolate with the "cream." Omit nutmeg and use 2 teaspoons vanilla.

Coconut Custard Pie

3	eggs	2	teaspoons vanilla
⅔	cup sugar	1	cup coconut
¼	teaspoon salt	Pastry for a single-crust pie	
2¼	cups "milk" or "cream"		

Make as Simple Custard Pie, adding coconut before pouring into pie shell.

Peach Custard Pie

3	eggs	1	20-oz. package frozen peaches, thawed
3	tablespoons "milk"		
½	cup sugar	1	teaspoon "butter"
¼	cup flour		Pastry for double-crust pie

1. Preheat oven to 400°. Beat eggs and "milk"; thaw peaches if frozen, combine ingredients and mix well; pour into shell, dot with "butter"; add top crust and cut slits in it.
2. Bake at 400° for 40–50 minutes.

Pecan Pie

3	eggs, lightly beaten	¼	teaspoon salt
1	cup corn syrup	1½	cups pecans
2	teaspoons softened "butter"		Pastry for single-crust pie
½ to ⅔ cup sugar			

1. Preheat oven to 350°. Mix pie ingredients together thoroughly.
2. Pour into pastry-lined pie pan. Bake at 350° for 55–60 minutes, or until knife inserted near center of pie comes out clean.

Vary by replacing pecans with walnuts or other favorite nuts, or peanuts if tree nuts are a problem for you;
Or add 1 teaspoon vanilla;
Or vanilla + ½ teaspoon maple flavoring.

"Ice Cream" Pie

*1½ pints nondairy frozen dessert **

1½ cups raspberries or other fruit

*Coconut or graham cracker pie crust ***

1. Soften nondairy dessert in refrigerator.
2. Bake and cool your choice of pie crust; combine fruit with the softened dessert. Freeze until firm, 2–3 hours.

Note: *For the above dessert use berry-flavored nondairy frozen dessert and unsweetened raspberries, fresh or frozen.*

Chocolate Coconut "Ice Cream" Pie: *Chocolate nondairy frozen dessert combined with 1½ cups coconut, plain or toasted.*

Peach "Ice Cream" Pie: *Vanilla nondairy frozen dessert and peaches. Pastry for single-crust pie baked and cooled. Arrange peach slices in pie crust, cover with nondairy frozen dessert, softened so that it will fill in around fruit. Freeze until firm.*

** **See** page 15. Mocha Mix® is not the only milk-free frozen dessert available. If you find another one you prefer, go with it.*

*** Some prepared pie crusts **do** have milk by-products in them. The one I found that doesn't has a lot of salt, so if you are watching your salt intake it may be best to make your own crusts.*

✖ ✖ ✖ ✖ ✖ ✖ ✖

Orange Pudding

¾ cup sugar	3 egg yolks, lightly beaten
3 tablespoons cornstarch	1 orange rind, grated—optional
¼ teaspoon salt	1 teaspoon "butter"
3 cups orange juice	

1. Combine sugar, cornstarch, and salt in saucepan. Add orange juice (if desired, add grated rind of one orange with the juice) and mix thoroughly. Add egg yolks and bring to boil while stirring constantly
2. When mixture reaches full boil, boil for 2 minutes, remove from heat and stir in "butter." Pour into individual serving dishes.

Orange Chiffon Pudding: *Make Orange Pudding; make meringue of the egg whites, fold in after the pudding has cooled.*

Orange-Coconut Pudding: *Add 1 cup coconut to either Orange or Orange Chiffon Pudding before pouring into serving dishes.*

Lemon Pudding

⅔ to ¾ cup sugar	6 tablespoons fresh lemon juice
3 tablespoons cornstarch	1 teaspoon "butter"
2⅔ cups water	Rind of 1 lemon, grated
3 egg yolks	

1. Combine sugar and cornstarch in saucepan; add water and mix well. Add egg yolks and bring to boil; boil 2 minutes. Remove from heat and stir in lemon juice, "butter," and lemon rind.
2. Pour into serving dishes.

Lemon Chiffon Pudding: *Fold meringue into cooled Lemon Pudding before pouring into serving dishes.*

Fruit Juice Pudding: *Follow instructions for Orange Pudding, except use a favorite fruit juice instead of orange juice. Be creative!*

Pudding Meringue

  3   egg whites   ¼   cup sugar
  ¼   teaspoon cream of tartar

1. In bowl beat egg whites and cream of tartar until foamy. Add sugar gradually, beating until stiff peaks form and all the sugar is dissolved.
2. Fold meringue into cooled puddings to make chiffons. This is a light and delightful treat.

For citrus puddings: Replace the cream of tartar with 1 teaspoon lemon juice. Or add ½ teaspoon vanilla or other flavoring.

Vanilla "Cream" Pudding

  ¾   cup sugar   3   egg yolks, lightly beaten
  3   tablespoons cornstarch   1   teaspoon "butter"
  ¼   teaspoon salt   2   teaspoons vanilla
  3   cups "cream" or "milk"

1. Mix the dry ingredients in a saucepan; add "cream" or "milk" and stir until thoroughly mixed. Bring to boil over medium heat, stirring constantly; boil 1 minute and remove from heat.
2. Slowly stir about half the hot mixture into the egg yolks, then blend yolk mixture into hot mixture in saucepan. Return to boil, stirring constantly and boil 1 minute longer.
3. Remove from heat and stir in "butter" and vanilla; pour into dessert dishes and serve warm or cold.

Coconut "Cream" Pudding: Add 1 cup coconut to basic pudding. Pour into dishes.

Chocolate "Cream" Pudding: Add ½ cup cocoa with sugar and cornstarch, or 3 squares melted semi-sweet chocolate, to basic pudding before cooking.

Banana "Cream" Pudding: Place banana slices into dessert dishes, pour basic "cream" pudding over them.

Cranberry Mousse

1	cup cranberry juice	1	16-oz. can cranberry sauce
1	3-oz. package raspberry gelatin	2	cups nondairy topping (read the label)

1. Allow whipped topping to thaw in refrigerator.
2. Place juice in saucepan and bring to boil; remove from heat; stir in gelatin until it dissolves.
3. In mixing bowl beat cranberry sauce until foamy; blend in gelatin mixture and chill until thickened, 2–2½ hours in refrigerator.
4. Fold in whipped topping, blending well, and spoon into dessert dishes or prepared pie shell.
5. Chill until firm, about ½ hour.

Chocolate Mousse

1	teaspoon unflavored gelatin	6	tablespoons sugar
1	tablespoon cold water	¼	cup cocoa
2	tablespoons boiling water	2	cups nondairy topping (read the label)

1. Allow whipped topping to thaw in refrigerator.
2. Sprinkle gelatin over cold water in small bowl stir and let stand a minute to soften. Add boiling water and stir until gelatin is completely dissolved and mixture is clear.
3. Sprinkle sugar and cocoa over topping in mixing bowl and blend thoroughly with mixer; add gelatin mixture and beat until blended. Pour into dessert dishes or prepared pie shell.
4. Chill until firm, about ½ hour.

Baked Apples

Apple(s)	1 teaspoon "butter"
1 to 2 tablespoons brown sugar	¼ teaspoon cinnamon

1. Preheat oven to 350. Choose, wash, and core the number of apples needed.
2. Spray appropriate-sized baking dish with vegetable spray.
3. Place the prepared apples in baking dish; fill center of each with 1-2 tablespoons brown sugar (depending on taste), 1 teaspoon "butter" and cinnamon.
4. Cover bottom of dish with water to ¼" depth and bake at 350° for 30-40 minutes, depending on size of fruit.

Fruit Cobbler

1 cup flour	⅔ to ¾ cup sugar
1 tablespoon sugar	1 tablespoon cornstarch
1½ teaspoons baking powder	1 cup water
¼ teaspoon salt	3 cups fresh fruit *
3 tablespoons shortening	1 teaspoon "butter"
½ cup "milk"	½ teaspoon cinnamon

1. Preheat oven to 400°. Spray a 1½-qt. baking dish with vegetable spray. Measure flour by sifting; combine dry ingredients; set aside.
2. In a saucepan mix sugar and cornstarch well; stir in water and bring to boil, stirring constantly. Boil 1 minute. Add fruit and pour mixture into baking dish; dot with "butter" and sprinkle with cinnamon if desired.
3. To the dry ingredients add shortening and cut in until well blended; stir in "milk." Drop by spoonfuls into hot fruit and bake at 400° for 25-30 minutes.
4. Serve warm.

* Use seasoned fruit or berries of your choice. Wash and drain berries before beginning. Amount of sugar will be determined by tartness of fruit and your taste.

Fruit Shortcake

1 quart fresh berries *	3 teaspoons baking powder
½ to ¾ cup sugar	¼ teaspoon salt
2 cups flour	⅓ cup shortening
2 tablespoons sugar	1 cup "milk"

1. Preheat oven to 450°. Mix the berries and ½–¾ cup sugar; allow to stand at room temperature while making cake. Crush the fruit if preferred.
2. Measure flour by sifting and combine dry ingredients; cut in the shortening; stir in the "milk" just until blended. Spread dough in two 8" layer pans or one 8" square pan sprayed with vegetable spray. Bake at 450° for 12–15 minutes for layers, 15–20 minutes for square pan. Tops will be crusty.
3. Serve by covering a layer with berries; add top layer and cover it with berries (you will split the square into layers). Top with thawed nondairy whipped topping, read the label.

Use seasonal fruit or berries of your choice. Wash and drain berries before beginning. Amount of sugar will be determined by tartness of fruit and your taste.

Meringue Shells (Tortes)

3 egg whites	1 cup sugar
¼ teaspoon cream of tarter	

1. Preheat oven to 275°. Beat egg whites and cream of tartar until frothy; beat in sugar a little at a time; be sure sugar is mixed in and dissolved; continue beating until very stiff and glossy. Tint if you like.
2. Cut brown paper to fit baking sheet. Then place shells, by ⅓ cup of meringue for each, on the paper and shape a hollow with the back of a spoon to form each shell. Bake at 275° for 1 hour. Turn off oven and leave shells in oven until cooled. Don't open the oven door after turning

off until the oven is completely cooled. If you open it while warm, shells will crack.

3. Fill as desired with "ice cream," fruit, pudding, sauce, etc.

- 8 tortes or shells -

Note: This can be baked as one large torte, also. Just make one large shape hollow and proceed as directed.

Milk-Free Candies & Treats

Peanut Clusters

2 12-oz. packages semi-sweet chocolate chips (read the label)	3 cups peanuts

1. Line cookie sheets with waxed paper.
2. In double boiler or heavy sauce pan on low heat, melt chips,* stirring until smooth. Stir in peanuts until well coated and drop by teaspoonfuls onto waxed paper.
3. Chill in refrigerator until set.

Use any favorite nuts, raisins, or coconut to make these milk-free candies.

* See "chocolate," pg. 15.

Mari and Mom's Mint Fudge

4 cups sugar	1 tablespoon "butter"
1 cup cocoa	1 teaspoon vanilla
1½ cups "milk"	1 teaspoon peppermint flavoring
4 tablespoons corn syrup	1 cup coarsely chopped nuts
¼ teaspoon salt	

1. Spray 9 x 13" pan, or equivalent, with vegetable spray.
2. In a large saucepan mix the sugar and cocoa, then the next 3 ingredients and cook over medium heat, stirring until a smooth liquid is formed. Then, without stirring, cook to 234° on candy thermometer or to soft ball stage.
3. Remove from heat; add "butter" and cool to 120°, lukewarm, do not stir. At 120°, or lukewarm, add flavorings and mix in well; add nuts if desired, then beat with spoon until mixture begins to thicken.
4. Pour into pan while still glossy (otherwise you may not be able to) and cool in pan until hardened. Cut into squares.

For plain fudge: *Use 2 teaspoons vanilla and omit mint flavoring and nuts.*

Quick Coconut-Nut Fudge

1 package semi-sweet chocolate chips (read the label)	1 package (2 pounds) powdered sugar
¼ cup "butter"	⅓ cup cocoa
½ cup warm water	¼ teaspoon salt
2 teaspoons vanilla	1 cup coconut
	1 cup chopped nuts

1. Melt chocolate chips and "butter" in double boiler, or heavy saucepan over low heat; add warm water and vanilla.
2. Mix sugar, cocoa, salt, coconut, and nuts in large mixing bowl; stir in chocolate mixture and blend well.
3. Press into 13" ungreased pan, refrigerate until set; cut into squares.

Vary *with choice of nuts and use dark chocolate for variety, but be sure to read the label for any product you use.*

Peppermint Wafers

1 egg (or 2 egg whites)	1 tablespoon "butter"
3 to 3½ cups powdered sugar	¾ to 1 teaspoon mint flavoring

1. In a mixing bowl combine all ingredients and blend well. Tint in color or colors desired and knead on surface dusted with powdered sugar until smooth. Make ½" balls, place on waxed paper and flatten with tines of fork, or roll out to ¼" thickness and cut with a small cookie cutter.
2. Allow to dry for 16–24 hours.

Chocolate Mint Wafers: Melt 6 ounces semi-sweet chocolate; dip hardened wafer in chocolate; place on "buttered" waxed paper to set.

Peanut Brittle

3	cups sugar	2	cups peanuts
1	cup water	1	teaspoon soda
½	cup corn syrup, light	1	teaspoon vanilla
¼	cup "butter"		

1. Bring sugar, water, and syrup to boil until it threads (separates into brittle threads); add "butter" and peanuts. Cook slowly to 300°, stirring occasionally.
2. Add soda and vanilla, which will cause a foam.
3. Pour onto 2 "buttered" baking sheets; spread out on the sheets as it cools.
4. When cooled, break into pieces with a knife handle.

Peanut Brittle II

2	cups sugar	1½	cups peanuts
1	cup light syrup	1	teaspoon soda
1	tablespoon "butter"		

1. In saucepan combine sugar, syrup, and "butter"; bring to rolling boil. Add peanuts and cook to a golden brown, stirring constantly.
2. Remove from heat and stir in soda, return to low heat and cook until mixture is a dark golden brown color, this will take a while; stir occasionally.
3. Pour into "buttered" rectangular pan; crack when cooled.

Chocolate Bars—Milk Free

12 ounces semi-sweet
chocolate (read the label)

1 cup chopped or halved nuts

1. Melt chocolate over low heat; do not get it too hot. When melted on the outside, remove from heat and stir to finish melting. Stir in the nuts.
2. Line a baking sheet with waxed paper. Pour the chocolate into bar shapes or pour out to ¼" thickness and cut into bars when cooled.
3. Chill until firm and wrap each bar separately.

Vary by using raisins and chopped nuts;
Or coconut and slivered almonds;
Or or use dried fruit to make a chocolate fruit bar.

Sea Foam

2 cups light brown sugar
½ cup water

2 egg whites
Walnut halves

1. Place light brown sugar and water in a saucepan; cook to soft ball stage. Remove from heat and add the two well-beaten egg whites; beat the mixture together until thickened.
2. Drop onto "buttered" waxed paper by spoonfuls and place a walnut half on each.
3. Let stand until hardened and wrap individually.

Caramel Popcorn

2 cups sugar
2 tablespoons vinegar

1 cup molasses
½ teaspoon soda

1. Bring sugar, vinegar, and molasses, to a boil; boil to the crack stage, 290° on a candy thermometer. Meanwhile, in a large bowl mix 9–10 cups

popped corn with 2–3 cups peanuts. When the syrup has reached the cracking stage remove from heat; stir in the soda and beat briskly.
2. Pour over the peanuts and popcorn and stir to coat all.

Note: If it's raining or very humid, cook just a degree or so above temperature reading in the recipes.

Frozen Pops

1	3-oz. package gelatin	1	cup boiling water
1	envelope soft drink mix, sugar free *	3	cups cold water

1. Dissolve gelatin and soft drink mix in boiling water, mixing well. Add cold water; pour into molds, small paper cups, or ice cube trays. Insert wooden sticks, or plastic spoons in each pop as a handle.
2. Freeze until firm, about 2–3 hours.

* If extremely lactose sensitive read the label on drink mix or omit!

Fruit Pops

Use fruit juice and omit water; proceed with directions.

Creamy Fruit Pops

1	3-oz. package fruit gelatin	3½ cups nondairy
1	cup boiling fruit juice	whipped topping (read the label)
3	cups cold fruit juice	

1. Dissolve gelatin in boiling fruit juice, add cold juice, and cool until partially set.
2. Add thawed nondairy whipped topping, using a mixer if you like, and blend thoroughly. Pour into molds, add handles, and freeze.

Creamy Choco-Orange Pops

1   3-oz. package orange gelatin
1   cup boiling orange juice
2   cups cold orange juice

3 to 4 ounces semi-sweet
    chocolate, melted
3½ cups nondairy topping
    (read the label)

Follow directions above, except add melted chocolate to the dissolved hot gelatin, then proceed as directed.

Variation: Make the above recipes, then place in dessert dishes and chill in the refrigerator. Serve as mousse—very nice.

Orange-Lemon Ice

2   cups water
¾ to 1 cup sugar
1   cup orange juice (or
    concentrate)

¼   cup lemon juice, fresh
1   tablespoon grated lemon rind
1   tablespoon grated orange rind

1. Bring water and sugar to boil and boil 5 minutes; cool to room temperature.
2. Add juices and rinds; pour into 8" square pan. Freeze 3–4 hours, stirring every half hour to increase volume.

Note: Milk-free frozen commercial products are available, but be certain to read the labels. Sherbets for instance are not milk-free. Commercial sherbets are milk-based.

> ## SORBET
> *is a commercial product made of blended fruit and juice. It does not contain cream or milk fat. So sorbets are a dessert that you should be able to enjoy.*
>
> ✶ ✶ ✶ ✶ ✶ ✶ ✶ ✶

Beverages

✖ ✖ ✖ ✖ ✖ ✖ ✖ ✖ ✖

HOT COCOA ✖ HOT CHOCOLATE ✖ EGG NOG ✖ LEMONADE ✖ "MILK SHAKES" ✖ TEA ✖ SODA ✖ AND MORE . .

✖ ✖ ✖ ✖ ✖ ✖ ✖ ✖ ✖ ✖

When you think of beverages, the first that usually come to mind are coffee and tea. There are a variety of instant products available, but I prefer to use tea leaves and whole or ground coffee.

Coffee

There are truly only a few secrets for making good coffee. For starters, find a coffee brand that suits your taste and your water. If the quality of the coffee you usually buy is not consistent, switch brands for a while, or for good. Also, use the same amount of coffee per cup of water each time—be consistent.

It's important to keep ground coffee fresh. Keep a small supply on hand; store the rest in a tightly covered jar in the freezer until needed. Also, be sure to keep the pot clean! That means the pot, stem, basket, and pump area, if a percolator. The pot, filter, water tank, and bottom of water tank, if a drip pot. Keep all the components free of coffee oils, water, sediment, and mold build-ups. (Yes, I've seen some office coffee makers.) Run vinegar through, or a commercial pot cleaner, on a regular basis. And wash the pot daily in between major cleanings. Do these things and you will enjoy great tasting coffee all the time.

The amount of coffee to water will depend on your preference, of course. For regular or drip grind begin with 1 tablespoon of coffee per 1 cup water. Remember, a regular coffee scoop is 2 tablespoons. If using a fine grind, use less.

If you wish to try flavored coffees or teas, remember to *read the labels*. If you like coffee or tea with cream, the nondairy creamer we use as "milk" is very good. Avoid the powdered nondairy creamers, and if you use them, read the label!

> *To enhance the flavor of a cup of coffee, try stirring it with a cinnamon stick.*
>
> ✖ ✖ ✖ ✖ ✖ ✖ ✖

Tea

When making tea, preheat the cup and pot with hot water. Use 1 bag, or about 1 teaspoon of loose tea, per cup of hot water. Place the tea in the heated receptacle and pour water that is just coming to a boiling point over it. Do not boil the water unless it is from a river, lake, or contaminated well. That said, if you do, it's no big deal.

Allow the tea to steep to your satisfaction, 1–5 minutes; remove the bag(s), or tea house, but do not squeeze the excess water from the bags into your cup or pot. The bitter tannic acid will also be squeezed into the cup if you do that. Don't squeeze the water out whether for hot or iced teas, simply remove the dripping bags and discard.

Find the tea brand(s) that suits your tastes and water. Water differs from area to area of the world and even in different parts of a state. If you have salt-softened water and must watch your salt intake, don't use the hot water from the tap for making coffee or tea.

Other Milk-Free Beverages

For the following drinks use fat-free, liquid nondairy creamer to replace milk. If you use a regular nondairy creamer, there will be more calories. If you're a weight watcher, use the fat-free, though neither is without calories.

To make a flavored "milk" drink, to an 8-oz. glass of "milk" add:

> *2–3 tablespoons chocolate sauce (see pg. 138)*
>
> *2–3 tablespoons butterscotch sauce (see pg. 137)*
>
> *2–3 tablespoons caramel sauce (see pg. 138)*
>
> *2–3 tablespoons maple syrup, read the label*
>
> *⅓ cup orange juice*
>
> *Add jam, ice cream topping, or thawed berries*
>
> *Add ½ banana, mashed well*

Mix thoroughly, or use a blender to make these drinks.

"Milk" Shakes

Combine choice of flavoring and "milk" in a tall glass, stir to combine; add one scoop of nondairy frozen dessert, mix well and enjoy.

Thick Shake

To ¾ cup flavored "milk," add ½–¾ cup nondairy whipped topping * (thawed). Blend well. Pour into tall glasses and enjoy.

* See pg. 16.

A WORD ABOUT COMMERCIAL SOFT DRINKS

*If you are lactose sensitive, this is important. Some soda (pop) has lactic acid; even in this area you must read the labels. Some well-known brands have lactic acid in the diet varieties but not in the regular and vice versa. Some of the powdered soft drink mixes also have milk by-products other than lactose in them, **read the labels**.*

Any soda that is free of milk by-products is good for the previous recipes. I drink sugar-free soft drinks as a general rule because the sugar in the regular sodas makes me uncomfortable. I also do not drink alcohol because of the sugar content. I don't tolerate alcoholic beverages well, and this could possibly be lactose related.

✗ ✗ ✗ ✗ ✗ ✗ ✗ ✗

Sodas

For each soda, combine 3 tablespoons flavored syrup, or ¼ cup crushed fruit in a tall glass with soda or tonic water. Add 1 scoop of nondairy frozen dessert and stir well. Fill to top with soda or tonic water and enjoy.

Mix a light soda and orange juice; serve over ice.

Mix a light soda and grapefruit juice; serve over ice.

Mix a light soda and cranberry juice; serve over ice.

Mix a cola with cranapple or apple juice; serve over ice.

A drink that is very refreshing is tonic water with quinine and a squeeze of fresh lime, or lemon, in a tall glass with ice. For some, the quinine acts to help prevent the cramping, so if you suffer from muscle cramping, you might try it. However, some people feel itchy after drinking tonic water with quinine. If you begin to feel itchy, especially on the bottoms of your feet, after drinking it, you may not want to use quinine water.

Fill a tall glass half full with unsweetened grapefruit juice and ice. Fill with tonic water.

Most dry beverage mixes have a form of sodium caseinate.

✖ ✖ ✖ ✖ ✖ ✖ ✖

Be willing to experiment with juices and soft drinks, you can come up with some interesting tastes!

Hot Cocoa

1 serving	4 servings
2 teaspoons sugar	¼ to ½ cup sugar
1 tablespoon cocoa	⅓ cup cocoa
Dash salt, optional	Dash salt, optional
2 tablespoons "milk"	⅓ cup "milk"
1 cup hot "milk"	4 cups "milk"

For a single serving, place the first 4 ingredients in a mug and stir until smooth. Fill mug with 1 cup hot "milk." Stir again and enjoy.

For 4 servings, place the first 4 ingredients in a saucepan, stirring until smooth. Add 4 cups "milk." Stir and heat, but **do not** boil. Serve hot.

Hot Chocolate

3 to 4 squares unsweetened chocolate	¼ to ½ cup sugar
	Pinch salt, optional
1 cup water	3 cups "milk"

1. Melt chocolate with water in saucepan, stirring until mixture is smooth. Add salt and sugar and bring to boil, stirring constantly. Boil 2 minutes.
2. Stir in 3 cups "milk" and heat just until hot.
3. Serve and enjoy.

Egg Nog

1 egg, well beaten	1 cup cold "cream"
1 teaspoon sugar	½ teaspoon vanilla

Beat egg and sugar well; add "cream" and vanilla and beat thoroughly. Serve immediately sprinkled with nutmeg if desired. (Keep in mind—this is not pasteurized.)

Lemonade

3 medium to large lemons   6 cups cold water
½ to ¾ cup sugar

Wash and cut lemons in half; squeeze juice and remove seeds. Combine lemon juice, pulp, and sugar in container and mix well. Add cold water, stir well. Chill and serve over ice. (Size of lemons and amount of sugar are an individual preference. Taste and, if you must, add more sugar.)

Hot Lemonade: *Follow above recipe but heat the lemonade. Excellent on a cool day.*

Milk & Lactose Reference Guide

x x x x x x x x x x x x x x x x x x x x

Lactose intolerance is a problem with assimilating milk sugars. It is usually an inherited trait but can be a side effect of taking certain antibiotics, abdominal radiation, or treatments that affect the gastrointestinal tract. Remember, people react to milk and lactose differently. An amount that does not affect one person in the least may make someone else very uncomfortable.

High-lactose foods are: milk and milk products such as dried milk, cheese, yogurt, sherbet, ice cream, sour cream, etc; most chocolate beverages that are commercially made; commercial foods that list milk products of any kind on the label; and some foods that simply don't reveal the inclusion of milk or milk by-products on the packaging. You needn't wonder if packaging says "milk chocolate"—the product does have milk in it! Below are some other foods you may want to avoid. Keep in mind that this is not a complete list, so always *read the label* (RL).

brain, liver, and other organ meats *
breads and baked products
candies
coffee creamers, powdered
cold cuts with milk, or whey, etc.
cordials
custards or caramels
diabetic preparations (RL)
dietetic aids (RL)
dips, party
eggs, powdered
frankfurters with milk, whey, etc.
french fries, commercial (RL)
green olives
liqueurs
meats, pre-breaded or creamed

maraschino cherries (RL)
margarines, milk-based
mayonnaise, low-cholesterol (RL)
mixes for pancakes, biscuits, cakes,
    cookies, etc.
nondairy whipped toppings (RL)
pickles
potatoes, instant or mashed, commercial (RL)
salad dressings (RL)
sausages & other prepared meats
sherbets
sodas/pops (RL)
soft drinks, powdered (RL)
soups, dried
spice blends (RL)
yogurts

Organ meats contain high levels of lactic acid because lactic acid is present in the animal's tissue. Avoid these meats or at least be aware of their potential problems. (Yes, we also produce lactic acid in our systems, but producing and ingesting are two entirely different things.)

The foods listed on the previous page are commonly known to have some form of lactose or milk in them. Work with these foods until you find which ones you can, or cannot, tolerate. If you can tolerate something, how often?

If you suspect that you might be more comfortable with no milk or milk by-products, avoid high-lactose foods and read all food labels for other names that lactose and milk proteins go by, including:

ammonium caseinate	lactoglobulin; lactalbumin
artificial butter flavor	lactose; lactic acid *
butter	milk
butter solids or butter fat	milk derivative
calcium caseinate	milk fat
casein *	magnesium caseinate
caseinate	margarine
cheese	potassium caseinate
delactosed whey	rennet casein
demineralized whey	skim milk
dried dairy blend	sodium caseinate **
dry milk solids; dried skim milk	sour cream solids
dry or dried milk; milk solids	sour milk solids
evaporated milk, concentrated/condensed	whey
hydrolyzed casein	whey powder
hydrolyzed milk protein	whey protein concentrate
lactalbumin phosphatel	yogurt
lactoferrin; lactate	

Also watch for: "may contain traces of dairy"; artificial flavorings; natural flavorings; or just flavorings—what's in them? Watch for fat replacers: Simplese and/or Opta, and others which may have milk protein in them. There is a high-protein flour available in some areas, be sure to check it if you're lactose intolerant.[10] Also watch for ghee, a clarified butter. In respect to any of the above, you may or may not react—*you* decide.

* Lactose, casein, lactic acid, and perhaps other milk by-products are in some prescription and over-the-counter medications. Ask your doctor or pharmacist if you're milk/lactose intolerant and read the labels on over-the-counter products.

** Sodium caseinate is in many processed foods and is being pushed for more and more uses.[11]

Calcium

✖ ✖ ✖ ✖ ✖ ✖ ✖ ✖ ✖

The question most asked of milk- and lactose-intolerant people is: If you're not drinking milk, or consuming milk products, how do you get enough calcium? Answer: By choosing foods carefully.

Between animal and vegetable protein, vegetable proteins are more readily absorbed by our bodies. Ingesting large amounts of animal protein, including dairy products, can cause a calcium loss in humans.[12] Excessive intake of animal protein leeches calcium out of the system via the urine and other means.[13] While it is true that a given portion of vegetables has less protein than the same size animal portion, the vegetables are more useful to us nutritionally because with less animal protein in the diet, the calcium we do take in is more readily available and utilized by our systems.

You should also be aware that caffeine and sodium cause loss of calcium and that alcohol inhibits calcium absorption. The recipes in this book address our overall nutritional needs. Where calcium is concerned, keeping bones strong is *not dependent* on increasing calcium intake, but on *preventing* calcium loss. Our body's calcium is replaced by the calcium in food, and the nonanimal proteins are the more effective calcium source.[14] Green leafy vegetables and beans are good sources of calcium, very low in fat, and moderate in protein. They are especially beneficial when combined with moderate exercise.

Most medical opinions state that weight-bearing exercise, on a regular basis, is as important as calcium for keeping bones healthy and strong. Many health professionals feel that exercise is a must to prevent osteoporosis.[15] To reap the full benefits of a healthy diet, moderate exercise should be part of a normal daily routine. Walking, running, or aerobic dance are good choices for bone maintenance. In short, a diet with a modest amount of animal protein—no milk products or lactose if intolerant, or very little—together with exercise, will insure healthy bones and overall good health for most anyone.

There are food sources other than milk that provide us with all the nutrition, vitamins, and minerals our bodies need. And we don't need to be vegetarians to be healthy. I have lived with the inability to tolerate milk products for sixty years, and I am very happy with my life. In some ways I am healthier than many people my age. Who's to say what's perfect and what's normal?

Where do you find calcium other than in milk? Some of the most accessible sources are listed below. The first list is from a paper for the Physicians' Committee for Responsible Medicine and is listed in order of highest amount of calcium.[16]

Calcium-rich foods:

collard greens	blackstrap molasses	kidney beans
bok choy	amaranth	black beans
turnip greens	great northern beans	okra
kale	dried figs	acorn squash
broccoli	vegetarian baked beans	pinto beans
kelp (seaweed)	navy beans	tofu, set with calcium
mustard greens	corn tortillas	soybeans
wakame (seaweed)	fortified orange juice	

Other good sources of calcium:

almond butter	eggs, boiled	salmon with bones
almonds	figs	sardines
apples	kohlrabi	sesame seeds
baked cod fillet	onions	shrimp
beet greens	oranges	spinach*
Brussels sprouts	potatoes	swiss chard *
cabbage	rhubarb*	tahini
cauliflower	rutabaga	watercress
cranberries		

These contain a substance called oxalates. There is some disagreement as to whether or not the calcium in them is readily absorbed. I eat them because I like them, and I suspect that more research needs to be done to be absolutely certain of the affects of oxalates.

Conversions & Size Guide

✖ ✖ ✖ ✖ ✖ ✖ ✖ ✖ ✖ ✖ ✖ ✖ ✖ ✖ ✖ ✖ ✖ ✖ ✖

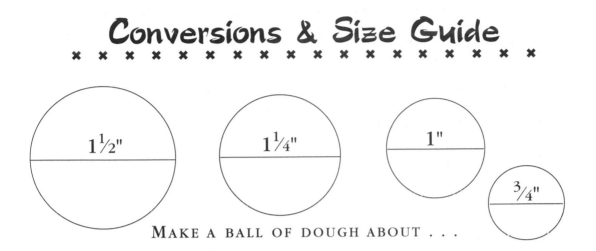

$1\frac{1}{2}"$ $1\frac{1}{4}"$ $1"$ $\frac{3}{4}"$

MAKE A BALL OF DOUGH ABOUT . . .

3 teaspoons	=	1 tablespoon
2 tablespoons	=	⅛ cup
4 tablespoons	=	¼ cup
5⅓ tablespoons	=	⅓ cup
8 tablespoons	=	½ cup
10⅔ tablespoons	=	⅔ cup
12 tablespoons	=	¾ cup
14 tablespoons	=	⅞ cup
16 tablespoons	=	1 cup
1 cup	=	½ pint
2 cups	=	1 pint
4 cups	=	2 pints
2 pints	=	1 quart
4 quarts	=	1 gallon

⅛"

¼"

⅓"

½"

INCHES GUIDE
FOR ROLLING DOUGH

Additional Information

✖ ✖ ✖ ✖ ✖ ✖ ✖ ✖ ✖ ✖ ✖ ✖ ✖ ✖ ✖ ✖ ✖

Just a few years ago, you couldn't find information on milk/lactose intolerance. Now there are thousands of sites on the internet and dozens of books about lactose and milk. My opinion? It has become the "in" thing. Please use common sense when going through all the material available. It isn't necessary to do all the things the various books, sites, and sources tell us we must. Certainly buying all the odd stuff that is touted as essential to lactose-intolerant people is not necessary. As an example, two sets of cooking pans and utensils are not necessary, and certainly not separate sets of dishes for those in your family who are milk or lactose intolerant. Dishes and pans should be washed thoroughly whether one is milk sensitive or not; this will remove the milk proteins. Expensive specialty foods, if a child is intolerant and not severely allergic to milk, should be considered carefully. Question the need for it and ask your doctor's opinion; then purchase it only if *you* agree it's needed.

It is the tendency of commercial interests, with stuff to sell, to frighten us with all manner of horrible possibilities. They want us to think the worst and assume the intolerance will get worse. It won't get worse; it won't get better. It just *is*. You or your child will feel better with no, or less, lactose. Period. From personal experience I can tell you that if you are just finding that you, or your child, are lactose sensitive, you will be amazed at how much healthier and happier you, or they, will feel when you reduce or eliminate, if necessary, milk and milk by-products from your diet. Not ingesting milk and milk by-products is okay. This is our normal life—and it's a good one.

I did a lot of looking at sites on the internet for information and for corroboration of my opinions. There are some interesting sites you may want to look at. I've referenced some on the opposite page. Of the thousands of web sites, most are non-medical and many are maintained by dairy industry affiliates or people who wish to sell lactose-intolerant "necessities." The medical sites that are easily available to the public did not post any evidence of a definitive study on milk in the human system. They all say the same thing: Avoid milk and milk by-products to the extent that makes each individual comfortable.

Notes

Most of what is in this book are my opinions based on my experiences. Following are some of the sources where I found medical or scientific information as of this writing. Please remember that due to the ever-changing nature of the internet you may or may not be able to access the links below at any given time.

1. http://www.diagnosishealth.com/lactose1.htm
   http://www.pcrm.org/health/Info_on_Veg_Diets/lactose_intolerance.html
2. http://www.nlm.nih.gov/medlineplus/ency/imagepage/18112.htm
   http://www.pcrm.org/health/Info_on_Veg_Diets/lactose_intolerance.html
3. http://www.nof.org/prevention/calcium.htm
   http://www.cc.nih.gov/ccc/supplements/vitd.html#food
   http://www.pcrm.org/health/Info_on_Veg_Diets/dairy.html
4. http://www.vrg.org/nutrition/calcium.htm
5. http://www.enyadatta.com/Misc/nomilk.html
   http://www.peta.org/mc/facts/fsveg6.html
6. http://www.afpafitness.com/MILKDOC.HTM
   http://www.drmcdougall.com/science/arthritis.html
   http://www.bestlifeint.com/articles/cure_for_rheumatoid_arthritis.htm
   http://dialspace.dial.pipex.com/town/park/gfm11/
7. http://www.members.tripod.com/~josquin/milk.htm
   http://www.naples.net/health/lactose.html
8. http://www.members.tripod.com/~josquin/milk.htm
   http://www.pcrm.org/health/Info_on_Veg_Diets/milk.html
9. http://www.nutramed.com/children/kidsmilk.htm
10. http://www.smallgrains.org/WHFACTS/nutrflrs.htm
    http://www.premiernutrition.com/products/protein.html
11. http://www.dmv-international.com/index2.htm
    http://www.dmv-international.com/proteins/LITERAT/pdf/16532_final.pdf
12. http://www.vegsource.com/klaper/optimum.htm
    http://www.vrg.org/nutrition/calcium.htm#need
13. http://www.vegsource.com/talk/health/messages/12359.html
    http://www.kaapeli.fi/eko.fi/chat/disc1/m-98-04-10-18.42.56-10914
    http://www.best.com/~juliemb/Mics/nomilk.html

14. http://www.vrg.org/nutrition/calcium.htm#need
15. http://www.vegsource.com/articles/calcium_update.html
16. http://www.pcrm.org
   Physicians Committee for Responsible Medicine
   PO Box 6322, Washington, DC, 20015, Tel: 202-686-2210

Additional web sites:

http://www.osteoporosis.ca/OSTEO/D02-01e.html#chart *(about calcium/vitamin D)*
http://vitamind.ucr.edu/index.html *(about vitamin D)*
http://www.cc.nih.gov/ccc/supplements/vitd.html *(about vitamin D)*
http://dialspace.dial.pipex.com/town/park/gfm11/ *(a UK site for the milk allergic and lactose intolerant)*
http://www.gastro.org/public/lactose.html *(Information about lactose intolerance from The American Gastroenterological Association)*
http://www.enviromed.org/food_allergy/CUMULATIVE___ADDITIVE_EFFECTS_OF_FOOD.html *(about food additives)*
http://www.foodproductdesign.com/archive/1997/1097AP.html *(about sodium caseinate)*

Index

✖ ✖ ✖ ✖ ✖ ✖ ✖ ✖ ✖ ✖ ✖ ✖ ✖ ✖ ✖ ✖